BOBBY KENNEDY

— A RAGING SPIRIT —

CHRIS MATTHEWS

SIMON & SCHUSTER

New York   London   Toronto   Sydney   New Delhi

Simon & Schuster
1230 Avenue of the Americas
New York, NY 10020

First Simon & Schuster hardcover edition November 2017

SIMON & SCHUSTER and colophon are registered trademarks
of Simon & Schuster, Inc.

For information about special discounts for bulk purchases, please contact
Simon & Schuster Special Sales at 1-866-506-1949
or business@simonandschuster.com.

The Simon & Schuster Speakers Bureau can bring authors to your
live event. For more information or to book an event contact the
Simon & Schuster Speakers Bureau at 1-866-248-3049
or visit our website at www.simonspeakers.com.

Manufactured in the United States of America

10 9 8 7 6 5 4 3 2 1

Library of Congress Cataloging-in-Publication Data has been applied for.

ISBN 978-1-5011-1186-0
ISBN 978-1-5011-1188-4 (ebook)

For Michael, Thomas, and Caroline,
to learn from this man's faith and
share his lived compassion

CONTENTS

CONTENTS

Man is Spirit

—Winston Churchill

I long ago came to realize that movies are always about the present. It doesn't matter whether the wardrobe is Elizabethan or cowboy. The story is told by and for the living, those who'll be there to see it.

The same is true of biography. Jack Kennedy said the reason we read about famous people's lives is to answer the question: What was this person actually like? Can I imagine being in their presence? Can I make the personal connection? Are they a hero to root for?

This book is about the Bobby Kennedy we'd want to have today, the kind of leader we lack today.

The years of Bobby's public life were my times, too—when the Kennedys first emerged in 1956; the excitement of that great presidential campaign of Kennedy vs. Nixon; the championing of equality for every American; and the campus unrest over Vietnam. All that youth and hope and sense of change: you couldn't be alive and not feel it.

In 1968 I joined the Peace Corps, spending two unforgettable years in Africa. That adventure took me to a new and a larger world. This, of course, I owe to the Kennedys' arrival in Washington and the ideas they brought with them. For me, as for everyone I knew, those years were a shift from looking backward to gazing ahead.

The books I've researched and written on Jack brought home to me again and again the essential role Bobby played in those historic moments. Those accounts appear here as a starting point for showing that the younger brother's role was indispensable to history. Among them: getting his brother elected to the Senate and then the presidency; handling the Cuban Missile Crisis; and pushing the Civil Rights Act to the national forefront of the Kennedy agenda.

And then there was Dallas.

And then there was Los Angeles.

To honor his life in politics, to mark the half century of his loss and the hope that our country can find its way back to the patriotic unity he championed . . . for all Americans, this is my story of Robert F. Kennedy.

BOBBY KENNEDY

Those who loved him stand in salute of Bobby Kennedy's funeral train.

PROLOGUE

On March 16, 1968, Robert F. Kennedy stood in the high-ceilinged, marble-walled Senate Caucus Room where, eight years earlier, his brother Jack had announced for president. Bobby now was doing the same. After months of agonizing and second-guessing, he'd decided to step up and make the commitment he'd been hanging back from, fearful the timing at this moment was wrong for his future political career.

Walking into the Caucus Room that Saturday morning was for something more than a simple announcement. It was, in fact, a declaration of all-out political war. It would see him doing battle for the Democratic presidential nomination not just on one front, but two.

The first enemy Bobby was facing down was Lyndon Johnson, the president who'd taken his oath of office in the shadow of Jack's assassination. His aggressive prosecution of the U.S. war in Vietnam had generated a dire national conflict, especially on college campuses.

But besides LBJ, Bobby had a second adversary, Democratic senator Eugene McCarthy, who was now holding aloft the banner of the growing anti–Vietnam War movement. The Minnesota law-maker, with his cool professorial manner, had just, four days earlier, simultaneously thrilled the young while frightening Lyndon John-son with a strong showing against the sitting president in the piv-otal New Hampshire primary.

Thus, two very different men now obstructed the path to a Ken-nedy nomination.

Nonetheless, standing there at the lectern, surrounded by family members along with loyalist veterans of his brother's campaigns, the forty-two-year-old Robert Kennedy was about to take on both men. He began his statement by paying homage to his brother, a tribute clear to many listening. The opening words he'd chosen were the ones Jack had spoken in that very place: "I am announcing today my candidacy for the presidency of the United States."

With the sentence that followed, Jack's steadfast brother left the past behind and went straight to the heart of the troubled moment that was early 1968: "I run because I am convinced that this country is on a perilous course and because I have such strong feelings about what must be done—and I feel that I'm obliged to do all that I can."

But it's what he said next that held such power and still would today: "I run to seek new policies—policies to end the bloodshed in Vietnam and in our cities, policies to close the gaps that now exist between black and white, between rich and poor, between young and old, in this country and around the rest of the world. I run for the presidency because I want the Democratic Party and the United States of America to stand for hope instead of despair, for reconcili-ation of men instead of the growing risk of world war."

Watching intently from his hotel suite in Portland, Oregon—where he himself was campaigning—was Richard Nixon, the Re-publican Jack Kennedy had narrowly beaten in 1960. Now certain of gaining the Republican nomination and having expected to face

Johnson, the two-term vice president turned off the TV set only to continue staring at the blank screen.

He felt a foreboding. "We've just seen some terrible forces unleashed," he pronounced grimly. He knew the force of the Kennedy magic, its power to thrill but also its power to disturb. "Something bad is going to come of this. God knows where this is going to lead."

For LBJ, witnessing this scene at the Senate Caucus Room, it was a nightmare taking life. Since being sworn in on the 22nd of November 1963, just two hours after the death of John F. Kennedy, he'd occupied the Oval Office in the shadow of Dallas. Now, the younger Kennedy, having served just three years as New York's junior senator, was ready, in Johnson's words, to claim "the throne in the memory of his brother."

There were millions of other attentive witnesses. All across the country, young people were obsessed with the daily spectacle of a war—glimpsed in all its horrors on the nightly news—a conflict that their country could neither win nor end.

But the news of Kennedy's decision to run struck many antiwar activists as both threat and insult to those already in the fight. I had this reaction myself. Despite having spoken out boldly against Johnson's war, Bobby Kennedy had for months refused to match Gene McCarthy's courage by committing himself as a candidate. That's the way I saw it as a grad student in economics at the University of North Carolina at Chapel Hill. For me, along with others of my generation facing the draft, Gene McCarthy had become a hero.

Let me put this feeling of ours in the simplest, most human terms. McCarthy galvanized us and claimed our loyalty by being the lone grown-up with the courage to assert that the Vietnam War was ill-conceived and that he, Gene McCarthy, meant to stop it. In this escalating conflict between sons and fathers—Gene, a guy of my own dad's era, was on our side. He told us we were right, and not just selfishly opposing a war because we were personally afraid to fight in it. We understood the patriotic call to duty our dads and uncles had answered in World War II, but Vietnam was different. They wouldn't admit it. McCarthy had.

Starting that Saturday with Bobby Kennedy's declaration, there began a fight within the antiwar ranks. Why, we wanted to know, was Bobby Kennedy, having hesitated to strike first at Johnson, now jumping in? Was it because that close call in New Hampshire had revealed LBJ as electorally mortal? And if so, hadn't Gene now showed himself capable of being more than a symbol? Wasn't he the one man to take down Johnson? Why was Bobby coming in to steal his thunder?

But whatever had held him back before, Bobby's entry into the race was compelling. That he'd taken up the mantle of his slain brother was both its power and its pathos. The great achievements of JFK's New Frontier—the robust economy, the Peace Corps, the space program, the historic commitment to civil rights, the superb leadership during the Cuban Missile Crisis—remained cherished by his countrymen.

Five years after Dallas, Bobby's popular appeal was also for the younger brother himself and what he'd come to represent. Beyond his vocal opposition to the war, he was seen as a champion of the underdog. He spoke out on behalf of the poor blacks of the Mississippi Delta, the youth of the inner city, the isolated whites of Appalachia, the California farmworkers, the forgotten Native Americans on reservations. He just seemed to care. When he saw people in trouble, he wanted to help. Only Bobby Kennedy said the conditions facing this *other* America were, to use his word, "unacceptable." As a politician, he often seemed out there alone in his insistence that America, which he believed deeply to be great, needed also to be good.

Then, eighty days after announcing for the presidency, Robert Kennedy was killed by a bullet just as his brother had been.

There are two main characters in Bobby's story. One was his father. When Joseph P. Kennedy, one of the country's richest men— arrogant, outspoken, autocratic, widely disliked—came even himself to realize that he was politically unacceptable, his single-minded goal was to propel his firstborn all the way to the White House. He put all his ambitions into his oldest and namesake. Positioned from birth as the ultimate American winner, Joe Jr. became the vessel of every bit of glory his father could dream of, the one chosen to inherit the family claim on history.

Yet American involvement in World War II—a prospect Joe Sr. had opposed to the point of villainy—would take from him this oldest boy upon whose future he had set his heart.

Robert—seventh of his children, third among his sons, born between two world wars—found himself from an early age enmeshed in his own life's struggle. In the eyes of his demanding dad, he simply lacked the qualities the father believed to be of any value.

From childhood on, Bobby showed a large heart and generous spirit, both traits believed by Joe Kennedy to count for nothing. As utterly chilling as it sounds, a close family friend—Lem Billings, Jack's boarding school roommate—recalled, decades later, Joe's response when he'd praised young Bobby as "the most generous little boy." Replied the senior Kennedy dismissively, "I don't know where he got *that*."

Bobby's true nature was known to those up close, his mother, Rose, among them. "It's pretty easy to watch somebody compete fiercely and see the grimace on his face," Jack's close friend Chuck Spalding observed of the younger brother he'd known since his boyhood. "You see that and then you translate it into terms of ruthlessness. But what you don't see is the softness, because it's been disciplined not to show." Jack's bride, Jacqueline, newer to the family, could discern nonetheless that Bobby, of all his children, was the *least* like the father.

Even when trying hardest not to show his different side—playing Harvard football, or serving in the navy—the younger Kennedy couldn't help but reveal himself if circumstances evoked it. When he heard a popular Boston priest preaching the doctrine of "no salvation outside the Church"—he openly challenged him from the pews, later writing a letter of complaint to Boston's Cardinal Richard Cushing. The devout Rose Kennedy worried that her boy had gone too far—until she saw the intolerant priest excommunicated.

But Rose Kennedy worried about her third son. She saw how open and vulnerable Bobby was, how his natural sweetness might work against him. With four sisters between him and his next-oldest brother, Jack, she feared his winding up "puny," even "girlish." The father's judgment was harsher. It bordered on outright dismissal. Bobby could feel it. It didn't take this young boy long to realize he needed to show his father—and show him repeatedly—how tough he was.

The other main character in Bobby's life was Jack. Though their shared heritage was on both of their map-of-Ireland faces, the two brothers hardly made for a match. For obvious reasons of age as well as personality, they'd never been close when young. "All this business about Jack and Bobby being blood brothers has been exaggerated," their sister Eunice once revealed. "They didn't really become close until 1952, and it was politics that brought them together."

Jack and Bobby simply were different, always. And by the scorecard of the day, the advantage went to the older. Jack was elegant, Bobby awkward. Jack was charming, confident socially, jaunty as Joe Jr. had been. Bobby was smaller and quieter, less naturally gifted at athletics than his brothers and sisters. He was moodier and more anxious. He liked being alone.

Jack, meanwhile, was one of this world's sunny princes. His longtime close friend Chuck Spalding—they'd met in 1940, when in their early twenties—once offered to me a wonderfully vivid description of the effect Jack had on companions. He made you feel, Spalding said, as if "you were at a fair or something."

Bobby Kennedy, for his part, came to reveal a definite aptitude, as his mother put it, "to make difficult *decisions*." That is to say, tough calls, favoring one person's interest over another, saying *no* as well as *yes*; even cutting people out of the action altogether. This tendency wouldn't, as time went on, win him friends.

In 1946, when Jack was just starting off in politics and running for Congress, he didn't even like having his brother around. "Black Robert" he called him, viewing him as too serious, too earnest, too much the straight arrow. One strategy for keeping him out of the way back then had involved sending this twenty-year-old family member off to work in an East Cambridge Italian neighborhood where the campaign didn't expect to get many votes. It worked out surprisingly well. Bobby ended up spending his time playing softball with the local kids and making a hit. Later, the campaign would credit Bobby's own style of community outreach with cutting the rival candidate's margin in those wards.

In the seventeen years they had left together, the brothers' political partnership saw them linked and striving ever higher and achieving ever-greater success—from the House to the Senate to the White House.

The question has long been what the loss of Jack—which Bobby could only bring himself to call "the events of November 1963"— did to him. As a close family member once suggested to me, the effect on RFK in the public sphere amounted to a shift in emotional focus. Before Dallas, he'd focused on going after those he saw as villains. After Dallas, he threw himself into making a difference for those he recognized as life's victims.

Today, a half century after his death, Robert Kennedy is remembered with an emotion very different from the afterglow enshrouding the memory of the brother he'd served. The endurance of the *idea* of "Bobby" is, I believe, because he stood for the desire to right wrongs that greatly mattered then and which continue to matter every bit as much in the twenty-first century. Let me state that more starkly—now more than ever.

When his body was carried south by that twenty-one-car train, leaving New York for Washington—his final destination where he'd join his brother at Arlington National Cemetery—it's estimated that a million admirers lined the route to pay tribute. News footage recorded those mourners, and in my mind's eye I still can see clearly the expressions on their faces—young, old, black, white, men and women, few well-off, all caught up in their shared devastation.

That outpouring along the New Jersey rail tracks captured what the idea of Bobby Kennedy would come to mean. He was, for so many, the one American leader of our lives who refused to turn his eyes from the people swept aside in our country's rush for economic prosperity and global prominence.

Over my years in Washington, I've seen the rarity of hero worship. You'll hear little of such talk in this capital city. In the newsrooms and after-hours watering holes of Washington—where veteran political writers are to be found and where sentiment is kept to oneself—few are recognized. Yet Robert Francis Kennedy is quietly revered as the genuine article. As difficult as he was to figure out, and even at many times to deal with, what thrilled his supporters and scared the hell out of his opponents was that, in matters of justice, they believed he'd do exactly what he said he would.

Following our country's politics has been my passion since the early 1950s. I was a young boy when General Dwight D. Eisenhower—the World War II commander who had received the Nazi surrender in 1945—entered the White House as our thirty-fourth president.

Then in 1960, after Ike had served his two terms, I was riveted by the back-and-forth electoral combat between Senator John F. Kennedy and Vice President Richard Nixon. What decided that turbulent campaign wasn't the posthumously confected image of "Camelot" but rather the Democrat's stirring call to "get this country moving again."

Yet by 1967, with President Johnson in the Oval Office, the aura of the New Frontier was shrouded by the Vietnam body counts on the nightly news.

By the fall of that year, 100,000 Americans—I was one of them—convinced that Lyndon Johnson's continuing war policy had locked their country onto a disastrous path, gathered in the nation's capital to march from the Lincoln Memorial to the Pentagon. Five months later Robert Francis Kennedy stood in the Senate Caucus Room to declare his candidacy for president.

My goal here is to come to grips with his story, who and what he was and what lay beneath the man we saw. Born twenty years before me, he was from a different East Coast city and an environment far more privileged than mine. Yet the familiarities of our Irish Catholic world rang ardently through our everyday lives. I've discovered that the Kennedy family and the Matthews family shared the same conversations, with the same enduring public friends and foes—and, with them, our common triumphs and resentments. As with the other Americans in the melting pot, we found ourselves in a country explained again and again in the language of such handed-down stories.

Having grown up in Philadelphia, in 1963 I went to college at Holy Cross in Worcester, Massachusetts. There, fifty miles west of Boston, on a campus known for years as "wall-to-wall Irish," I learned about the ingrained social attitudes of New England Catholics and their historic friction with the Yankee elite. It was, in fact, a Holy Cross fellow who, back in 1910, had delivered this famous toast at an alumni dinner:

> *And this is good old Boston,*
> *The home of the bean and the cod,*
> *Where the Lowells talk only to Cabots,*
> *And the Cabots talk only to God.*

Like so many Americans of my generation, I've kept up my fascination with the Kennedys. Try to think of the era without them and see if you can do it. It's impossible, really. More than most countries, American politics has tended to the phenomenal, driven by the moment and the person. The national mood often seems to emanate from the White House. When Jack Kennedy was president in those upbeat years of the early 1960s, then again when Bobby ran for president, the special Kennedy atmosphere captured the day. There was a spring in the country's step, an excitement that could also, to those threatened, mean trouble.

Bobby was never to get his moment as the country's leader. There was no Robert Kennedy *era*. What there was—and what remains vibrant in his legacy—was *spirit*. I disagree with those who argue that the younger brother's true soul showed itself only after Jack. I've found good early evidence of that compassion which was later to reveal itself so vividly.

Even when acting the role of his brother's bare-knuckled enforcer, as Jack made his way from congressman to senator to president, he brought an intangible value to the partnership. Jack had the charm, Bobby the conscience.

The narrative running through these pages has been decades in the making. The portrait is that of the public figure I watched with a powerful interest. That said, the account comes from the list of witnesses I've come to trust. They include at the top his wife, Ethel, and oldest daughter, Kathleen, who answered my every question. I've relied, too, on the recorded accounts of his confidant Kenneth O'Donnell, which were made available to me by his daughter Helen.

Not all had known Bobby Kennedy up close. Some were caught up by his message. Among them were the other volunteers with whom I served for two years in the Peace Corps through 1970, those fifty of us who'd left together in late 1968 for Swaziland. Fading quickly behind us as we flew off was an America carrying on in the shadow of Los Angeles and the rioting at a Democratic convention Bobby never got to enter.

Spread out across the Southern African veld, we'd get together whenever we could and sometimes talk of life at home, especially politics. Looking back, I've decided, it was a good time to be away. The America we were missing for those couple of years was turning downcast and divided.

When I returned to the States in early 1971, I began my career in politics working on Capitol Hill for a liberal Democratic senator from Utah. The top aide who recruited me was a young Mormon, Wayne Owens, who had been Bobby's campaign director in the Rocky Mountain states. Wayne held a steadfast reverence for the fallen candidate that could only be termed remarkable. That Bobby's background was different from his own didn't matter; only his principles did. I remember, too, the Capitol engineer who one day reminisced to me about a behavior he'd noted daily. He'd realized one way the senator from New York differed from many other of his fellow liberal Democrats. While they would enter the building, walking past the Capitol Police avoiding eye contact, it was Bobby, he said, who made a point, always, of saying hello.

You might call that a small detail, but it's one that's stuck with me.

I've spent the best part of five decades not just working and living in Washington but also, I believe, intently observing it. I've been fascinated, on occasion repelled, but rarely indifferent. If you ever were to ask me what America needs in its leaders, my answer will vary with the times. When I spot indecision at the top, I'll say "conviction." When I watch a leader muddling through, I want "purpose." When I see hawkishness, I look for the peacemaker.

What is it that's missing today? Here's my straightforward answer. We've gotten so used to treating our politics as zero-sum that we've lost the faith that joint action by the people is capable of bringing joint success. Why can't there be a patriotism that joins us together instead of dividing us?

It's now the accepted wisdom, for example, that the interests of the discarded factory worker and the ignored inner-city youth cannot be met together, so why try? Don't we need leaders eager to champion the future of both? The faces and salutes of those thousands of Americans, white and black, lining the route of Bobby's funeral train make for moving testimony to the fact that this country once had a brave figure who they believed could.

I lived through the times of both Kennedy brothers and carry within me still the memory of those moments when we knew we had lost them. It's often said that we all remember where we were when we heard each was gone. But where are we now? And where are we heading?

I've written two books about John F. Kennedy. My need to know more about Robert pushed me to write this one. He was there at his brother's side, yet was always his own person, contributing and supporting but also taking charge and leading. No one who knew him was indifferent to him. No one who encountered him ever forgot him. In that, he was like his brother. His own path, however, led him elsewhere, into new places and new concerns that, most strikingly, became his heartfelt priority.

It was, after all, Bobby Kennedy of the two, who'd recognized the historic urgency of making civil rights a national priority, who saw how vital it was to elevate the struggle to a main goal of his brother's presidency. It was he who'd argued that ending segregation was a matter of American conscience. Over the following years, up until his own death, one can see clearly how—after that signal beginning, when serving as his brother's vigilant attorney general—he progressed further and further into the role of activist champion of the country's disinherited.

Recognizing the stubborn, burning passion that lay within him, I find myself now wanting to look into his life and understand both the origins and the evolution of that deepening commitment to a greater justice.

Bobby, 12, with younger brother Teddy.

CHAPTER ONE

ALTAR BOY

The Child is father of the Man;
And I could wish my days to be
Bound each to each by natural piety.

—William Wordsworth

The immense wealth and security of the Kennedy family in twentieth-century America must be measured against the horrid poverty of their immediate ancestors. For those who lived, worked, and died on the subsistence farms of mid-nineteenth-century Ireland, life itself hung on the annual harvest of a single crop—the potato, which was the basic food for much of the country. A family had to survive an entire year on those pulled up the previous fall. If a new crop failed, as it did in what's known as the Great Famine, the people starved.

Over a period of years beginning in 1845, owing to a spreading blight, a million tenant farmers and their families, making up much of the country's rural population, died of both hunger and disease.

They were not Ireland's only loss. More than a million others fled across the Atlantic, through what poet John Boyle O'Reilly would call "the bowl of tears."

The English government—at its head Queen Victoria, who'd assumed the throne eight years before at the untested age of eighteen—gave little sympathy, less help. In February 1847, it was announced in the House of Commons that fifteen thousand people a day were dying in Ireland. The young monarch "was so moved" by the ongoing tragedy, as a sarcastic Robert Kennedy would remark more than a century later, "that she offered five pounds to the society for Irish relief." All official assistance issuing from London came, in fact, with a terrible condition: any family accepting it must forfeit its land.

The occasion on which Bobby recalled that history was St. Patrick's Day 1964, in the Hotel Casey's ballroom in Scranton, Pennsylvania. The hundreds seated before Bobby, all wearing formal attire, were proud members of the Friendly Sons of St. Patrick of Lackawanna County. It was a significant appearance, the first speech Bobby had agreed to give in the shocked, grieving months after the killing of his brother in Dallas. Many listening were soon weeping openly.

What Bobby wanted was for the crowd, so close to him in heritage, to hear him explain his and his lost brother's commitment to ending another injustice. He wanted to engage them on an emotional level, connecting their shared past to that of another disadvantaged people: the African Americans. He reminded them how the Irish once had poured into America, escaping the heartlessness of their historic British rulers only to be confronted by the New World's dismissal of their basic humanity.

In Boston, for example, there were NO IRISH NEED APPLY signs everywhere to greet those seeking jobs. "Our forefathers," he pointed out, "were subject to every discrimination found wherever discrimination is known." Now, with Congress engaged in landmark legislation aimed at ending segregation in its Southern strongholds, Bobby was raising the well-known specter of Irish servitude and English disregard to enlist support for it.

It was not the Kennedys' only experience with victimhood. Throughout his life, a very different sort of Irish legacy—one he would never speak of yet would invoke in ways stronger than words—had been carried across the Atlantic by his forebears. This, too, had long been haunting the third son of Joseph P. and Rose Fitzgerald Kennedy. In much of Ireland, tradition had dictated that a farmer, facing retirement, would divide his land among his sons. In County Wexford, on Ireland's southeast coast, where the economy was better off, such rural inheritance was handled differently. There, the father kept his farm intact, awarding it when the time came to the son born first. It was this rule of primogeniture, carried on by Joseph Kennedy—already two generations settled in America—in *this* country that would leave its invisible stain on the young Robert. He was the Irish son who would not get the land.

Bobby's great-grandfather Patrick Kennedy, a third son himself, had arrived in Boston's North End in 1848. In this city the Kennedys stayed and prospered until 1927 when Patrick's grandson Joseph P. Kennedy moved his young family to New York. Again, the reasons had to do with rejection, though now upon a rarefied level.

Joe Kennedy was, by almost every measure, an American success story. A graduate of the prestigious Boston Latin School, he'd gone on to Harvard, class of 1912, where he majored in economics. At age twenty-five, having maneuvered his way to control of a bank, one of whose major shareholders was his father, it was his boast that he was the youngest bank president in the country. Socially, he advanced rapidly amid the Boston Irish elite, marrying the daughter of Boston's mayor, a colorful pol known as John "Honey

Fitz" Fitzgerald. From there, Joe proceeded to new heights, reaching past Boston, wheeling and dealing his way in Wall Street, Hollywood, and beyond. Yet there was a Gatsby quality to him—his rise so meteoric—that his success always carried in equal measure awe and suspicion.

What separated Joe Kennedy from the other Irish around him were the high ambitions deep inside him, ones that couldn't be satisfied by the usual scoreboard. He saw his destiny as grander than a law degree allowing him to put "Esq." after his name, with an income just enough to secure a cottage on the Cape. "The castle or the outhouse," he declared, "nothing in between." What drove him in those early climbing years was what he was prevented from achieving—namely, social acceptance by the gatekeepers of the old New England order.

The doors shut to the Kennedy family had to do with their very name—such an obvious giveaway—and the background it proclaimed. Joe's children—smart, lively, prosperous, attractive, well-schooled—were no different in their own eyes from their Protestant neighbors. They suffered from the basic handicap of their birth. Even if the rejections they faced were not those of employment opportunities slammed in the face of Irish immigrants seeking jobs, the reason was the same. The social gates closed to them were those through which the well-off if newly rich Kennedys believed they had a right to pass. It was not that they'd been given less in the new country; they wanted more.

So it was, in 1927, that the Kennedy family left Boston to settle eventually in leafy, moneyed Bronxville, a short drive from Manhattan. The move south from Massachusetts was hardly of the sort to earn sympathy from onlookers. The travails of the lace-curtain Irish clearly lacked the fearful drama of the exodus across the ocean. But that didn't stop the Kennedys from their refrain. Joe Kennedy and his children would, for the rest of their lives, continue to recount the saga of being forced from their hometown to seek social refuge elsewhere, even if sympathy from listeners was in short supply. As a friendly skeptic, a fellow Irish American, later would put it, Joseph Kennedy was the only person driven out of Boston "in his own railway car."

"Yes, but it was symbolic," his son Robert would insist until the end of his life. "The business establishment, the clubs, the golf course—at least that was what I was told at a very young age. Both my parents felt very strongly about the discrimination." For her part, Rose could rarely bring herself to such an admission. She'd claimed they'd made the move down to New York simply due to her husband's business. But even she would ask in dismay why the "better people" of Boston had closed their doors to them.

It was young Bobby who took the Kennedy self-banishment from Boston—lasting a dozen years, beginning when he was five—to heart. For him, it had the effect of creating a continuum, linking him to blood feelings stirred by stories of the Great Famine and the British indifference to his own family's latter-day exile. It made him more Irish.

The year following the Kennedy family's arrival in Bronxville was a presidential election year, bringing with it a fresh episode of rejection to bind together America's Irish Catholics in their apartness.

The 1928 Republican nominee for the White House was Herbert Hoover, whose name is known to us because he won. His Democratic opponent was Al Smith, a figure often and unfairly lost to history. Born into an Irish Italian family living under the shadow of the Brooklyn Bridge, Smith had been first a newsboy, then toiling long hours at the Fulton Street Fish Market. From there, rising steadily in accomplishments and status—he joined the Tammany Hall political machine, which enabled him to pass through a number of worthy positions, winding up as a four-time governor of New York. He was a city kid made good.

Yet the "Al Smith legacy" is the relevant story here. It's the one I grew up with, exactly as the Kennedy brothers and sisters had earlier. Nominated to head the Democratic ticket, Smith lost to Hoover in 1928, failing even to carry his home state of New York. Why was he beaten? Whatever the fuller, more complicated reasons, we Catholics all knew the answer: because he was one of us.

Others might say differently—that 1928 was still a time of roaring prosperity—and that his Republican rival, Herbert Hoover, had made for himself a first-rate reputation as an economic manager, earning praise for his distribution of U.S. food aid to post–World War I Europe.

Such an argument didn't carry water with us, not enough to displace the often taught belief that anti-Catholic sentiment was widespread enough in pre–World War II America to doom Smith's chances. In short, one reason for Smith's defeat was handed down as if part of the catechism. My mother, born Mary Theresa Shields, of whose five sons I was the second oldest, knew exactly what she believed. As, I'm quite sure, did the pious Rose Kennedy, even if her husband had voted for Hoover.

Being Irish Catholic has always meant a tribal as well as a religious loyalty. Back in Ireland, under British rule, it was "them" versus "us." In America, where it meant to stand in strength against the Protestant majority, it required loyalty to the clan as well as to the faith. Whatever their social ambitions and desire for higher acceptance, the ingrained habits of the Kennedys, as well as their fealty to their shared traditions and rituals, put being Catholic and Irish at its center. Even Jack, the least churchy, would go in and light a candle for his older brother or kneel—a physically painful act for him—at the gravesite of a beloved lost sister or for one of his two lost children.

Yet it wasn't the banishment from Boston alone that forged in the young Bobby such a lasting identification with the way his co-religionists had been overlooked and rejected. There was also a permanent scar left on him by his relationship with his father, which carried a personal experience of rejection. He yearned for Joe's attention and dreaded his disapproval, much as a faithful subject does with a ruler.

Bobby's childhood, already difficult, forced upon him the continual challenge of holding his own amid the pack. Once he raced so hard to get to dinner on time, in desperate fear of the senior Kennedy's wrath, that he smashed his head into a glass wall he thought might prove a shortcut. It left him bleeding. "I was very awkward," he'd later admit. "I dropped things and fell down all the time." Once, not yet having learned to swim, he jumped from a boat into Nantucket Sound to force himself to. That at least caught brother Jack's attention: "It showed either a lot of guts or no sense at all."

But in the way that families arrange themselves, Bobby, the odd child out, endeared himself to his mother and soon became her favorite. A devout Catholic, she took her third boy, overlooked by his father, to her heart, openly calling him her "pet." Responding to the emotional space she made for him, he reciprocated by fully accepting Rose Kennedy's devotion to the Church as his own. He could see that it was a way of making her happy. He would tag along with her to daily mass, not just out of shared piety but also to clearly demonstrate his concern for her—something his brothers decidedly did not. He was "thoughtful and considerate," his mother saw. "And probably the most religious of my sons." Also, others would discover, the least *assimilated*.

The most Irish of the Kennedy children, and always attached to exactly what that meant, it wouldn't be wrong to say he was, despite being a third-generation American, the least changed from the old country.

Bobby adored his older brothers, even if his desire for their company was one-sided. Joe Jr. and Jack were a world to themselves and kid brothers can, of course, famously be nuisances. At night from his room upstairs, hearing them and envying their closeness, he'd long to be part of them, even when the noise was that of a knockdown fight. It was also about the age gap that lay between them, not to mention the presence in between of sisters Rose Marie (nicknamed "Rosemary"), Kathleen, Eunice, and Pat.

As his older brothers matured and were invited to join their parents for political discussions at dinner, Bobby inevitably was marooned with younger sister Jean and later Teddy, the very youngest, at the "little kids' table." "He longed to explore the world with Dad," Jean has written, "and to engage in debate with Joe and Jack. But when he was a toddler the older boys were already headed into their teenage years."

Bobby, as we've seen, was a decade younger than Joe, eight years behind Jack. By the time he was old enough to imagine being at least tolerated as their companion, his big brothers were already off to boarding school. Thus, they seemed to keep widening their lead on him. According to Jean: "Bobby strove to be as near as possible to Joe and Jack every chance he got, and to be respected by them. At dinner time at the kids' table off to the side, Bobby strained his ear to their direction and longed to be their equal." Rose Kennedy, meanwhile, worried at the effect on Bobby of having his adored, if negligent, brothers gone nine months of the year.

Jean remembered how Bobby spent many a Hyannis Port summer playing with local Cape Cod pals of his own. They were the sons of a family maid. "Only looking back," she added, "does it occur to me how uncommon it was during that time in American history for children of different races to play together."

One could argue, of course, that I'm overdoing this emphasis on birth order and favorites. But anyone who's ever experienced the reality of rivalry for parents' affections while growing up will understand. I know very well that my own four brothers continue to have their own individual perceptions and convictions about the way it played out in our house. I sensed from the beginning I had my mom's love without effort, it was Dad's I felt I had to earn. Loving him, and I clearly did, wasn't enough to accomplish the job. I had to work for it.

Whatever else they were, the Kennedys were such a family, with each member contending for his or her space. Here, as elsewhere, life was unfair. While Bobby could comfort himself with his mother's love, Jack didn't have the same experience of Rose's maternal affection.

Unlike Bobby, Jack kept small regard for his mother. Looking back, he was cold in his dismissal of her, once saying she was, in his upbringing, "a nothing." She "never really loved him," Jacqueline Kennedy told author Theodore White a week after Dallas. "She didn't love him," she repeated for emphasis. Meanwhile, he kept a guarded distance from his father. Sick much of the time, and relying on books for escape, Jack would discover his own world. "History made him what he was," his widow believed. "This little boy in bed, so much of the time . . . reading history." As his sister Jean would put it, he was "funny and original, charting his own path regardless of what others thought." Thus, he was able to make a refuge for himself, away from family and doctors.

Bobby, we know, wasn't his brother. He found comfort in Rose's consoling embrace. When it came to his father, he had to keep making his case. It explains his emerging devotion to justice, if only for survival. To be unfavored, as Bobby was, forces you to put forth your claim based on what's right. Early on, his family would often hear him speak of what was "fair" and "not fair." Here he was, with all his family advantages, not yet a teenager, learning the language of the oppressed.

More than his brothers, Bobby clung to the black-and-white strictness of his church's moral order. For the Kennedys—and, a generation later, for me—Catholic instruction, certainly at the catechism level, was blunt when it came to moral teaching. A page in our religion textbooks—which we opened each day in our first-grade class at Maternity BVM—showed three milk bottles side by side. The white one, we were instructed, represented a person's soul in the "state of grace," that is, without sin. The darker bottle replicated a soul that had committed venial, or pardonable, sins. The third bottle was black, indicating mortal sin, which, if not cleansed through the sacrament of confession, meant you were going to hell.

This was Bobby's world. He was the one who took every bit of this to heart. When the time came, he eagerly became an altar boy. He would now be up there with the priest on Sunday morning, the eyes of the communicants on him and his fellow celebrants. These would be the first hours of his life he would be onstage, in this case a holy place. He was sharing his faith; though his body was small, his soul was now large.

His brothers and sisters would hear him in his room practicing his Latin: *Introibo ad altare Dei, ad Deum qui laetificat juventutem meam.* "I shall go unto the altar of God, the God who gives joy to my youth." This was the liturgy of the centuries, spoken in the ancient language of the early Roman Church. It carried with it the aroma of incense and the judgment of the divine. It was hierarchical and mysterious, and it was meant to be as strict in its observance as in its devotion.

Bobby loved it.

Jack and Bobby at U.S. ambassador's residence, London, 1939.

CHAPTER TWO

AMBASSADOR'S SON

"For the second time in our history, a British Prime Minister has returned from Germany bringing peace with honour."

—NEVILLE CHAMBERLAIN

Against the wishes of his staunchly Democratic father-in-law—the former Boston mayor, John Fitzgerald—Joseph Kennedy had quietly voted for Herbert Hoover in the 1928 national election. Kennedy was betting the Republican candidate, who'd served as secretary of commerce under the preceding president, Calvin Coolidge, might now continue the prosperity enjoyed during the course of that administration.

The more revealing truth is that Joe Kennedy's 1928 vote was as much *against* people like himself as it was *for* Herbert Hoover. Whatever else might be said about Kennedy, he had disdain for crookedness, especially in politics, and most especially the Irish kind. He regarded such local political characters as Honey Fitz—

his wife's father—and James Michael Curley not only as corrupt but embarrassing. They reflected badly on his people.

Kennedy lumped Al Smith, Hoover's opponent, in the same category, unfairly. Recognized as an honest and honorable public official, the New York governor nonetheless spoke in the street-corner language of New York City and when he addressed crowds, threw kisses to supporters as if he were a matinee star. To Kennedy, Smith's urban accent and lack of reserve made him the type of machine-turned-out pol he found most repellent.

The Crash of 1929—in a way few outsiders could imagine— was afterward viewed by Irish Americans as evidence the Lord, in fact, was looking out for us. Our reasoning went like this: had Smith won the election the year before, he undoubtedly would have had to shoulder the blame for the Great Depression that followed. And by extension, his fault would be ours as well. Had the first of our faith—in this case, Smith—won the election, the victory he'd achieved would have preceded a calamity, and that, too, would have belonged to us. Our first president would have been our last.

Events took a different course. So bleak was the economic outlook by 1932 that even tough businessmen like Joseph P. Kennedy recognized the need for the country to move left. Unless action was taken to stanch the massive economic bleeding, even a revolution might be possible. Just as Kennedy had voted Republican four years before, believing it would keep the country booming, he now was willing to look to a Democrat to keep it from failing. So worried was he in the spring of 1932, he later claimed, he would have given up one half his wealth as long as he could be sure of keeping the other.

He looked upon the new governor of New York, Franklin Delano Roosevelt, as that insurance policy. "I was really worried," Joe would later tell a Boston reporter. "I knew that big, drastic changes had to be made in our system and I felt that Roosevelt was the one who could make those changes. I wanted him in the White House for my own security."

So it was that he began enthusiastically drumbeating as an open supporter of the Democratic candidate. It wasn't only about the economy. He also viewed the patrician Roosevelt as the president most likely to present a responsive face to the American groups for so long shut out, the largest of whom were the Catholics. To Joe Kennedy, FDR loomed as a door opener.

His most effective maneuvering on behalf of Roosevelt's nomination took place behind the scenes. When his candidate failed to win the necessary two thirds' support on the first ballot at the Democratic National Convention in Chicago that summer, Kennedy quickly saw what he might do to remedy the situation. He went to his pal William Randolph Hearst, the press baron whose chain included newspapers in San Francisco and Los Angeles that had great influence over the California delegation. Hearst was backing Speaker of the House John Nance Garner for president. Kennedy now convinced him that his man had no chance and should instead throw his delegates to Roosevelt. To return the favor, FDR picked Garner as his running mate.

For what he'd so critically helped deliver, Joe Kennedy expected in return a swift and sizable patronage reward. Yet for months, throughout the whole of 1933, the new president held back, keeping him at bay, aware of his recent ally's impatience but ignoring it. The fast-buck men of Wall Street had brought on the Crash. Why welcome one of its most notorious figures into the new government?

It wasn't until the spring of 1934 that President Roosevelt relented. With his administration seen as moving leftward, he needed to signal balance by bringing on board a well-recognized symbol of Big Money and political moderation. The job he was offering to Kennedy was to be envoy to Ireland, which by then had gained a limited autonomy. For Joe it was a negligible posting, one hardly matching his ambitions. He refused it cold.

Not long after, however, a far better employment proposal was put on the table for Joe to consider. In 1934 Roosevelt had just created a federal body to regulate the stock market, to be called the Securities and Exchange Commission. He proposed making Joseph Kennedy its first chairman. Who better to protect American stockholders from men like him? Joe agreed to take on the challenge, and went on to head up the SEC for more than a year. Mandated to put a stop to the manipulation and deception that had brought on the Crash, he would prove himself just the right man for the difficult job.

When the time came for FDR's reelection push in 1936, Joe remained loyal. Using his own money, he published and distributed a book entitled *I'm for Roosevelt*. He argued that FDR's programs had saved the country and capitalism from the Great Depression. It was a sales pitch based on self-interest. By his accounting, the richer you were the more you benefited from FDR's progressive policies.

The country's wealthiest Catholic also made a sectarian case for the president. With Roosevelt's shift to the left branded by a faction of more conservative Democrats—including a resentful Al Smith— as "Communist," Kennedy defended him in a way that would appeal to his fellow Catholics. He argued that the New Deal programs, especially Social Security, actually had much in common with their own teachings. To reach a wider Catholic audience, including its proud and populous "subway alumni," he played the Notre Dame card. How, Joe would ask, could a Catholic question the worth of any man to whom, only the year before, that university had awarded an honorary degree, citing his "faith and invincible courage"?

With Roosevelt's 1936 reelection sweep, winning all but two states, he came to Joseph Kennedy again at the start of 1937, asking him to chair the new U.S. Maritime Commission. The position offered Joe the challenge of building up the country's merchant marine. It proved another success for both men. By the end of the year, the president realized a greater reward needed to come next. He sent his son James to learn what would satisfy Kennedy, who'd done such loyal service.

Kennedy's first pick, James reported back, was secretary of the treasury. But if he couldn't have that, he'd suggested ambassador to England. When FDR heard this, he "laughed so hard he almost toppled from his wheelchair." He sent his son back with a counteroffer: secretary of commerce. Kennedy turned that down flat.

The tough businessman knew it was time to close the deal. He would accept no appointment but the one on which he and Rose had set their hearts. Confronted with Kennedy's deal-or-no-deal insistence, Roosevelt agreed. He sent word to immigrant Patrick J. Kennedy's grandson that he was granting his wish. He was going to be U.S. ambassador to the Court of St. James's.

It was the reverse of their grandparents' forced journeys in steerage. Rose and five of her children were now, in triumph, heading across the Atlantic to join her husband in Britain, traveling in the full luxury due a wealthy tycoon's family. Young Bobby can be glimpsed in a newsreel interview expressing his pleasure at the trip ahead: "This is my first trip to Europe and I am very excited," he said from the New York pier as they were about to board the SS *Manhattan*. "I couldn't even sleep last night!"

Arriving in London, the Kennedys—particularly the golden trio of Joe, Jack, and sister Kathleen (known as "Kick")—found themselves in a glowing spotlight. Their new circle of upper-crust friends, perhaps enjoying their novelty, kept them out every night. They were the toast of London—in a city where worries of a coming war broke down inhibitions and made for a heightened gaiety. All the time Joe Sr.'s focus remained sharply on his oldest, now twenty-three, giving him the title of his "secretary." It became the mark of his emerging status.

The younger Kennedy children, entering British classrooms, saw London as a very different city than did their wined-and-dined elder siblings. Bobby, with no voice in the matter, found himself enrolled at the Gibbs School for Boys in Chelsea. Diplomat and Conservative politician David Ormsby-Gore—who first met Jack during this era and would become his lifelong friend—was a witness to how "acutely embarrassed" and unhappy Bobby was by the red cap all Gibbs boys were forced to wear as part of the school uniform.

During these months of 1938, the mood in London was watchful, its fate dangerously poised on the brink. The reality of Adolf Hitler's menacing rise was each day more unavoidable. Appointed German chancellor only a month before Roosevelt's first inauguration, he was the dark specter haunting the countries of Europe—and the world beyond. Leader of the increasingly dominant Nazi party, he made his path to power by emphasizing national pride and German identity, and vowing to redress the many grievances of the country's World War I defeat. His urgent goal was the annexation of lands on his borders, where lived large numbers of ethnic Germans. In order to make this happen, he committed himself to smashing the Versailles Treaty, which in 1919 ended the Great War between Germany and the Allied Powers, and placed postwar restrictions on German armaments.

Just days after the Kennedys established themselves in the ambassadorial residence in Prince's Gate, Hitler began keeping his promises. Marching into Austria, he bloodlessly claimed it for Germany, throwing the Jewish population there, as Germany's own was already, into imminent peril.

The new American ambassador seemed more concerned by the newspapers' reaction than the infamy itself. As far as he was concerned, the banner headlines back home reporting on Hitler's takeover were intended to spur the American public into accepting a war. Joachim von Ribbentrop—the German ambassador in London who was soon to be appointed his country's foreign minister—reported on a conversation he'd had with Kennedy. It concerned "the agitation against us in the American press." Ribbentrop felt that he now had insight into Kennedy's thinking. He concluded that his "main objective was to keep America out of any conflict in Europe." In Ribbentrop's view, Joe Kennedy's real enemy was what he saw as the war hawk press.

Kennedy soon repeated a similar sentiment to the Third Reich's new ambassador to America. What Herbert von Dirksen remembered being told was that "it was not so much the fact that we wanted to get rid of the Jews that was so harmful to us, but rather the loud clamor with which we accompanied this purpose. He himself understood our Jewish policy completely."

Kennedy explained how in Boston, where he came from, it was not only Jews but Irish Catholics, like himself, who had suffered discrimination. "Such pronounced attitudes were quite common," Dirksen quoted Kennedy, "but . . . people avoided making such an outward fuss about it." The Protestant majority back then, Kennedy allowed, didn't have to face, as Germany now did, an American press "strongly influenced by Jews."

In short, the United States ambassador in London, descended himself from a shunned and shunted-aside minority, told two different representatives of the Third Reich that their government's harassment and persecution of their Jewish citizens was not the issue. In Kennedy's view, public relations was the real problem. By repackaging their Jewish policies for outside consumption, they would solve it.

"While telling them what they wanted to hear about American anti-Semitism and Jewish media dominance," Joseph Kennedy biographer David Nasaw has observed, "he was not saying anything he did not believe himself."

Upon his arrival in London, Joseph Kennedy had swiftly established a strong relationship with British prime minister Neville Chamberlain. Both men were in agreement on what appeared to them the greater wisdom of letting Hitler play out his hand. They were willing to let him stretch Germany's borders in land grabs that could, with closed eyes and a bad conscience, be accepted as reasonable territorial demands, thereby avoiding another European war.

In the last week of September 1938 Chamberlain traveled to Germany several times. But not until the waning hours of the 29th did he and the three other European leaders with whom he was meeting—Adolf Hitler; the Italian dictator Benito Mussolini, who in 1936 had agreed to a treaty with Germany; and the French prime minister, Édouard Daladier—sign what is known as the Munich Agreement. There in the Führerbau, Hitler's Munich headquarters, Chamberlain, wanting nothing more than to keep Britain at peace, behaved expediently—thereby turning his name into a synonym for ignominious retreat: *appeasement*.

The deal to which he agreed said, basically, that neither the British nor the French would intervene in Hitler's imminent annexation of the German-speaking areas of Czechoslovakia, which stretched along the eastern German border and were known as the Sudetenland. It was a cold-blooded sacrifice, nothing less. No moral claim could cover it. What drove it was the hope, which Joseph Kennedy also clung tightly to, that this concession would avert a second world war, one that America would be again impelled to enter—and this time threaten his beloved older sons who were of an age to fight.

Winston Churchill, then outside government and not regaining any official position until the autumn of 1939, saw it very differently: "We have sustained a defeat without a war, the consequences of which will travel far with us along our road. And do not suppose that this is the end. This is only the beginning of the reckoning. This is only the first sip, the first foretaste of a bitter cup which will be proffered to us year by year."

But Ambassador Kennedy not only accepted the Munich accord; he went out of his way to offer his support. "It is unproductive for both democratic and dictator countries to widen the division now existing between them by emphasizing their differences, which are self-apparent," he said in a speech on that October day the British annually celebrate Admiral Horatio Nelson's 1805 victory over the combined French and Spanish fleets. "After all, we have to live together in the same world, whether we like it or not." The American ambassador to Britain was endorsing a policy of live-and-let-live with Adolf Hitler, the man who'd grabbed Austria and now part of Czechoslovakia.

Three weeks later came the horrors of Kristallnacht, the Night of the Broken Glass. Across Germany and Austria, violence against Jews raged through the streets, shocking the world. The American ambassador to Great Britain had just been trying to proselytize the notion that democracies and dictatorships needed to share the same world. But Kristallnacht decisively demolished such thinking. Kennedy was now a man fighting history.

In September 1939, Hitler invaded Poland. The new war in Europe was now a reality. Joseph Kennedy, having long opposed the conflict, now responded to Chamberlain's declaration of war on Germany with a personal genuflection to defeatism. Remaining in London himself, he began sending his family back to America and out of harm's way.

He could never shield them from the legacy of "Munich" and his own part in appeasing Adolf Hitler. Although barely a teenager at the time, his father's legacy from London would hang on Bobby Kennedy for the rest of his life.

Joe Jr., Jack, and Bobby with Ambassador Joseph P. Kennedy.

CHAPTER THREE

HONOR THY FATHER

"The most important obligation, binding on everybody, was the preservation, at all costs, of the good name of the family. It is much more powerful than any notion of good citizenship . . . stronger and more compelling than any ethical or moral law."

—Caoimhín Ó Danachair,
"The Family in Irish Tradition"

Returning to the States with his family, Bobby was, by his father's decision, packed off to St. Paul's in Concord, New Hampshire. An elite boys boarding school with Episcopal ties, its alumni list had on it Astors, Biddles, and Vanderbilts. The famed banker J. P. Morgan had gone there as well. It was an institution that meshed perfectly with Joseph Kennedy's ambitions—though not, as it turned out, with the reality of his third son's nature and skills and, more importantly, his needs.

Bobby would say that he was always "going to different schools, always having to make new friends." Only a kindergartner when the Kennedys left Boston, he'd been placed in a public primary school in Riverdale, New York, staying there through second grade. When they next moved—to Bronxville, only a few miles distant—he attended third through fifth grades. For sixth grade, he switched from public to private, enrolling at Riverdale Country School. After this, it was off to England and the despised red cap at Gibbs.

Bobby described himself as "quiet," never troubled by being alone. But at St. Paul's, his adjustment, from the start, was rocky, and his poor performance was a result of that. It was his first time living away on his own from the familiarity of all that he knew: his mother and father, his sisters and brothers, the rituals and rhythms of so many in the same house. Within a month, he was gone.

Whether or not he'd have adjusted—as fourteen-year-old boys often succeed at doing in such cases—his mother's response to her son's difficulties put the blame on the Protestantism of St. Paul's. Though her older sons both had graduated from the very similar Choate, a school also chosen by her husband, Rose's view was that it had none of the spiritual shelter necessary to her keenly faithful third son. Alerted to the fact—and not happy—that the St. Paul's chapel relied solely upon the King James Bible, she decided to remove Bobby and enroll him at Portsmouth Priory, a Benedictine-run school in Rhode Island. If only for the moment, she was able to follow her own wishes regarding the education of her "pet."

She could do so only because her strong-willed husband's attention—ordinarily bent on his boys being educated beside the heirs of the American establishment—was elsewhere. Still in London and still the United States ambassador, Joseph Kennedy was starting to contend in earnest with the challenge of his own diminishing credibility.

At this point, Kennedy needed a corrective PR campaign of the type he'd suggested to the Nazis. Seen as an "appeaser" on both sides of the Atlantic, America's man at the Court of St. James's had backed himself into a bad corner. He'd allowed himself to appear, certainly to his harshest critics, an apologist for Adolf Hitler.

Claiming that his sole concern all along had been to avoid war, it didn't square with his well-known remarks on the subject.

Kennedy had surpassed even Neville Chamberlain in his desire to appease the German chancellor. Britain's prime minister had realized at last the folly of trusting any deal with Hitler. In demanding the territory that was the Sudetenland, the Führer had spoken only of his goal to restore German-speaking populations to the Fatherland. He then trampled on that claim when the Wehrmacht marched into what was left of Czechoslovakia in the spring of 1939.

More even than an appeaser, Joe Kennedy was, from the start, a defeatist. Before Munich, he'd flown famed aviator Charles Lindbergh to England to argue that German airpower could devastate London and Paris. Then, with Hitler unchecked, Kennedy kept up the idea, against all the evidence, of reaching "good relations" with Germany.

In truth, Joe Kennedy was never a team player, and the less savory aspects of this self-interested maverick were now pushing through the polished surface he'd so carefully cultivated. He'd gotten where he was being exactly who he was—by relying upon his instincts and his own distinct vision of the world. "Ruthless"—the word so often applied to him—had fit him his entire life and still did.

But now he was floundering. On the most vital question of the day—whether his country should aid a beleaguered Britain against Adolf Hitler, the American ambassador was opposed. He had one thought, and one thought only: a sustained British resistance to Hitler only insured the inevitability of a United States entry.

On May 10, 1940, eight months after Britain and France declared war on Germany, the "Phoney War"—the name given to the period in which the belligerents held only to defensive positions—abruptly ended. Suddenly Hitler's panzers were racing through Belgium, the Netherlands, and Luxembourg, and on into France.

In July, Hitler prepared to invade Great Britain. His first target was Royal Air Force fighter bases, needing to crush them in order to permit a sea assault across the English Channel. For two months, German bombers struck at the British airfields and industrial targets. Starting in September, the target became London itself. And now came the Blitz. With unceasing attacks day and night, German bombers carried out raids aimed at crippling British morale. More than a million buildings were hit and tens of thousands killed. Walking along Piccadilly, Joseph Kennedy told a companion, "I'll bet you five to one any sum that Hitler will be in Buckingham Palace in two weeks."

Against this terrifying backdrop, with Europe and Britain in mortal struggle against a demoniac foe, the three adult Kennedy men each now continued on his path. Joe Sr., the father, carried on with his ambassadorial duties, even as President Roosevelt pushed him further to the sidelines, choosing to communicate directly with the new prime minister, Winston Churchill. Joe Jr., who'd graduated Harvard in 1938, the same year his dad received the ambassadorship, had returned there after his stint as his father's secretary to enter Harvard Law. Jack, for his part, finished his undergraduate degree at Harvard just as the war entered the deadly phase that would last over the next five years.

As his senior thesis, Jack—who the year before began taking seriously his studies for the first time—wrote "Appeasement in Munich." In it he offered his thoughts about the fateful decision made by Neville Chamberlain when he'd met with Hitler, Mussolini, and Daladier. Praised by professors, and encouraged by his father, he transformed the paper into a bestselling book, *Why England Slept*, published the year he graduated. He took the title from a recent book by Churchill, which was a collection of his speeches, starting in 1932, warning Britain about the rise of German military power and its own need to rearm.

Jack Kennedy took a nuanced angle on the Munich decision. He defended Chamberlain's failure to fight in 1938, but accepted Churchill's argument that Britain had been guilty of not being *prepared* to confront Hitler. He carried the argument further, writing that his own country must not make the same mistake. Jack was using his book as a megaphone, exhorting his country to prepare itself for war and, at all costs, to avoid finding itself in the same weak position as Britain in 1938.

In July of 1940, Franklin Roosevelt, breaking the two-term tradition set by George Washington, was again nominated to head the Democratic ticket in that November's presidential election. His opponent, Wendell Willkie, an Indiana lawyer and businessman, had been an active Democrat until the year before.

By October, FDR had reason to think his man in London increasingly a public problem, political and diplomatic both. Kennedy had continued to make abundantly clear his belief that the British would lose the war. Defiantly, he persisted in fighting Roosevelt's plan to send Churchill fifty destroyers in return for long-term leases on U.S. naval bases on British overseas islands.

FDR was worried also about Catholic voters defecting from the New Deal coalition. One was Kennedy's own son, Joe Jr., who as a

Massachusetts delegate to the Democratic convention had backed Roosevelt's opponent James Farley over the third-term issue. Roosevelt had hopes Kennedy senior would agree to one last timely service: a nationwide radio address urging his reelection. An election eve broadcast from such a prominent and successful Irish American would be an eleventh-hour boost.

Joseph Kennedy had been signaling his wish to come home, and now asked for a "consultation" with the president. Roosevelt obliged, summoning him back. Stopping over in Bermuda, he contacted the White House to say he'd be late arriving in New York. Getting on the phone, FDR was "very pleasant." He urged Joe—and Rose, who was joining him—to come directly down to the White House for the night.

Lyndon Johnson, then a junior Texas congressman and fervent New Deal supporter, happened to be in the room with the president when he spoke to Joe. Here's the version he left of the conversation he overheard as he sat there. First, there was FDR's brief opening retold LBJ style: "Joe, how are you? Been sittin' here with Lyndon just thinkin' about you, and I want to talk to you, my son. Can't wait. Make it tonight." After hanging up—again here in Johnson's telling—the president turned to him. "I'm gonna fire the sonofabitch," he announced with a grin.

LBJ took glee in sharing his rendering of that one-sided conversation. What gratified him most, obviously, was showing how close he'd been to his political hero, Roosevelt. But it also made clear his unabashed contempt for Joe Kennedy.

Like all good stories, it traveled wide, to be heard incessantly by friend and foe alike. For many of those listeners, it served only to burnish the notoriety of a man whose stubborn public positions—defeatist and even cowardly—in the lead-up to World War II had placed him forever on the wrong side of history. Getting wind of LBJ's gem of a story years later, Bobby Kennedy took it as an insult to his family.

President Roosevelt, of course, won the controversial third term he sought, carrying thirty-eight of the then forty-eight states. He exceeded Willkie's total by five million votes and carried the electoral college by a sweeping 449 to 82.

His task of firing Joseph Kennedy was then made easier by the ambassador's remarks that ran in a *Boston Globe* front-page story on Sunday, November 10, just five days after the election. "Democracy All Done in England" ran the headline on the Associated Press wire, which had picked up the story.

Joe had been interviewed at the Ritz-Carlton. It was Boston's most exclusive and luxurious hotel, expecting its guests to be in either *Who's Who* or *The Social Register*. There he greeted a *Boston Globe* reporter and two writers from the *St. Louis Post-Dispatch* while eating a slice of apple pie. With no ground rules set for the conversation and yet assuming the session was off the record, Ambassador Kennedy spoke frankly. "People call me a pessimist. I say, what is there to be gay about? Democracy is all done." He went on to add, "Democracy is all finished in England. It may be here . . ." He saw the Labour Party's inclusion in the British government leading the country to socialism. He believed American entry into the war would put us on the same road. "A bureaucracy would take over *right off*. Everything we hold dear would be gone."

Kennedy, later feeling the heat for what he claimed were "off the record" remarks, said that he was merely trying to keep the U.S. out of the war. It was too late. On December 1, Joseph Patrick Kennedy offered his resignation to President Roosevelt. His two years at the Court of St. James's were over. The dark stain he'd laid upon his own reputation became an indelible one. It would cast a shadow on his family that never quite went away.

Many of us today know the Kennedys only from the perspective of history. Yet others, like Chuck Spalding, then a new friend of Jack's, were around to see them as a real and lively family. Recounting to me his first visit to Hyannis Port that summer of 1940, Chuck painted an unforgettable picture. Greeting him as he arrived at the big house overlooking Nantucket Sound was a happy crowd of sisters and brothers all yelling down at him from a window. He couldn't tell for sure, but to him they all appeared to be naked. It took him aback. "I regarded myself as fairly sophisticated having gone to prep school and all that," he told me. Yet he hadn't been prepared, he said, for such unselfconscious high spirits. Eventually, he found his pal Jack sitting wrapped in a towel autographing copies of *Why England Slept* to an impressive set of world leaders—including one, he remembered, for the prime minister of Australia.

The Kennedys' joy in life would come, of course, to prove vulnerable. It was the following year, 1941, that brought what Rose Kennedy would call "the first of the tragedies." Her third child and oldest daughter, Rosemary—who'd suffered serious oxygen deprivation at birth—was then living at St. Gertrude's School of Arts and Crafts in Washington, D.C. There, "educable or mildly emotionally disturbed, handicapped girls" were looked after by a small but devoted staff of Benedictine sisters.

Rosemary, in her early twenties, was causing problems: she'd get angry, even violent, striking at people. Worse, especially for her protective father, was her tendency to disappear from the grounds and then be found wandering local streets. Hearing of an experimental surgery—known as a prefrontal lobotomy, a procedure necessitating the cutting away of brain matter—Joe made the decision, entirely on his own, to have it performed on Rosemary at George Washington University Hospital. His hope was, if not a cure, then at least an improvement in her behavior. But it was far from a success.

Greatly more handicapped—that is to say, more infantilized than she'd previously been—Rosemary now was unable to speak or walk. Even personality had been taken from her. From then on, only her father was allowed to see her. For her brothers and sisters, it was as if she'd stepped off the face of the earth. Joe Kennedy never told them the truth of what he'd done.

Rosemary's surgery had been performed in November 1941. It was on Sunday, December 7, that the Japanese air attack on Pearl Harbor naval base brought the war Joseph Kennedy had so feared and so struggled against to America. Joe Kennedy, Jr., and his brother Jack were both already naval officers when the Japanese struck that Sunday morning. Joe was down in Jacksonville taking flight training. Jack was assigned to Naval Intelligence in Washington.

Playing touch football along with Lem Billings on the Washington Mall, Jack got the word on the car radio on their way to his apartment. Up at Portsmouth Priory, Bobby soon caught a glimpse at the coming war when the USS *Ranger*, an American aircraft carrier, headed into Narragansett Bay. Its presence provided him and other students the thrill of watching American planes in their dive-bombing practice. Bobby stayed intent on what was happening in the world beyond his school walls if only to keep up to date for possible conversations with his father. His roommates would quiz him at his request on the latest stories in *The New York Times*.

For the same reason—caring what his father would think—he worried about his grades. "If he got a 77 he would argue for a 78 and not give up," a priest recalled. "He was remembered for that quality more than any other student in the history of this school."

Another way Bobby would likely be recalled by fellow students had to do with his mother's visits. When she came to see him—Portsmouth, after all, had been her choice—he'd courteously introduce her around. But then, once she'd left, he'd have to endure hearing himself mockingly tagged as "Mrs. Kennedy's little boy Bobby."

With the war only a few months old, in the spring of 1942 suddenly Portsmouth Priory joined the list of schools Bobby Kennedy no longer attended. Once again he had no choice in the matter. But this time it was different. Desperate to escape a failing grade, he'd peeked at a stolen exam being shared around the dormitory; he was caught and quickly confessed. Now came a dire warning from his father. It concerned his future. "Don't, I beg you, waste any time." It summed up the senior Kennedy's way of looking at life. For Joe, it was a race, you against the other guy. The earlier you began, the better your chances of winning.

His next stop would be Milton Academy—which, thankfully, would be the last school to go on the list. In November 1942, he transferred there, and the effects, over the next two years, were positive. Founded in 1798, Milton had been established originally as a Massachusetts land-grant coeducational school. But at the turn of the last century, it divided itself into two schools, with boys and girls separate. Though it would later change back, in Bobby's era it remained the traditional New England boys prep school it had become. There he was able to settle and be himself in a way he had not before.

Bobby Kennedy wasn't clever or bookish like Jack, nor did he have that brother's ready charm. He wasn't a classically well-rounded young specimen like his oldest brother, Joe. He lacked his brothers' gift for easy camaraderie, for athletics, for scholastic attainment, for impressing girls. What he had instead was a gut determination to hang in there, to overcome whatever stood in his way. Here's how one teammate described him: "Bobby ran every practice play and tackled and blocked dummies as if he were in a hard-fought game."

At the same time, he seemed to have no interest at all in whether his efforts were approved or not by his classmates. His sense of humor was caustic rather than wry. He had a chip on his shoulder and a short fuse. He was, and liked playing, "the Mick," embracing his Irish rebelliousness.

Most crucially at Milton, Bobby, as Jack had done at Choate with Lem Billings, would forge a lifelong friendship. The new pal's name was Dave Hackett, who lived in Dedham, a neighboring town. Hackett was both a legendary football and hockey star at Milton, in his own day and afterward. He would be a literary legend as well. That's because, having met him one year at summer school, writer John Knowles later used him as a model for "Finny," the prep school golden boy in his classic 1957 novel, *A Separate Peace*.

"I think we became friends right away," Hackett recalled of his first encounter with Bobby. "I think, maybe, my first impression of him was that we were both, in a way, misfits. I think he was a bit of a misfit because of coming in both late and also because of who he was, and so he didn't fit into Milton easily at that time. I think that was because his name was Kennedy and he was an Irish Catholic and Milton was basically an Anglo-Saxon, WASP school." Hackett could have added the father's notoriety, Joseph P. Kennedy's reputation as a "bootlegger."

What impressed Dave about Bobby was his impulsive fearlessness. Hackett couldn't believe it when he saw his new friend—who'd invited him one Sunday to join him at a nearby Catholic church—dart up to the altar. Kennedy was seventeen at the time. "There was no altar boy, and the priest said he needed somebody. So Bobby just got up and became an altar boy." It was this readiness to do what others would be afraid to do that Hackett so admired. "From the moment I met him I knew he would embarrass his friends," Hackett said.

"He would move into those situations where most of us would not. I think if anybody got into trouble he would just instinctively move right into it, whereas most people are too afraid to be embarrassed." He appreciated, too, the fact that Bobby refused to compromise in order to win acceptance, that he refused to tell or listen to dirty jokes, how he would step in when a bigger student was pushing around someone from a younger class.

Bobby loved that Hackett could see all this in him. His father certainly hadn't. He had once asked him if something could be done for the poor people they saw from a train window. The senior Kennedy simply dismissed the question. Dave Hackett, on the other hand, clearly liked what he saw in Bobby. "I think what he did have was always compassion for other people who had problems. I think part of this was that he did not find anything easy. Things did not come easy to him, so he was very sympathetic to other people who did not have it easy. I think what he never had compassion for was . . . wealth that was not used properly by the privileged. He had very little compassion for that."

Looking back to their time together at Milton, Hackett would recall the under-the-radar profile Bobby Kennedy kept there. "I think if you talked to most people who knew him at that time, there would be very few who would have said that he'd be a remarkable person." But if others didn't take notice of Bobby's soul, Hackett did. "I think that his basic character and characteristics were there that made him what he was later on." Here was a friend who valued Bobby's natural human charity and desire to intervene on behalf of the less favored, traits his father couldn't—and wouldn't—ever appreciate or respect.

The two would talk about how they'd never come in contact with people—the poor, especially—who faced lives without the same privileges they had. They also agreed how lucky they were to go to a school like Milton.

The bond held. As Bobby's younger sister, Jean, put it, "Once a person was his friend, Bobby was loyal for life."

Bobby with football teammates on the steps of
the Harvard Varsity Club, 1946.

CHAPTER FOUR

RITES OF PASSAGE

"After every charge and thud of the footballers . . . he felt
his body small and weak among the throng of players."

—James Joyce, *A Portrait of the*
Artist as a Young Man

During his two years at Milton, Bobby's thoughts were never far from the war and his brothers who were fighting it. Eager to get into action, Jack had asked to be transferred from Naval Intelligence to the PT boats. He was now on his maiden voyage as a skipper, headed down to Guantánamo Bay in Cuba. Joe Jr. was a naval aviator anxious to get overseas. "I want to go over there and bomb the hell out of those Nazis," he told one of his Choate classmates. It was a marked shift from the antiwar attitudes he'd shared with his father.

His mother, taking her husband's lead, played into this wartime rivalry between Jack and his older brother. She did this by conspicuously wearing Joe Jr.'s gold wings, which he'd given her, the recognition of his new status as a naval aviator. The fact that she never went anywhere without it prompted Jack to seek equal billing: he had her turn his PT boat silver tie clip into a brooch.

Meanwhile, the third brother was showing his spirited independence. In a letter to his mother he described talking to his father and hearing his latest scheme to have FDR call him into action. Since Joe's pre–December 7, 1941, posture on U.S. intervention had drawn wide scorn, Bobby couldn't resist a shot at the old man. "Dad just phoned from N.Y. and said he was going down to Washington . . . to see the president tomorrow which sounds pretty exciting for the president, but I suppose there are other almost as exciting things happening in life right now."

In February, Bobby's second semester at his new school, Jack shipped out for the South Pacific. While still aboard the transport USS *Rochambeau*, he had his first glimpse at the war he was about to enter. A Japanese pilot, shot down while attacking their vessel, now was floating off the side. Suddenly he threw off his life jacket, pulled out his gun, and started shooting up at the bridge, clearly attempting to kill the captain and other officers. For the first time, it sank into Jack that with enemies like this, the war was going to be a long one.

Lieutenant (junior grade) Kennedy and his twelve-man crew were assigned to the Russell Islands at the end of May 1943. Their dangerous job was to attack the Japanese convoys regularly passing through. In the dark early morning hours of August 2, an enemy destroyer cut Jack's wooden-hulled boat in half, killing two of his men. Kennedy then led his crew to a tiny deserted island nearly four miles distant. Their endurance reaching it was remarkable, his own even more so—for he swam four hours in enemy waters while pulling a badly injured crewman, Patrick McMahon, by a strap clenched in his teeth. For six days, Jack held his men together, on two different islands, towing engineer McMahon a second time, never quitting his duty to signal possible rescuers. He would later downplay his extraordinary heroism, saying, "It was involuntary. They sank my boat." But no one believed it.

Thrilled by his brother's courage at sea, Bobby was now eager to join Jack in the South Pacific. This struck Jack as a horrible idea and he let his parents know it.

> I don't think he should. By the time he's ready to get out here the usefulness of the boats will be done, I think. I think he should go into that V-12 [the naval officers training program] and stay there for a good long time. He's too young to be out here for a while. When he has at least a year of college he'll be more effective and he will be better able to handle a job. The war will last long enough for him. . . . Try to come steaming out here at 18 is no good. It's just that the fun goes out of war in a fairly short time and I don't think Bobby is ready yet to come out.

That October, about to turn eighteen, Bobby went on his own and enlisted in the Naval Reserve as an apprentice seaman. It was what he wanted most to do. His father, however, had other ideas. Through the senior Kennedy's hasty intervention, Bobby was quickly released from active duty and ordered to enter the officers training program as Jack had recommended.

In March 1944, leaving Milton early, Bobby began the V-12 officers training program at Harvard. In a letter to Dave Hackett, he wrote: "We haven't really had too much action here on Harvard Square, but we're on the alert at every moment. Wishing I were still back at Milton where, although I might not have any friends, I had a radio I could listen to and had pictures of my family I could look at." He also joked "the hope still remains in the family that the navy will make a man out of me."

Then he added mischievously, his tribalism coming to the fore: "Say hello to all the Irish Catholics for me and tell 'em that next to John F. Fitzgerald and J. P. Kennedy, I'm the toughest Irishman that lives which makes me the toughest man that lives." It was a boast about his grandfathers they both could enjoy, since Milton's "Mick" population was quite small.

In the summer of 1944, Bobby was on the Cape. Jack, returned to the U.S., was still laid up in Boston's Chelsea Naval Hospital recovering from back surgery. That June he had been awarded the Navy and Marine Corps Medal. It cited him for "extremely heroic conduct as Commanding Officer of Motor Torpedo Boat 109." Strangers, seeing Bobby in Hyannis and mistaking him for Jack, would stop him on the street to offer their congratulations. He loved it!

Brother Joe, however, had a more conflicted response to Jack's "outstanding courage, endurance, and leadership." At a farewell dinner in his honor—he was heading off to Britain to start duty as a naval aviator—he had to listen to the following toast: "To Ambassador Joe Kennedy," a guest proposed, "the father of our hero, our own hero, Lieutenant John F. Kennedy of the United States Navy."

The tribute the guest intended and what Joe heard were two different things. His father repeatedly told his children, "We don't have any losers around here. In this family we want winners—and don't come in second or third—that doesn't count." How could the younger Joe feel any different?

Later that night, Joe was seen lying in his bed, clenching and unclenching his fists, saying loudly to himself, "By God, I'll show them." It wasn't an idle boast. By that August, he'd already completed his designated number of missions, along the way losing a copilot as well as a number of other close friends. Yet he'd kept refusing to accept the leave due him. Instead, he'd obstinately continued to fly combat missions through June and July. When his crew took leave and headed for home, he stayed behind.

One reason he remained was the news he'd heard of an upcoming mission both secret and highly dangerous. "He had already written us a letter telling us that he was on his way home," Jean recalled. "But then another letter arrived. He'd volunteered for just one more assignment before coming home."

Joseph Kennedy associate Arthur Krock was one of those who believed the motive driving his eldest son to further risk was a desire to rescue the family name. "I share the opinion of some," Krock wrote, "that Joe had been influenced to undertake his fatal final mission—after having completed all his scheduled flights and well knowing the hazard—to disprove a slander, common among the British of that time of their resentment against the Ambassador's Boston interview, that the Kennedys were 'yellow.'"

The lieutenant's assigned target was a V-2 rocket-launching site in Normandy. When approaching it, the mission called for him to bail out, leaving his plane filled with high explosives over to the remote control of a pair of bombers flying alongside. Before he could do this, his plane exploded.

In his last letter to his son in Britain, Joe told him that he'd figured out why he kept delaying his departure from Europe. "I can quite understand how you feel about staying there because the worst of it is certainly better than anything in the Pacific." Grotesquely, he was telling his son, who was facing the most terrifying mission of his life, that it was all his way to avoid the *real* fighting.

Jean remembered that when the tragic news arrived in Hyannis Port that Sunday the voice of Bing Crosby was rising from the phonograph, crooning the wartime standard "I'll Be Seeing You." It was after the arrival of two priests at the house that Joe Kennedy made the announcement all had been dreading. "Children, your brother Joe has been lost. He died flying a volunteer mission. I want you all to be particularly good to your mother." He then told his surviving children that they must proceed with their plans for the day. Since they intended to go sailing, they did, Bobby obeying along with the others. Jack, never one to take orders, went for a walk alone on the beach.

Here now was mortality in their midst. "Success was so assured and inevitable," Jack reflected, "that his death seems to have cut into the natural order of things."

He understood instantly that buried in the announcement they'd just heard was news addressed to him personally. The torch had been passed.

In November of 1944, Bobby found himself transferred from Harvard's V-12 group to the one at Bates College in Lewiston, Maine. During this period, Dave Hackett—who'd left Milton Academy during his junior year to become an army paratrooper—received an update from him, confessing that he felt his "usual moody self." Bobby went on: "I get very sad at times. If I don't get the hell out of here soon, I'll die."

In Europe, with the Allied forces having reached into Germany, his concern over missing out on wartime action was real. Hearing stories of their Milton classmates' exploits overseas, he told Dave, made him feel "more and more like a draft dodger. I suppose somebody has to be in the V-12, but the attitudes of some of these guys really makes me mad, especially after Joe being killed."

One night at supper, a fellow trainee declared, "I won't be the last man killed." Bobby couldn't let it pass: "That's not the right attitude to have. My brother didn't feel that way." "Your brother is a jerk," the man said, causing Bobby to leap from the table and grab ahold of him by the neck. A witness said it took a group of them to pry Kennedy off.

In March of the following year, 1945, Bobby wrote Hackett again about how much he hated the whole setup at Bates, or as he called it, "this G. D. place." Keeping up his morale was the hope he would soon be a naval aviator like Joe. "It looks like I will fly like a bird and attempt to get my wings of gold. That all sounds very grand, but you know me. . . . I wish to hell there weren't so many problems and that people would have let me alone to do as I wished. But I suppose I simply must be an officer." What he really wanted to do was jettison all the protective family advice, quit all the training, and get into the war, *pronto*.

In April, Franklin Roosevelt, the man who led the country back from the Great Depression and on to victory in World War II, died. He was succeeded in office by Vice President Harry Truman, just months before a mildly known Missouri senator.

By month's end, Hitler and Eva Braun were facing the end in his Berlin bunker. In San Francisco, meetings were being held to plan the postwar order. From every victorious capital came delegates to attend the founding conference of what would become the United Nations. To cover the event from a "serviceman's" perspective, the *Chicago Herald-American* had hired PT boat hero Jack Kennedy.

Back in Maine, Bobby was continuing to be frustrated in his attempts to get into the war. The war in Europe ended on the 8th of

May, V-E Day. Soon after, Bobby dispatched further discouraging news to friend Hackett. He'd not succeeded, after all, in his latest ambition. "Am not going to fly. I found out yesterday as I failed a test in Flight Aptitude. This, of course, hurts me, but everything bad that happens now people say it's God's will so I guess I will chalk that up to it also. I guess the rest of this war is going to have to be won by you and your brothers for I think the Kennedys have all about shot their bolt."

But for the Kennedy family, there now came a stirring moment. On July 26, the U.S. Navy launched a new destroyer, the *Joseph P. Kennedy Jr.* Jean Kennedy was chosen to christen it. "My heart is with it and will stay aboard as long as I live," Joseph P. Kennedy, Sr., said.

With Hitler dead and the war in Europe over, what remained was the war in the Pacific. To end it, President Truman made the decision to use the newly developed atomic bomb on the Japanese cities of Hiroshima and Nagasaki. The result, following a devastation the likes of which the world had never seen, was the Japanese surrender. V-J Day came on the 2nd of September.

Without telling his father, Bobby headed alone to Washington, hoping to convince Secretary of the Navy James Forrestal to release him from officers training and assign him as a regular seaman on the new ship named for his oldest brother. His request accepted, he was scheduled to report for duty in February of the new year.

It was then, in early 1946, that Bobby—now a swabby, or regular seaman—headed off on the *Joseph P. Kennedy Jr.*'s maiden voyage in the Caribbean. It must have been an extraordinary experience, to sail aboard a destroyer bearing the name of the brother who'd been such a vital force and influence for the first twenty years of his life.

From Guantánamo Bay, he sent a sympathetic view of his ship-mates, who were mostly Southerners. They possessed, he wrote family friend Lem Billings, "a lot of something a lot of those guys at Harvard lacked." In a letter to his parents, he phrased it differently: "I certainly am meeting people with a different outlook & interests in life."

Though his active service aboard the *Joseph P. Kennedy Jr.* would be brief, his impulse to give up officers training and enlist as a common seaman had been a first—large—step toward being his own person.

What was hard to deal with was his sense of failure at having seen no action in the war. It counted for little that it had been largely his family's decision and not his own. That didn't work for him as a man. He couldn't help feeling forever open to the charge he might have found a way to risk himself in combat, but hadn't. There would always be that question he dreaded most, "Where were you in the fighting?"

When Bobby returned to dry land in the spring of 1946, he joined a conflict of a different sort. Few were not aware that Joseph Kennedy had long wanted his namesake, Joe Jr., to enter politics. Fate had intervened, making Jack now the bearer of that ambition. Yet what happened next was not, as often portrayed, a case of his being press-ganged into service. Bobby, as Jean observed, was the obliging one, forever wanting his father's approval. Jack did what *he* wanted to do.

After his brief foray stringing for the *Chicago Herald-American* at the U.N. conference, Jack had realized what he wanted was to make news, not cover it. His experience in the South Pacific had changed him. "The war makes less sense to me now," he wrote, "than it ever made and that was little enough—and I would really like—as a life's goal—in some way at home or at some time to do something to help prevent another."

His old friends weren't surprised. It was only partly, the way they saw it, the acceptance of a family obligation. Here's Lem Billings's view: "I think a lot of people say that if Joe hadn't died, Jack might never have gone into politics. I don't believe this. Nothing could have kept Jack out of politics. I think this is what he had in him, and it just would have come out, no matter what."

By the spring of 1946, when Bobby received his honorable discharge, his older brother was already headlong into his race for Congress in Massachusetts's 11th District, which comprised Cambridge, Charlestown, and East Boston.

Jack's courageous military service was a big advantage. Still, in the language of politics, he was a carpetbagger. "I had never lived very much in the district," he admitted later, at the start of a planned memoir. "I had lived in New York for ten years and on top of that I had gone to Harvard, not a particularly popular institution in the 11th Congressional District."

To overcome this handicap, he spent months walking up and down the steps of "triple-deckers," those three-story Boston dwellings with families living one on top of the other. For larger groups, he'd pause before entering, putting on what he termed his "BP," the Big Personality, which others would one day call his "charisma."

No one would ever deny the benefit of his father's bottomless war chest. Still, it was Jack himself who was the major selling point of that first campaign. And magnifying the power of his BP—which soon became more natural to him—was the local knowledge of his war record. To reinforce his appeal, of course, the Kennedy money bought saturation exposure in newspapers, on radio ads, in widely distributed campaign literature, and even newsreels featured in local theaters.

Family members threw themselves into the fray with pride and enthusiasm. The youthful vitality of his attractive sisters, especially, who were up from New York, made Jack's home team an eye-catching bunch. Jean looked back on these early days: "Eunice and Pat and I rented an apartment on Beacon Street and took a film around. People would call up and have twelve of their friends and whomever they wanted and then we'd show the film. Instead of getting too much into the nitty-gritty of the questions because none of us were politically astute, we would say what he was like as a brother and things like that."

Bobby Kennedy was just as excited about his brother's campaign. His Harvard friend Kenny O'Donnell remembered it as the first time he'd ever heard him *mention* Jack. "I didn't realize how Bobby worshipped him, could not stop talking about him. I think it was the first time Jack had paid any attention to him."

In truth, Jack wasn't as eager to have Bobby hanging around as his brother was to be a part of it all. The far-from-outgoing Bobby clearly lacked the upbeat nature for dealing either with voters or volunteers. Making an executive decision that his gung ho effort might be better off without his "Black Robert," the candidate fobbed him onto his navy buddy Paul "Red" Fay, who'd arrived from California to pitch in.

"It's damned nice of Bobby wanting to help," Jack told Fay, "but I can't see that sober, silent face breathing new vigor into the ranks." He said the best plan was to make known to the press that the younger brother had arrived to help, but then get him quietly out of the way. "One picture of the two brothers together will show that 'we're all in this for Jack.' Then you take Bobby out to the movies or whatever you want to do."

The photo taken, Fay did as suggested and led Bobby off to a local theater that offered both a film and a live performance. Fay thoroughly enjoyed himself and couldn't stop laughing. For his companion it was a different story. "From his expression," Fay remembered, "he might have been paying last respects to his closest friend."

The next of Jack's buddies to have Bobby handed off to him was Lem Billings, who smoothly dispatched the younger brother out to knock on doors in enemy territory. He'd chosen three wards in East Cambridge, an area where one of Jack's several opponents was expected to dominate. It was here that Bobby's naval experience—the ability to be at ease with people from different backgrounds—came into its own. Instead of doing what was expected, appealing to actual registered voters, Bobby won neighborhood fans by playing softball with the local kids. By being himself, the candidate's brother managed to subvert the reputation of his family. Said a local political figure, "It had the effect of proving the Kennedys weren't snobs."

Bobby, it turned out, had made another conquest. On a group skiing trip to Quebec that Christmas, his sister Jean had brought along her roommate Ethel Skakel from the Manhattanville College of the Sacred Heart in New York City. She had noticed Bobby with more than casual interest. "Wow!" is how she remembered him on first sight. On weekends that spring, she again joined the Kennedys, this time, to help in Jack's election. The campaign "was really fun," she remembered. "We'd ride up to Boston and lick stamps." But she also put in time, when he was around, keeping an eye out for Bobby. Unfortunately for her, "he took a left turn" and started dating her sister. "Ah, that was a black period," she ruefully admitted.

Ken O'Donnell's reaction when Bobby introduced him to his older brother was less breathless. "He asked me to work on the campaign. I said yes, but never followed through. I wasn't that interested in him politically. I just didn't think he had much future in politics."

Thomas P. "Tip" O'Neill, Jr., then a state legislator representing Cambridge, had even less interest in the young Kennedy now running so vigorously, and so visibly. He was backing Jack's top rival, former Cambridge mayor Mike Neville, a political ally. Finally meeting Jack for the first time, Tip was incredulous: "I couldn't believe this skinny, pasty-faced kid was a candidate for anything!"

In Tip O'Neill's old-school world, politics required an approved rise in the ranks, time loyally served, dues paid, and credits amassed. You didn't just come walking in one day, looking boyish and carried aloft by Dad's money, and ask to be elected a Member of the United States Congress. War hero or not.

Tip was far from alone among his fellow Dems and their supporters in his disapproval. Watching the daily outpourings of cash spent on Jack, the backers of one candidate, Joe Russo, began pinning $20 bills to their jackets and calling them "Kennedy Buttons." This mockery would cost him. Locating another Joe Russo, the Kennedy operation got him to put his name on the ballot, too—making for a confusing pair of Joe Russos and siphoning off votes from the original.

But when it came to getting his own name on the ballot, Jack nearly didn't. When the deadline for filing voter petitions of candidacy arrived and then passed, the crucial documents remained in a stack atop a filing cabinet in the campaign headquarters. It was Red Fay who suddenly spotted them after having seen a late-edition newspaper item reporting John Kennedy had failed to file. It was 6:30 p.m. The government offices were closed. Here's Fay's account of what happened next: "Then, very quietly, the candidate and some loyal public retainers went down, opened up the proper office and filed the papers."

In the end, what counted for more than the middle-of-the-night saves, the dirty tricks such as fielding phony candidates, or even the bankroll being spent, was a simple, gripping story told by a masterful writer. In *The New Yorker* for June 14, 1944, the young John Hersey wrote "Survival," chronicling the saga of PT-109 and its commanding officer, Lieutenant (junior grade) John F. Kennedy, who'd made such an extraordinary effort to keep his crew together in a desperate situation. Abridged in the *Reader's Digest*, the article was reprinted by the Kennedy campaign and mailed first class to every household in the 11th Congressional District.

His story set Jack completely apart from the other three candidates for the nomination. None of the others had done anything like it. Only he had the war record, the looks, the charm, and, with all that going for him, the willingness, even with his often crippling back, to climb the stairs of every triple-decker in the district.

Though only twenty-nine, Jack's medical records had already grown voluminous. And now the strains of the effort he'd been making drove him to the edge of his endurance. "He was as thin as a straw," said one onlooker who watched him marching in the annual Bunker Hill Day Parade, held the day before the primary. "We didn't think he'd last the parade." And he didn't. Near collapse, he wound up being taken to the hospital.

The next night, when the results came in Jack had taken 42 percent of the vote and, with it, the Democratic nomination for the U.S. House of Representatives. With few Republican voters in the 11th District, he had, in effect, won a seat in the United States Congress, the same one his mother's father had held.

In September Bobby returned to Harvard, now as a regular student. He was given credit for the two years he'd served in the V-12 officer-training program, leaving him just his junior and senior years to go. But what he cared most about right now was making the football team.

At five-ten and 165, he was an unlikely candidate. But he made it on grit. He would come to practice an hour early, stay an hour later. Knocked down, he would get up again. In friend and biographer Arthur Schlesinger's words, "His real field of concentration at Harvard was football."

Though their father had been a star of Harvard baseball, and Jack had been a splendid swimmer, both winning letters in their sport, none of the Kennedys had won that distinction in football. Jack wasn't healthy enough for the game, and Joe had been kept on the bench in the all-important 1937 Harvard-Yale contest, which kept him from earning his letter. Bobby was determined to do what neither older brothers had done: win that "H" in football.

Ken O'Donnell was certain to get one. His older brother Cleo was captain of the Harvard team in the 1946 season. The brothers had grown up in Worcester where their father had for a decade coached Holy Cross, a team that had just made it to the Orange Bowl. Ken and Bobby had quickly found they had much in common. "I didn't even realize he was Ambassador Kennedy's son," O'Donnell said later. "I read in the *Boston Post* one day that his son had done very well in a scrimmage." They shared, incidentally, an antipathy toward Harvard coach Dick Harlow. Bobby couldn't forgive him for keeping his oldest brother off the field in the Yale game. Ken dismissed Harlow as nothing more than a drillmaster, an erratic one at that.

Like his brother Jack—likely because of it—Bobby was accepted into Spee, a final club. But upon seeing Spee reject another Irish Catholic classmate—he lacked Bobby's Milton Academy stamp of approval—he resigned, and began spending his social time at the Varsity Club hanging around with O'Donnell and the other jocks.

"Bobby began to meet other kinds of people, people who didn't give a damn who he was," O'Donnell recalled. "For Bobby Kennedy the choice of friends could have been very simple. He was obviously one of the more desirable social types. I mean, all the girls would like to have gone out with Robert Kennedy. He was a handsome boy then and very wealthy and from a well-known family. But he made his choice clearly from the beginning. He made a decision about the fellows he wanted to be with, a very irreverent, disinterested group of fellows just out of the service. They had been all over the world. One fellow who hung around with us was a fighter pilot in China who'd just come back from serving with General Chennault."

It should be added here that Ken O'Donnell himself was a figure of heroic stature. In World War II, he'd flown numerous missions over Europe as a bombardier. In one legendary exploit, he'd climbed down into the open bay to loosen a bomb that had gotten stuck. For a few wild moments, he'd been hanging out there over the open sky.

"At first they didn't like him very much," O'Donnell reported of the guys to whom he introduced Bobby. "They didn't want to pay any attention to him; they didn't think he was that good a football player, and they thought he was just a rich kid who happened to be hanging around. But after about six months, he became one of the group."

As O'Donnell described them: "These were fellows returning from the war, ones who could never have gone to Harvard before but had been recruited as football players. Ten or twelve of us lived in the Varsity Club. Bobby spent most of his waking hours there."

His friend also proved himself on the field. "I can't think of anyone who had less right to make varsity than Bobby," O'Donnell said. But he found a way, working his way up from the lowest squad. "He'd come in from his end like a wild Indian. If you were blocking

Bobby, you'd knock him down, but he'd be up again going after the play. He never let up. He just made himself better."

He faced serious competition for a slot on the team. It was before the Ivy League was formed, when Harvard was still offering athletic scholarships, still engaged in big-time football. The team went 7 and 2 that season, reaching 18th, at one point, in the national rankings.

Bobby's new crowd talked often about politics. Ken was a steadfast defender of the New Deal and Roosevelt. Bobby was just as tough on offense, taking his father's skeptical position on FDR.

In November, at the end of the season, Bobby invited the entire football team out to Hyannis Port, the occasion being his twenty-first birthday. In recalling the scene, O'Donnell paints a vivid picture: "Quite bluntly, they weren't the type of fellows Joseph P. Kennedy was used to his son associating with—or any of his children. I think he was a bit taken aback. Jack's friends were the Lem Billings type: elite, educated. Bobby's crowd, myself included, were rough, tough fellows, returned war vets, hardened by what we'd seen."

Bobby's friends were even less impressed with their host and let him know it. "Helping themselves to his alcohol, testing his cigars and pulling out books, all without being asked or invited to." O'Donnell was replaying the scene in his memory. "None of us liked him because of what he had done in the war, and he had to know that by the way he was being treated. I don't think he was used to that . . . certainly not in his own home."

The one person most appreciating these two worlds colliding was Bobby. He understood only too well what he was watching. And he savored it. Joseph Kennedy had wanted his third son to toughen up. Well, look at him now . . . the boy his father had called a "runt" was showing him who he'd become.

"I remember being kind of disgusted because at that party his father presented him with an enormous check for keeping the pledge," O'Donnell recalled, which was not to drink or smoke until he reached twenty-one. It was a promise neither of his older brothers had succeeded in keeping. "I thought it was fairly disgusting if that's the best your father can do is write you a check as opposed to spending time with you. But, again, I realized Bobby had a fairly tough relationship with the old man."

There was one person Bobby most wanted Ken to get to know. "We arrived earlier than the others because Bobby wanted me to meet Jack." Meeting the newly elected congressman in person came as a surprise to O'Donnell. He spotted in Jack a quality he hadn't before. It was mutual. "Jack seemed quite astonished that this rough, tough crowd were not only Bobby's friends but that Bobby fit in with us so well." The older brother quickly became the center of the party.

Jack Kennedy had won the general election that November with 73 percent of the vote. That same night, two other war veterans were among the many who won seats in Congress in that first postwar election: Richard Nixon, a California Republican who'd been a navy officer, and the new senator from Wisconsin, Joseph R. McCarthy, a marine. The latter boasted that he possessed the electoral advantage of being "a Republican with a Democratic name."

Bobby Kennedy began his senior year by scoring a touchdown in Harvard's 52–0 opening-game trouncing of Western Maryland College. Days later, he appeared to be out for the season, with a broken leg. Valiantly, he'd tried to continue playing until it became obvious he couldn't.

As a salute to his guts, Coach Harlow ended up putting him in, despite his condition, in the final game, against Yale. Because of that gesture, Bobby reached the goal on which he'd set his heart. "He had a broken leg; he had a cast on his leg," his future wife, Ethel, later looked back admiringly at her Bobby. "He really wanted to get his letter."

By season's end, Bobby was not only hanging out with the hardened jocks, he was one of them. No longer the sensitive soul of his altar boy days, he'd earned his father's respect—but at a price.

Bobby and Ethel on their wedding day, June 17, 1950.

CHAPTER FIVE

COMMITMENT

*"For anyone to achieve something, he will
have to show a little courage."*

—ETHEL KENNEDY

World War II, which began for Europe in 1939 and for the United States two years later, came to its final awful end by late summer 1945. But the state of euphoria felt by the victors after the long conflict soon started its retreat.

Three months before V-E Day, Franklin Roosevelt, Winston Churchill, and Joseph Stalin met in Yalta, a resort city on the Black Sea, to plan the landscape of postwar Europe. Stalin had insisted on holding on to military and political control of the countries of Eastern Europe—above all, Poland—as a buffer against possible German aggression. What Americans at the time would remember is that the Soviet dictator soon reneged on his promises of "democratic institutions" and free elections "responsive to the will of the

71

people" in all these lands. It was obvious that, whatever he'd agreed to across the conference table, his word could not be trusted.

President Truman, alert to Stalin's westward ambitions, now signaled the U.S. resolve to restrain them. Henceforth, America's policy would no longer be détente with Russia but containment. The Cold War had begun.

The spring of 1947, as Bobby was finishing his junior year, had seen the early stirrings of conflict between the United States and the Soviet Union. Coinciding with this historic shift in American foreign policy, two newcomers to Washington—freshmen members of Congress, a Republican and a Democrat—found themselves one April night traveling in the same train compartment. One, the Democrat, was Bobby's brother Jack. He and the Republican, Dick Nixon, both serving on the House Education and Labor Committee, had been invited to western Pennsylvania by fellow congressman Frank Buchanan for what would be their first public debate. Returning to D.C. at the end of the evening on a sleeper, Jack Kennedy and Dick Nixon spent hours lying in their berths, debating the emerging conflict with Russia.

That conflict would come to an early reckoning in late June of 1948 when the Russians cut off ground access to Berlin, a city entirely surrounded by Soviet-occupied East Germany. The United States and Britain both responded by sending in planes to provide the marooned population of West Berlin with food and necessary provisions. The Berlin "Airlift" would continue for almost a year.

Two tragedies—the arranged "disappearance" of Rosemary in 1941 and the death of Joe Jr. three years later in 1944—had reduced from eight to six the number of Bobby Kennedy's siblings. Bobby's family, essential to who he was, had begun to fall around him. In the summer of 1947, it was his brother Jack whose life was on the line. Taken seriously ill in London, he was discovered to have Addison's disease, a chronic disorder of the adrenal glands. The attending physician wondered if Kennedy would even live out the year. Arriving back in New York, he was given the last rites of the Catholic Church.

Then, in May of 1948, came tragedy. His sister Kick—christened Kathleen—was taken from them. Five and a half years older than he, she'd been 1938's "debutante of the year" when presented at court in London during her father's ambassadorship. She'd been the high-spirited American girl, a third of the sought-after "Golden Trio," as they were dubbed, along with her dashing, charming brothers Joe Jr. and Jack.

Then, in 1944, while working for the Red Cross in London, she married—it was a civil ceremony with only her brother Joe in attendance—a titled Protestant whom she'd met when she first came to the country. It was against her family's wishes then; four months later, her husband, William "Billy" Cavendish, the Marquess of Hartington, was killed in action in Belgium. It came a month after the death of Joe Jr.

In 1948, she herself would perish in a plane crash over the South of France. A grieving Bobby made his way to London. While there, he saw the long-running West End comedy *The Chiltern Hundreds*, in which one of the characters is an American millionaire's daughter who captures the heart of an Englishman like Hartington. Infatuated with the actress, he began taking her out, with the relationship growing serious enough for him to bring her along for a visit to his sister's gravesite at Chatsworth, Billy's ancestral estate. The relationship wouldn't survive Bobby's return home, his father's disapproval, most of all his growing commitment to another.

By the fall of that year, it was time for the first presidential election since the end of the war. Running against Truman was a strong challenger, New York governor Thomas E. Dewey, the favorite to win and end the Democrats' lengthy hold on the White House. But what happened next was a stunning upset.

Truman won his come-from-behind victory that November thanks to an extraordinary Democratic sweep in the Midwest farm belt. Minnesota's young Eugene McCarthy, who'd defeated the left-wing faction in the primary, won election to Congress. A former Benedictine seminarian running as an anti-Communist liberal, he had won the party primary over a "popular front" Democrat. He was described in the press as "the new type of Catholic politician, the intelligent Catholic whose judgments and acts stem from a consistent social philosophy based on the natural law and who is working for the right ordering of society for the good of everyone." For McCarthy and other Catholic progressives, New Deal–style social justice and anti-Communism worked hand in hand.

The Cold War was only getting icier and more dangerous. Bobby Kennedy, deciding he had graduated from Harvard "without knowing anything" and rejecting the alternative of business school, was starting his first year of law school at the University of Virginia. Like many of his fellow Catholics, he took the view that Roosevelt's agreements with Stalin had been betrayals of American values. He believed a failing FDR had been taken in by his wartime ally's assurances, throwing the small defenseless countries of Eastern Europe to the mercy of Soviet commissars. For him, the Catholic Church would stand now as the lone reliable bulwark against the advancing menace.

Bobby became especially vehement when he read reports of Hungary's Communist government arresting the staunchly anti-Nazi and also anti-Communist Cardinal József Mindszenty on the day after Christmas, 1948. Driven by outrage, he put together a denunciation of the cardinal's imprisonment and torture to run in a Boston Sunday paper. America should demand, he argued, that Mindszenty be released.

"We can look back over the last four or five years," he wrote, broadening the argument, "and see the colossal mistakes that we have made. . . . Every day someone is heard to say, 'How could anyone be so stupid as to act like that? Yalta, Potsdam, how ignominious!'" His call to arms concluded: "Here is a great opportunity for forceful action. . . . Let us not now once again grovel in uncertainty. LET US NOT FAIL."

His global anti-Communism would be rivaled by a more personal passion. He was seeing Ethel Skakel regularly, and with deepening interest. But he soon faced a daunting adversary. The one who held his heart was tempted to become a nun. For such a devout Catholic girl, educated by Sacred Heart sisters, the call of such a vocation was not only common but received by many Catholic families as a blessing. That didn't make it less tragic for her boyfriend. "How can I fight God?" he asked a pal. Fortunately for Bobby, she chose him.

Bobby was now in his second year at UVA Law. By now the sense of confidence America had gained by winning the war, its assumptions of invincibility wrought by Hiroshima and Nagasaki, were turning to a public nervousness. The danger that had loomed so recently from Berlin and Tokyo now arose from Moscow. At the end of September 1949, shocking America and the world as well, President Truman announced that the Soviet Union had exploded an atom bomb. In just four years from V-J Day, America's nuclear monopoly was no more.

The Cold War news continued to be disquieting. On October 1 the revolutionary leader Mao Zedong declared the establishment of the People's Republic of China, his Red Army in total control of the

Chinese mainland. China, our heroic, long-suffering ally in World War II, had been taken over by the Communists.

Jack Kennedy was among those now blaming the Communist victory on the Truman administration. "The responsibility for the failure of our foreign policy in the Far East rests squarely with the White House and the Department of State. So concerned were our diplomats with the imperfection of the democratic system of China after twenty years of war and the tales of corruption in high places that they lost sight of our tremendous stake in a non-Communist China."

That January, during the law school's winter break, Ethel and Bobby celebrated their engagement at a party hosted by the bride's parents in Greenwich, Connecticut. Before returning to Charlottesville, they headed off to ski at Sun Valley.

Meanwhile, public concern over the Communist threat began to center on the home front. In January, a New York jury convicted American diplomat Alger Hiss—a Harvard Law graduate and protégé of Supreme Court justice Felix Frankfurter—in his second trial for perjury. A prince of the American liberal establishment—Hiss had served as executive secretary at the UN founding conference in San Francisco—he had denied under oath passing government documents to Moscow. The jury, and much of the country, was now convinced otherwise. Richard Nixon, the congressman who'd brought forth convincing evidence against the prominent diplomat, seized upon the jury's verdict as evidence of a far broader, ominous danger.

On the Senate floor, Nixon railed against FDR and Truman both: "The conspiracy would have come to light long since had there not been a definite effort on the part of certain high-level officials in two administrations to keep the public from knowing the facts." Continuing, he declared that "the great lesson to be learned from the Hiss case is that we are not just dealing with espionage agents who get thirty pieces of silver to obtain the blueprint of a new weapon . . . but a far more sinister type of activity, because it permits the enemy to guide and shape our policy."

Taking his cue from Nixon's words, Wisconsin senator Joseph McCarthy now exploited the country's fears of subversion at the top. McCarthy had won his seat three years earlier, earning over 61 percent of the vote by tagging his Democratic opponent as "communistically inclined." He now went national with his claims.

Soon after Nixon's speech, at the beginning of February 1950, the little-known McCarthy was booked to address a GOP women's club in Wheeling, West Virginia. There, spurred by the bold insinuations of the California Republican and appropriating chunks of Nixon's own language, the Wisconsinite claimed to know the names of 205 Communists holding jobs in the Department of State. Pacing the stage, he singled out as the "most traitorous" those "bright young men who are born with silver spoons in their mouths" and denounced the "whole sorry mess of twisted, warped thinkers [who needed to be] swept from the national scene."

"Today we are engaged," he declared, "in a final, all-out battle between communistic atheism and Christianity. The modern champions of communism have selected this as the time, and ladies and gentlemen, the chips are down—they are truly down."

For McCarthy, the Wheeling speech, the first stop on what was scheduled as a routine Republican Party speaking tour, became a galvanic event: it was as if he'd shot himself out of a cannon. Yet McCarthy would continue to juggle the number of "loyalty risks"— 205 one minute, 57 the next, 81 another—and reveled in making exorbitant claims of the present danger.

In fact, the official assessment of the Communist danger was dire enough. The National Security Council report No. 68—or NSC-68, as it became known—was overseen by a distinguished study group, whose members included Secretary of State Dean Acheson and Charles E. "Chip" Bohlen, a diplomat of considerable Russian experience. Presented to President Truman in April and labeled "Top Secret," it would not be declassified for a quarter century. Among its conclusions: "The Soviet Union is animated by a new fanatic faith, antithetical to our own, and seeks to impose its absolute authority over the rest of the world. With the development of increasingly terrifying weapons of mass destruction, every individual faces the ever-present possibility of . . . destruction not only of this Republic but of civilization itself."

NSC-68, which warned of the Soviet plan for "complete subversion" of Western governments, soon became the underlying philosophical rationale for the Cold War as waged by the United States.

That June, Bobby Kennedy married Ethel Skakel at St. Mary's Catholic Church in Greenwich, Connecticut. Congressman Kennedy was his brother's best man, the eighteen-year-old Teddy one of the ushers. For his part, Jack professed himself in awe of his brother's willingness to make such a lifetime commitment to another human being.

Over twelve hundred guests were invited to the ceremony, and more than that attended. Afterward, the newlyweds set off on a trip to Hawaii where, as they were enjoying its waters, a startling incident occurred. Already a distance into the ocean themselves, they suddenly heard a voice shouting for help. As Ethel described it, "Bobby turned and saw the person in trouble. He swam out—it was a long way—got him and brought him back." The swift action exhibited by her new husband made for a lasting memory of his courage, quick-wittedness, and obliviousness to danger when someone needed help.

Leaving Hawaii, the newlyweds returned to the mainland where they made a leisurely road trip east across America to Charlottesville. Bobby would now complete his final law school year at the same time as he and Ethel began their married life.

One week after the Kennedy wedding, the United States found itself at war in Korea. Occupied by Japan for most of the century, since V-J Day the country was now divided between a Soviet-allied North and a pro-Western South along the 38th Parallel. On June 25, without warning, Northern forces—ninety thousand of them—swept across the border. Within hours, news reports cited attacks all along the 38th Parallel, and within four days Seoul had been taken. At the United Nations in New York, the Security Council voted to come to South Korea's assistance, with the United States to provide the main military force. The Soviet Union hadn't been present at the voting, thus forfeiting their chance to veto the action. For the first time since World War II, American men were called back to the battlefield, this time against the Communists.

Our GIs were once more on the battlefield, this time feeling a sense of betrayal. In the minds of the soldiers, as well as their families waiting for them, there were questions. Why did a nation that had vanquished both Nazi Germany and the Empire of Japan now find itself slogging its way up a country that, two months before, most fighting men had never heard of? Why had we fought a world war to protect Czechoslovakia and Poland only to see them become Soviet satellites? And why did we "lose" China? Most terrifyingly, after having invented the atomic bomb, how did we have it stolen from us by the Russians in just four years?

Soon, there started to be answers to these questions. And they were found close to home. It had started in February with furious headlines that began to explain how America's biggest secret had reached enemy hands. A scientist named Klaus Fuchs was arrested. A physicist who'd been a Communist Party member in Germany before he fled the Nazis, he'd spent time involved on the Manhattan Project, the covert U.S. effort to build the atomic bomb. It now was revealed that from the moment he'd arrived in America, he'd been passing information about the atomic bomb program to the Soviets. In June, the trail led from Fuchs to the American Julius Rosenberg—recruited as a Soviet agent in 1942—who then was arrested for his role in the conspiracy.

With the breaking of the Rosenberg story, the country's suspicions about internal threats became real. That November, Congressman Jack Kennedy, speaking to a seminar at the Harvard Graduate School of Public Administration, offered his own opinion on Joe McCarthy. "He may have something," he told his listeners.

That spring, Bobby had been elected president of the UVA Student Legal Forum. Now, in the fall, he invited his father to address the group. The talk Ambassador Kennedy gave showed once again his readiness to spit in the face of mainstream opinion. Echoing his pre–World War II isolationism, he called for the U.S. to withdraw from Korea, end its occupation of West Berlin, and, for all intents and purposes, let the Communists have Europe. Having opposed Roosevelt when it came to stopping Hitler's march across the face of Europe, he saw no reason to support Truman in his efforts to aid countries targeted by the Communists.

Not surprisingly, a number of Bobby's classmates—many of them returning World War II veterans proud of their service—took exception. Objecting to the values Joe stood for, *The Cavalier Daily*, the university's daily newspaper, ran a derisive editorial titled "Mr. Kennedy, the Dinosaur Is Dead." Furious, Bobby set off for its offices ready to punch out the author. The only thing stopping him was that the person he confronted denied that he'd been the one to write it.

The other invitees that year were a varied group, including Justice William O. Douglas, Joe McCarthy, Arthur Krock, and brother Jack. In the spring of 1951, his final semester, Bobby took the bold step of inviting the distinguished United Nations envoy Ralph Bunche to speak. The previous December, Bunche had been the first African American to win the Nobel Peace Prize.

On hearing of what he'd done, a number of Bobby's classmates, many of them Southerners, objected. They feared this would be a taint on their future—likely, political—careers. And Bobby could see this. In a rage, he called them "gutless."

It soon became clear to Bunche that if he were to come, his audience would, under state law, be segregated. At this stage, he informed the student organization that he wouldn't speak to such a group. Bobby's response was an eloquent five-page letter to the university president, Colgate W. Darden. Here is a key passage:

> Ever since its inception the lectures sponsored by the Student Legal Forum, while primarily designed for law students, have been open to the public at large. At no time did it occur to us that it would be possible or desirable to have Dr. Bunche lecture under any other arrangement. Indeed it did not appear to us then, and does not occur to us now, that there is any problem calculated to embarrass the University, unless the University should decide that it is necessary to create the issue itself by invoking an educational segregation policy which, as we shall attempt to point out later, is, in this instance, legally indefensible, morally wrong, and fraught with consequences calculated to do great harm to the University. There is no question but that Dr. Bunche will feel compelled to cancel his engagement if an educational segregation policy is invoked.

He went on to make his argument in Cold War terms:

> We have previously suggested that the failure to invoke an illegal segregation policy is not likely to create any issue of consequence. On the other hand the invocation of such a policy is, we believe, calculated to harm the University, the Commonwealth of Virginia and, because of its propaganda potential, the United States. Publicity attending Dr. Bunche's lecture is necessarily limited in its appeal. Publicity attending the cancellation of his lecture is not so limited. The implications are obvious. At a time when the United States is battling a daily propaganda war with Russia, the racial issue would probably be spread across the headlines in its most damaging aspect. We believe the results would be catastrophic.

Darden agreed, ruling that seating at the Bunche lecture would be fully integrated.

Despite Bobby's prediction of three to four hundred people coming to the lecture, fifteen hundred turned up to hear Bunche make campus history. Afterward he stayed the night with the Kennedys. It was the "safest place," Ethel said, even if it didn't end up seeming that way. "They threw things at the house all night."

In a pair of final-year papers, Bobby revealed his more conservative tendencies. One of the papers dealt with the Ninth and Tenth Amendments to the Constitution, both of which limit the power of the federal government. He accused the Supreme Court of failing to honor these restraints on the power of Washington. He argued the need to restore "effective control of the great Leviathan, the federal government."

His other major project that last year looked at Yalta. He charged

Franklin Roosevelt with forfeiting our country's moral position by yielding over Eastern Europe. He called FDR's concessions "the final step from which there was no salvation." By allowing Stalin to subjugate Poland, whose sovereignty had been the cause of World War II itself, America had behaved "to our everlasting dishonor."

Eunice, Pat, Bobby, Jack, and Jean together at Senate campaign headquarters.

CHAPTER SIX

BROTHER

*"Every politician in Massachusetts was mad at Bobby after
1952, but we had the best organization in history."*

—Jack Kennedy

That September, John F. Kennedy was readying himself for the next
step of his career, preparing to run for the U.S. Senate against the
Republican incumbent, Henry Cabot Lodge, Jr.

In Massachusetts, the name "Cabot" produced an automatic respect, its origins in the state stretching back to the *Mayflower*. The
family's political lineage had begun with George Cabot, chosen to
represent Massachusetts as U.S. senator from 1791 to 1796. The
current senator owed his first name to his grandfather, Henry Cabot
Lodge, who'd been a friend of Teddy Roosevelt's, and represented
his state in the United States Congress for thirty-seven years—six
in the House of Representatives, thirty-one in the Senate.

The current Lodge had followed his grandfather into both of

those chambers. He'd first served as a congressman in Washington for two terms starting in 1932. Moving to the Senate in 1936, he was an Army Reserve officer who went on active duty in 1941, despite still holding elected office. In 1942, his tank unit, fighting in North Africa with the British Eighth Army, was the first to engage with Hitler's Afrika Korps.

Reelected in 1942 and still in uniform, a directive issued by President Roosevelt forced him to pick between politics and the active military. He chose front-line duty, becoming the first senator to do so since the Civil War. Serving in Europe, he won acclaim in 1944 by singlehandedly capturing a four-man German patrol. Ending the war as a lieutenant colonel, he returned home and bravely resumed his political career.

This aim required him to take on Senator David I. Walsh, a four-term incumbent. Lodge managed not only to defeat his Irish Catholic opponent, but to carry the Democratic stronghold of Boston. It was solid evidence that here was a patrician Yankee who enjoyed an unusual popularity among Irish voters.

With the approach of the 1952 election year, Lodge had enhanced his national prestige with his successful recruitment of General Dwight Eisenhower. He persuaded the Supreme Commander of the new North Atlantic Treaty Organization to enter the presidential race as a Republican.

Could John F. Kennedy beat such a man as Lodge? Historical precedent seemed to predict otherwise. In 1916, Jack's politician grandfather, John F. "Honey Fitz" Fitzgerald, had lost that year's Massachusetts Senate race to the first Henry Cabot Lodge.

Despite Lodge's seeming advantages, the younger man believed he could match them with his own. One significant card he held was the strength of his party, with FDR and Truman both having carried Massachusetts. As Jack had recently pointed out on the weekly news program *Meet the Press*—then in its infancy—it was "essentially a Democratic state." That electoral truth meant Jack Kennedy, still only thirty-four, was able to see a fallback position. He could either go for the Senate now, or else run for governor and await the next chance.

What irritated him, however, was the hard fact that it wasn't up to him which office he might run for. Governor Paul Dever, a Democrat now serving his second term in the State House, still hoped to follow the career route taken by an earlier governor, Leverett Saltonstall. He wanted to move on to the United States Senate. But Dever had a genuine dilemma: if he made the Senate run against the formidable Lodge, it could become a career-ender. On the other hand, if he took the safer route and ran for reelection, he could well be stuck in place.

Kennedy couldn't make his move until Dever made his.

Whichever the governor's choice, Kennedy had great faith he could pull off a statewide win. His easy reelections in 1948 and 1950—with his heavily Democratic district never in doubt—had allowed him the freedom to go out into the commonwealth and make himself known. He'd seen the way voters responded to him; if he could get to them, he believed he could win them over.

Jack's increasing focus was on foreign policy. To give himself credible experience as well as to seem more senatorial, he went off on a month-long trip early in 1951—starting in England and ending in West Germany—to study Western European rearmament. Then, to further strengthen his grip on the world situation, his father staked him that fall to a seven-week tour through the Mideast and the Far East. It would be a 25,000-mile trip that would take him to Israel, then Iran, Pakistan, India, Singapore, Thailand, and Indochina, finishing up in Korea, where the war the U.S. was fighting was in its second year.

Rather than have Jack set out alone, however, Joe Kennedy insisted that Bobby accompany him. This was far from welcome news to Jack, an extra piece of extra baggage he didn't think he needed. As far as he was concerned, brother Bob was still "a pain in the ass." But here was Bobby, married hardly a year and with a two-month-old daughter, always ready to answer his father's call.

Reaching Vietnam, five years into a war for independence, the travelers couldn't venture safely beyond Saigon for fear of the Vietminh insurgents. The stubborn fervor of their fight to liberate themselves from their French colonial masters impressed the Kennedy brothers. Had a fair election been called, Bobby could see Vietminh leader Ho Chi Minh taking 70 percent of the vote. Always drawn to underdog causes, he learned—and it struck at his own patriotism—that the Vietnamese now regarded the U.S., who supported the French, as equally their enemy.

En route to Korea, they were forced to abandon their schedule. Jack suddenly had become frighteningly ill. It was his Addison's disease. Bobby immediately took charge. With his brother running a dangerously high fever, the only choice was to make an emergency detour. "We flew to the military hospital in Okinawa and he had a temperature of over 106 degrees," Bobby recalled years later. "They didn't think he would live."

Under enormous pressure in such a frightening emergency so far from home, the younger brother proved himself quick-thinking, resourceful, and, above all, protective. As Jack's condition appeared to worsen, Bobby did what was natural for him, praying all night for Jack to survive. For the second time in his life—the first had been the Addison's episode four years earlier, in England—John Kennedy was given the last rites of the Church.

In February 1952, Bobby Kennedy, having signed on as an

attorney in the Criminal Division, was presenting to a Brooklyn grand jury the Justice Department's case against some former Truman officials charged with corruption. At the time, this mission constituted, as he later said, "one of the biggest tax prosecutions ever held." Meanwhile, Jack, now recovered, was back in Washington, still unsure of his next political move.

Thanks to Bobby, Ken O'Donnell was working for Jack. Married in 1947 and the father of three children, he'd spent a year in law school after graduating from Harvard, then becoming a salesman for a Boston paper company. Always an avid student of Massachusetts politics, he was paying attention to the possibility of Jack's going for the Senate and calculating the odds. Front and center, he saw, were Lodge's solid electoral strengths: his strong statewide organization, his first-rate staff, and his high reputation for integrity. "He was a war veteran, he was smart, rich, handsome, and a Yankee politician who could deal with the Irish. The Irish liked him and he appeared to like them."

But O'Donnell's assessment of Lodge's many positives didn't paint the whole picture. He understood that the political landscape in Massachusetts was changing. And he sensed that his fellow World War II veterans were looking for an alternative to what amounted mostly to the same old choice—the patrician Lodge or Saltonstall model and the machine-backed hacks and crooks typified by Boston's four-time mayor James Michael Curley, who'd served part of his mayoralty in prison. Speaker Tip O'Neill, Jr., whom I worked for in the 1980s, once gave me an insider's estimate of Curley. "He was crooked even by the standards of those days."

Young guys like Ken, with roots in the working class, had come back from the war and taken advantage of the GI Bill. An FDR-created federal initiative, it was a program that made an enormous difference to the postwar American world. Enacted as the Servicemen's Readjustment Act of 1944, it offered returning servicemen a college education, something their fathers and mothers never had.

These voters, O'Donnell thought, who no longer slotted into the category of "reliable" Democrat, might well find a figure like John Kennedy appealing. Jack seemed to meld the new and the old, emerging with his own fresh tradition. "He started getting our attention because he made statements and did things that weren't the norm for politicians in Massachusetts," was how O'Donnell looked at it.

However, when Ken went to the meeting Bobby had set up, he was still in the dark about the brother's intentions. The question hanging in the air was which office Jack would be going for. It was a source of more than a little irritation to him when O'Donnell raised it.

"I'm seriously considering running," he confirmed to Ken. "But I'm not sure what exactly I'm going to do." When O'Donnell pressed him further, he watched the congressman quickly turn cold, not liking to be asked a question to which he himself didn't know the answer.

To defeat Lodge, the Jack Kennedy campaign needed to win a two-front war: excite those new-generation voters, adding them to the ethnic, working-class base any Massachusetts Democratic candidate already counted upon. It would need to attract those voters ready to support the popular Eisenhower for president, convincing them to split their ticket and send Congressman John F. Kennedy to the Senate.

Only in that way might young Jack win in a state that had consistently placed its confidence in Henry Cabot Lodge. It was clear, too, that Lodge would now make every effort to benefit from his close ties to the Republican now likely headed to the White House.

Jack's campaign so far consisted mainly of the speeches he gave each weekend to whatever groups across the state would have him. He'd gotten these speaking engagements with that most basic of appeals, by offering to pay his own expenses. Afterward, he'd return to his Bowdoin Street apartment and head straight to the wall where he'd hung a large Massachusetts map. Sticking a pin into each locale where he'd now introduced himself sustained his confidence that he was making progress.

The problem with the campaign—O'Donnell could see the trouble right away—was that no one was in charge. You had Joe Kennedy, who was paying the bills. He'd occasionally show up and bark orders. And then you had Jack, who'd fly back from Washington. When neither was around, the headquarters went lifeless.

Mark Dalton, who'd held the title of campaign manager in the 1946 race, assumed he'd now get it again. Primarily a speechwriter, however, he was incapable of the necessary leadership. Most vitally, he couldn't stand up to Joe Kennedy. Whenever the senior Kennedy made an appearance at the headquarters, Dalton simply avoided his glare. He was afraid to take even the minimal step toward building a statewide organization, reluctant even to begin naming "secretaries"—those community figures who'd be the links in the Kennedy-for-Senate network.

Nothing, in other words, was getting done—for the basic reason that Jack himself was waiting for someone to come along and take charge of the campaign even as his dad was ensuring no one else did. The basic trouble was that Joseph P. Kennedy *thought* he understood politics. He didn't. His notion of getting a political campaign up and running was to hire a roomful of campaign veterans and keep them under his thumb. But intimidation wasn't the same as leadership. What he lacked was any strategic vision. With all his smarts for making money, he had no idea what moved the voter.

Except for Jack's weekend forays into the state, the only campaign events being planned were the Kennedy "Teas." Back in 1946, a first tea party hosted by the ambassador to the Court of St. James's and his wife had been a grand success. Their war-hero son had been the star attraction on the receiving line—and now, that formula was being repeated.

But while the Teas were extraordinarily effective, they were a tactic, not a strategy. It was still necessary to get more happening. The postwar landscape was different, offering tremendous opportunity, but it needed to be cultivated. There were those upwardly mobile World War II vets now building new lives in those mostly Republican towns like Braintree and Malden, Melrose and Weymouth. A well-targeted approach would be needed to make them Kennedy supporters. The campaign needed a stronger taskmaster to help organize this, along with meeting its other goals.

Watching closely, Ken O'Donnell thought he saw the solution. Only a Kennedy, he decided, could push the interfering father to the side and get the campaign moving forward. As it stood, Jack couldn't do either. O'Donnell believed he knew who could: Bobby.

In O'Donnell's view, the younger brother had learned how to handle the father. Unlike his brother, who kept his distance, Bobby was now practiced in maneuvering him, while Jack never could . . . nor did he especially want to.

Curious, Ken once had asked Bobby to explain why he never told his father to back off. The reply he received startled him. Bobby explained that he liked their relationship the way it was. While Jack wasn't invested in his father's feelings, Bobby had grown up with his heart set on winning them. Achieving even a measure of his dad's attention was, for him, a victory. The son who'd worked the hardest to gain the father's attention and respect now knew just how to do it.

"I knew Bobby was the one with enough sense, who was tough enough and a regular enough guy to run the campaign. And he'd be the only one able to turn to the father and say, 'No, Jack won't do it.'"

Meanwhile, the weeks were passing. And there was still the question of whether the Senate was the goal. If Governor Dever decided to go for it, that would close the door to Jack. But early in April, Jack got word the governor wanted to meet with him. "Jack," he said, "I'm a candidate for re-election."

"Well, that's fine," the younger man shot back. "I'm a candidate for the Senate."

But the conversation wasn't over. Dever had more to say. Putting Jack on notice, he told him to expect no help from the regular Democratic organization. What he said carried an unmistakable subtext that wasn't lost on Jack. *I know this state, and I believe Lodge is unbeatable. You're on your own, buddy.*

Jack heard every word, the unspoken warning included. But it didn't matter. All that counted was that he was in the race he wanted. What he needed now was a way to win it.

Bobby checking vote returns, Senate election night 1952.

CHAPTER SEVEN

THE KENNEDY PARTY

*"He was a Kennedy, which was more than a family
affiliation. It quickly developed into an entire political
party, with its own approach, and its own strategies."*

—Thomas P. "Tip" O'Neill, Jr.

Over the half dozen years I worked for him, I heard Tip O'Neill—a
storied figure in Massachusetts politics—give a great many campaign fundraising speeches. Tip had started as a fifteen-year-old
campaigning for Al Smith in 1928 and would go on to a long career.
Serving thirty-four years as a U.S. congressman, he spent the last
ten of them as U.S. speaker of the house. There was little he didn't
know, or hadn't seen, when it came to the ambitions and strategies
involved in running for office.

In those speeches I'd listen to him delivering, one rule he
preached applies neatly to John F. Kennedy's 1952 Senate run.
"Every campaign," Tip would declare, "needs three elements to
succeed: the candidate, the money, the organization." The problem

for Jack was the conflict *among* all three factors. The man with the money was keeping the campaign from building the organization, and the candidate was unable to stop him.

Jack had the ability, most of the time, to keep his father at a distance, but not always. There were occasions when he'd get under Jack's skin—for example, when they played golf together. Ethel Kennedy knew that her father-in-law had the nasty habit of trying "anything to distract you when you were putting." Jack, she said, was thrown off his game by Joe. "But Bobby wasn't," she added.

Thus it was that, at this critical moment, Ken O'Donnell, acting on his own, summoned Bobby. "I told him you've got to come up here. It's chaos. You've got to take over."

Ken's summons caught Bobby by surprise. He'd been fully occupied with his assignment at the Justice Department. He hadn't paid much attention to what was happening up in Massachusetts.

For O'Donnell, this was a window into the complex family relationships. "Bobby didn't talk to Jack. Bobby didn't know what Jack was doing. And Jack didn't know what Bobby was up to. Neither cared very much what the other was doing." He added, "I'd been under the impression that they were peas in a pod. They certainly were not."

Bobby was annoyed at Ken for attempting to rope him in. How could he, with no experience in politics, take charge of a campaign for the United States Senate? It made no sense; he didn't know the state at all. And, he reminded Ken, what about his own life? He was working a big anti-corruption case in Brooklyn, and had a job where he could see a career ahead.

"He just made it very clear that he didn't want to come. He didn't feel he was necessary or would be helpful. He just did *not* want to do it." The irony, of course, was that if Bobby had never gotten O'Donnell the job, he'd never have been facing his pressure, nor would he have been forced to reckon personally with Jack's dilemma.

In the end, Bobby took a few days to think about it before phoning to tell Ken, "Okay, I guess I'll have to do it."

But only half the battle was won. Now came the task of convincing Jack Kennedy to put his political future in the hands of his twenty-six-year-old brother. Even for a broken campaign, it was an unlikely notion of how to fix it.

The trick would be getting the two of them together. The opportunity came in a car ride from Quincy, a suburb south of Boston. Now, for the first time, O'Donnell was really sticking his neck out, having summoned Bobby north. With both brothers as his audience, he laid out his views. And they weren't pretty. The campaign was stalled for lack of a leader, with Mark Dalton too scared of their father to do his job.

Jack didn't like hearing any of this, especially from a non-Kennedy. "He felt," Ken said, "that I'd been telling tales out of school to his brother . . . instead of telling him, whom I was really working for."

Angry or not, Jack listened. He sat there, in that car, as O'Donnell let fly with the unwanted truth. Then it was Bobby's turn. The moment had arrived: he offered to help.

"Why don't you come up?" Jack responded. And that was that.

Ethel would later say that it was that moment, in the car headed to Boston, when Jack met the essential condition. Bobby Kennedy would now quit his job, leaving Washington to take charge of the campaign, for one reason, and one reason only: "His brother asked him."

"He loved his brother," Ethel told me. "It was a very tough thing for him to do because he felt like he was on his way to making a name for himself. He went up, and it was a big sacrifice." In truth, it can't have been that easy for her, either. Their daughter, Kathleen Hartington Kennedy, named to honor the memory of her late aunt Kick, was now nine months old, and Ethel was three months pregnant with their next child.

It was mid-April when Bobby took over, from the very start working eighteen-hour days and making it clear who was in charge. Handling their father was at the top of the agenda. Charlie Bartlett, one of Jack's closest friends, recalled overhearing a phone conversation. "Yes, Dad," Bobby kept repeating. "Yes, Dad." He was keeping the father out of the decision making by convincing him it all was being done exactly his way.

From Jack's political beginnings in 1946, recruiting volunteers had been key to his efforts. The idea was to hand any newcomer an immediate, achievable task, such as writing thank-you notes on behalf of the family. It was a way to make them part of what Tip O'Neill called "the Kennedy Party."

In his new role, Bobby controlled the campaign's finances, deciding, among other bottom-line issues, who'd be paid and who wouldn't. "How much money is the candidate going to give us to spend in our district?" he was asked at one early meeting. The questioner was referring to what's commonly known as "street money," the cash campaign workers expect for getting voters to the polls on election day.

The Kennedy for Senate campaign, Bobby now made clear, was a strictly volunteer operation, no exceptions. "Listen, kid," the man demanded, "you want campaign people out working for you, you gotta pay 'em—and you can afford it. The Kennedys are rich."

Hearing this, Bobby got up, grabbed the fellow by his collar, and hustled him out the door, saying as he did: "Would you mind getting lost . . . and keeping yourself lost!"

Later, after that victim of Bobby's wrath had gone to Jack to complain, Bobby set the candidate straight. "Look, you get one guy like that crying, then you have to pay him and his volunteers to work. Then other people hear about it, and they want to be paid to volunteer, and then we'll end up spending a million dollars in Boston alone. I'm not going to have him around. You asked me to run this campaign. I didn't want to, but now I'm here, so I'll run it my way."

Decades later, Ethel would defend her husband's conduct. As she saw it, Bobby was simply making sure everyone knew who was boss. He was now saying, "I'm the one." So don't go running to Jack. It's just going to backfire on you.

Jack Kennedy would one day famously say that a person gets only one reputation in life. It was from occasions like this, to be widely talked about, that won Bobby his. The word used was "ruthless."

"Bobby has taken over the management of the whole campaign," his father wrote with obvious relish to twenty-year-old Ted, his fourth son. "He works fifteen hours a day and is showing remarkable good sense and judgment." But it was Bobby's toughness putting the campaign back on track that gratified him most.

As Jack's campaign ramrod, Bobby soon learned how suited he was to the part. Those who met him for the first time saw a hard-driving, take-no-excuses street fighter. He seemed to them that way—and he was. He wasn't in the friend-making business; that was Jack's job.

But O'Donnell was cheered at having his old roommate as his new captain. "Any decision you needed, Bobby made."

Here's Bobby describing what he *wasn't* doing: "I didn't become involved in what words should go into a speech; what should be said on a poster or billboard, what should be done on television. I was so busy with my part of it that I didn't see any of that."

What he actually did, working those eighteen-hour days, was the equivalent of commanding an army in battle.

Since Governor Dever had made it clear to Jack that he was on his own, the Kennedys had proceeded to build a total political network of their own. It was entirely divorced from the entrenched Democratic organization controlled by Dever. "Our secretaries were making weekly reports to me," Bobby would say, "and they were growing more sophisticated from week to week. For a long time neither Lodge nor the Democratic regulars realized what we were doing."

Having constructed a Kennedy operation unto itself, Bobby insisted on total loyalty. There could be no dual allegiances even to Democrats in other races. He was the unassimilated Irishman forever on the lookout for *traitors and trimmers*. He didn't mind making fierce judgments even if it meant making enemies. What mattered to him was winning, and the only way to do that was to keep people in line.

Jack was learning how to use Bobby. He could do what the candidate could not. Bobby's role was to be the bad guy, and to be seen as such. Few realized the campaign's profound secret: that candidate Jack, favorite of all who encountered him, was capable of the most heartless call. His easy charm belied his interest at winning at all costs.

Looking at Jack's hard-nosed dealings with Paul Dever gives a useful illustration. Back in the spring, the governor had figured it was smart to cut the Kennedy campaign loose. He'd been fearful of being held back by an effort he saw as doomed—no matter how attractive the young candidate or admirable his war record. A factor influencing him, too, was his high regard for the political strength of Henry Cabot Lodge. The two were contemporaries, and the governor had watched Lodge's rise since they'd served together in the 1930s as Massachusetts state representatives.

By autumn 1946, the ground had shifted. The growing popularity of Eisenhower had put all Democrats onto the defensive. With the Kennedy campaign now smartly organized and energized, Dever thought joining forces might be a good idea. Why not do it?

His relationship with Joe Kennedy was good, with Jack less so. While the father was for an alliance with Dever, Jack resisted. He regarded himself as better off running an independent campaign, pitching himself to those voters in the suburbs and small towns who saw him as a new kind of politician. Knowing that this meant crossing both the governor and his father, the trick was cutting Dever loose with the minimum of damage.

"Don't give in to them," he instructed Bobby, now tagged as the bad guy. "But don't get me involved with it." Cold-bloodedly he wanted the *bearer* of the bad news to be the bad guy.

Another ploy the Kennedy campaign used was a pincer maneuver. It attacked Lodge from the left on economic issues. It struck him on the right on foreign policy, playing on that front to the growing conviction, especially among Catholics, that FDR had sold out Eastern Europe at Yalta and Truman had given away China. For this particular call to arms, the Kennedys were the ready and perfect messengers.

"Kenny and Bobby would go out at night and make speeches," Rose Kennedy recalled. "Eunice and Pat and Jean would be out making calls and showing the terrific interview Jack had given on 'Meet the Press.' All of us were doing something ten or fifteen hours a day. Usually everyone would be back and in bed by twelve. Then we were up again before eight. We just had a wonderful summer."

That September Bobby and Ethel became parents for the second time. Joseph Patrick Kennedy II, like his older sister, Kathleen, was named to celebrate a lost Kennedy child and sibling. Bobby was keeping their memory close.

There was disturbing news as well on the family front. As it had before, the spotlight turned to Joe Kennedy's notorious anti-Semitism. The Lodge campaign recruited New York Republican congressman Jacob Javits to lead the attack. Javits—his own father a Talmudic scholar who'd earned his living as both a janitor and a Tammany Hall gofer—had chosen to join the Republican Party in reaction to the Democratic corruption he'd seen in New York City as a boy.

As a rare Jewish Republican in Congress, he cut a distinctive figure. When he told a Jewish audience in Mattapan that his Democratic colleague now running for Senator Lodge's seat was "the son of his father," they understood. As Tip O'Neill put it years later, "He didn't have to be any more explicit."

There was also the matter of Joe's ties to Senator Joe McCarthy. A friend, in fact, of the entire family, he had dated two of the candidate's sisters, Eunice and also Pat, who found him charming when he hadn't had too much to drink.

Almost three years after the Wheeling speech, the word "McCarthyism" now had meaning around the world, and carried more than a hint of menace. Still, Massachusetts, with its large number of Irish American voters, remained his strongest area of support nationally. Any criticism by Jack would cost him on election day.

McCarthy knew Jack and liked him, indeed counted him as a covert backer. How Jack regarded him had remained a matter of speculation until the appearance on newsstands, less than a month before the November 4 election, of the October 13, 1952, edition of the liberal weekly magazine *The New Republic*.

It revealed how, back in 1950, Congressman Kennedy had told that audience of Harvard grad students it was his belief McCarthy "may have something" with his mission to uncover Communists in the government. On that same occasion, according to the *TNR* article, Jack Kennedy had also admitted to preferring his Republican colleague Richard Nixon, now his party's nominee for vice president, over liberal Democrat Helen Gahagan Douglas in their 1950 California senatorial contest.

Nixon had tried—successfully—to turn Congresswoman Douglas's progressive activism into a scorching negative, saying, among other accusations, that the three-term congresswoman was "pink down to her underwear." What Kennedy revealed, speaking to those students in that post-election seminar, was that he'd actually *rooted* for Nixon.

It was all true. Jack had indeed maintained friendly relations with Dick Nixon. The cordial rivalry among Nixon, George Smathers (D-FL), and himself—after the other two had moved up to the Senate in 1950—made, in fact, for a friendly prod to his own efforts to join them. *The New Republic* writer had also nailed him ideologically: Jack Kennedy was no liberal. "His position cannot exactly be called 'liberalism'; it might be referred to as 'popularism'—a willingness to give the people what they want in specific situations while shunning the generalities of a liberal philosophy."

Jack Kennedy had actually made a point of separating himself from the Democratic liberals. "Tell them I'm not a liberal," he ordered his top congressional aide, Ted Reardon, in answer to a charge that he'd failed to fall in line with certain sectors of his own party. "I never joined the Americans for Democratic Action or the American Veterans Committee. I'm not comfortable with those people."

Earlier that year, at the hundredth anniversary of his Harvard club, a member was talking about the spirit of Harvard College and saying how glad he was that the school had produced neither "a Joseph McCarthy *or* an Alger Hiss." On hearing that coupling, Kennedy jumped from his chair. "How dare you compare the name of a great American patriot with that of a traitor!" and left the room.

As for his father, the very thought of expediently separating himself or his family from Joseph McCarthy was unacceptable. When one of Jack's campaign aides, the progressive activist Gardner "Pat" Jackson, passed around a draft "Declaration of Conscience" condemning "the twin evils of McCarthyism and Communism," Kennedy senior went wild. "You and your . . . sheeny friends . . . are trying to ruin my son's career."

As the campaign drew to a close, a big challenge became the

need to keep Joe McCarthy, running for easy reelection in Wisconsin, out of Massachusetts. Getting nervous, Lodge was now desperate enough to enlist his Senate colleague's "help." Would McCarthy consider coming into Massachusetts on Lodge's behalf?

McCarthy richly enjoyed Lodge's predicament. He agreed, with one condition: "I told them I'd go up to Boston to speak if Cabot publicly asked me to. And he'll never do that; he'd lose the Harvard vote." McCarthy never entered the state.

On the night before the election, General Eisenhower, the front-runner to be chosen the next day as America's thirty-fourth president, arrived in Boston. His presence there was a five-star general's salute to the man who'd served him in both war and politics. Eisenhower wasn't one to forget that if it hadn't been for Lodge he wouldn't be headed to the White House.

The early returns on the next evening showed Ike winning big in Massachusetts. By midnight, his plurality over Adlai Stevenson stood at 200,000. The word on radio and TV was that the state's entire Democratic ticket—Stevenson, Dever, and Kennedy—would be going down together. Calling campaign headquarters from his apartment, Jack was frantic.

When he got Bobby on the phone, he wanted to know what the hell was happening. But Bobby cut him off, telling him, "Look, on the basis of our numbers and our chart and the basis of what we have and our computations, we're winning the race. And if the trend continues, even with a little drop-off, we'll defeat Lodge. The television predictions are wrong."

Hearing but not believing him, Jack headed to the headquarters on Kilby Street and began working the numbers himself. "He went town by town—and we walked him through it," Ken O'Donnell recalled. "But it became confusing to him and he just kept telling us the reports on the television and those we were giving him simply didn't square."

At this point, Governor Dever called, saying they'd both lost and should concede together. Outside the window, rowdies—"Irish bums" O'Donnell called them—were shouting "Jack Kennedy, you're a loser and a faker! You're in the shithouse with your old man!"

Their main target was Bobby. For those out in the street, he'd been the gatekeeper against the hacks and wannabes, the enforcer whose job it had been to bounce the nonproducers.

For Bobby Kennedy, the campaign had been both a blooding and a bonding—with both the rough-and-tumble of politics, and with his older brother. Additionally, he'd learned an important truth about himself. It was that ability to *make decisions.*

Finally, at six or six-thirty in the morning, Lodge, who'd been a personage on the Massachusetts political scene for twenty years, conceded. John F. Kennedy had beaten him by seventy thousand votes, each vote going against the Eisenhower landslide.

Walking to Kennedy headquarters to offer his official concession along with his congratulations, Lodge looked his polished patrician self.

As he saw him approach, Jack Kennedy couldn't help but feel the formality of the moment and of the man about to face him. "What a bunch of bums we all look like," he said. "Put a tie on, for God's sake!" he instructed Bobby.

As disheveled as they may have appeared to the outsider, the two brothers had performed a masterful feat. In an uphill contest they'd outpointed Lodge, the regular Democratic Party, and the historic odds. Bobby had made Jack a United States senator. The two of them could never forget what they'd been able to do together.

Bobby confers with Joseph McCarthy and other senators.

CHAPTER EIGHT

CLAN

"Bobby going to work for Joe McCarthy was as natural as a Jewish kid from CCNY joining the Communist Party in the nineteen thirties."

—JACK NEWFIELD

Having taken on the challenge of running his brother's race for the Senate, making many of those tough decisions that secured Jack's surprise victory, Bobby now faced hard ones of his own. "What are you going to do now?" his father demanded to know, pointing out that his recent law school graduate son hadn't, himself, been elected to anything.

One thing he knew for sure—having seen the campaign battlefield from inside the trenches—was that seeking elected office for himself was out. He didn't enjoy making speeches, nor did he have the patience for the continual backslapping. And he'd had more than enough of dealing with those hangers-on forever underfoot.

He particularly despised the opportunists who'd stayed away during the fight, then had no qualms about showing up on election night. Whatever it was they wanted, those fair-weather types were never going to get it from him.

It's reasonable to assume Bobby regarded Lyndon Johnson as one such self-server. The Texas senator had phoned Jack with crack-of-dawn congratulations just as soon as the news hit the wires that he'd won. Johnson had gotten up especially early just to make sure his voice was one of the first new Democratic senators heard.

Lurking behind Johnson's message of welcome to each incoming freshman senator was a very real agenda, and one easy enough to spot. For the previous two years the Senate majority leader had been Ernest McFarland, who'd represented Arizona in the Senate since 1941. Unable to surmount the Eisenhower-led Republican landslide, McFarland now was out, and his opponent, Barry Goldwater, was in. It was this vacancy in the leader's office that Lyndon Johnson was ready and eager to fill.

The newly elected Jack Kennedy, well able to see what Johnson had been up to with his ingratiating telephone call, didn't mind. Coolly political himself by this point, he wasn't turned off by Johnson's obvious angling for the leadership position. Bobby, though, had no such tolerance for it, and made clear his contempt for Johnson's self-serving gesture.

Despite Bobby's reluctance to become a candidate himself, there were those around him, including Ken O'Donnell, who felt otherwise. Eager to keep alive the Kennedy organization, which had now proven itself so well, they fixed on a possible race for Bobby to enter. Republican Christian Herter had just narrowly beaten Paul Dever in what was for then a two-year term as governor. Herter would be up for reelection in 1954. The idea was for Bobby to take him on.

To the loyally committed O'Donnell, it made perfect sense for Bobby to try to move into the State House and take charge in Massachusetts exactly as he had in his brother's campaign. No longer as intimidated by Joe Sr. as he once had been, O'Donnell asked for a meeting, only to find out they were thinking along the same lines.

When confronted with their plan, Bobby just as quickly let them know he was having none of it. "I'm tired of it," he explained to Ken. "Tired of all the infighting and the lying. I'm much happier in Washington, quite honestly, just doing my own thing in my own way. I think Dad's very frustrated with me at the moment. But I'm glad to get out of Massachusetts. I don't like politics."

Down in Washington already—his seventh year in the nation's capital—brother Jack was settling into his new office on the third floor of the Senate building. Needing to hire new staffers, Kennedy looked around and found himself impressed by Theodore Sorensen, a young attorney from Nebraska working on Capitol Hill. Would he come be his legislative assistant?

For his part, the liberal Sorensen wanted to hear more about Kennedy's connection to Senator Joseph McCarthy, which to him was a problem. Kennedy said that McCarthy was a friend of his father and his family and was enormously popular among Massachusetts Irish Catholics. Jack added that he didn't approve of all McCarthy's tactics, nor did he believe in all his accusations. Sorensen listened, and, obviously responding to Jack personally, decided to come on board.

McCarthy himself had just landed a new job. Owing to the coattails of the Eisenhower-Nixon ticket, the number of Republicans and Democrats in the Senate was now equal. This meant that, as vice president, Richard Nixon's tie-breaking vote would give his party control. This put the GOP into the majority, controlling the chairmanships of all committees and subcommittees. Senator Joseph McCarthy, the country's most celebrated pursuer of Communists, became the head of the Committee on Government Operations and, by his choice, also its Permanent Subcommittee on Investigations. The subcommittee held sweeping jurisdiction to probe any federal activity it chose. That meant anywhere the new chairman set his sights.

A critical hire for him would be the naming of subcommittee counsel. As it turned out, he didn't have to look far, since his old friend Joe Kennedy was working to convince McCarthy to give the position to his son Bobby.

There were ways in which the forty-four-year-old senator and the twenty-seven-year-old Bobby Kennedy fit together better than one might have supposed. The older man was a farm boy from rural Wisconsin who'd dropped out when he was a young teen though later resumed his education. And while the younger went to elite private schools, it had now been clear for a long while that Bobby was the opposite of a snob. Both, moreover, were from large Irish Catholic families, with the McCarthy family's seven to the Kennedy nine. That meant that taking McCarthy's job would involve battling on behalf of the clan.

McCarthy's sense of mission carried an appeal as well. Above all, both he and Bobby were fighters. The idea of joining his staff, therefore, wasn't a difficult notion. For Bobby, it was about flying the Kennedy flag alongside an old friend of his father's. It also had the appeal of standing alongside one of those pugnacious sorts to whom he was drawn. And there was the cause itself, purging spies and traitors from the U.S.

Bobby was hardly alone in this pro-McCarthy sentiment. Many American Catholics believed from the start of Joe McCarthy's notoriety that any and all establishment attacks on him were evidence of the same bigotry that had brought down Al Smith back in 1928. A Catholic rising to prominence in American life, they suspected, would find himself—at the behest of people who weren't their own—put back in his place.

Catholics also held to the belief that the war against Communism—an issue made passionate after the loss of Eastern Europe—was, essentially, their own conflict. Fully supported by Catholics around the world, the Church saw itself as the leading challenge to Soviet aggression.

I grew up hearing that call to American Catholics to rally against Communism. Though only a young boy at the time, I remember how we prayed each Sunday "for the conversion of Russia" and my classmates arriving at school with five-dollar donations to help "ransom" Chinese babies from the Communists.

Another prominent Irish Catholic voice during this era was Bishop Fulton Sheen. Ordained in the Diocese of Peoria, Illinois, in 1919, he made his early career as a respected theologian and author. Reaching his first national audiences through radio in the 1930s, he moved on, in 1951, to the new medium of television. His Tuesday-night broadcast from New York City, called *Life Is Worth Living*, reached as many as thirty million viewers.

Sheen's weekly ministry gained historic currency with a program airing in late February 1953. "Stalin must one day meet his judgment," Sheen pronounced. As it turns out, the Soviet leader soon had a stroke and died. When Sister announced the Russian dictator's demise in class and asked us all to pray, I remember wondering at the time what the intention was. Were we praying for him to go straight to hell? Or for an unlikely deathbed conversion? Or simply out of gratitude at his demise?

As it turned out, Senator McCarthy didn't select Bobby Kennedy to be the committee's chief counsel. He appointed him, instead, to a subordinate position—as assistant to the committee's general counsel, Francis "Flip" Flanagan. For the job Bobby didn't get, he picked Roy Cohn, a whiz kid a year younger. Graduating from Columbia Law School, he'd been named an assistant U.S. attorney when only twenty-one. A New York City judge's son, Cohn made his name early on as part of the team prosecuting Julius and Ethel Rosenberg—the husband and wife both convicted of conspiracy to commit espionage and sentenced to death.

Lyndon Johnson, meanwhile, had gotten his wish and became the newly elected Senate Democratic leader. One morning in the Senate cafeteria, McCarthy and his subcommittee staffers stood to greet the Texan as he passed their table. Only Bobby, the newcomer to the group, stayed seated. When Johnson stuck out his hand on being introduced, Bobby very deliberately refused to extend his own in return. Only after an embarrassing stretch of time did he grasp Johnson's hand.

"It's about Roosevelt and his father," Johnson told aide George Reedy by way of explaining the scene that had just occurred. For years, Johnson had dined out on his having sat there and witnessed FDR's 1940 vow to "fire the sonofabitch," namely Bobby Kennedy's ambassador dad. Now, a dozen years later, that January 1953 breakfast-time encounter revealed, the Texan believed, the younger man's bitter attitude toward him, one that was never to lessen.

"Did you ever see two dogs come into a room and all of a sudden there's a low growl, and the hair rises up on the back of their necks?" was how Reedy described the scene. "It was like that. Somehow he and Bobby took one look at each other—and that was it."

As his sister Eunice would politely phrase it, her brother had "a gift for estrangement." Thus Roy Cohn, too, was poised to join the list of those on Bobby's enemies list. The chief counsel, like his boss, was a limelight seeker, now making headlines when he suddenly set off on a self-assigned seven-day, seven-country European tour. Its supposed purpose was to purge State Department libraries in capitals like London and Paris, Bonn and Athens, of books by Communist writers.

To accompany him, Cohn decided to invite a new friend, G. David Schine. The Harvard-educated son of wealthy hotel owners, Schine had recently self-published a pamphlet titled *Definition of Communism*, copies of which were left, like Gideon Bibles, in the company's hotel rooms. After meeting the good-looking Schine, Cohn had wangled a job for him on the subcommittee staff as an unpaid "chief consultant."

The watching press didn't take such a peculiar junket seriously. Reporters mocked the two young men in print at every dateline.

It was difficult for Bobby to watch Cohn's seemingly insatiable appetite for attention grabbing. Bobby took himself seriously, also the job he was doing. In Bobby's mind, Cohn had pegged him as a daddy's boy—and, worse still, no more than a gofer.

Frictions were eased, if only temporarily, when a subcommittee assignment handed him in early 1953 sent him off on his own course. He was put in charge of investigating the shipping being carried on openly by Great Britain and other Western countries with Communist China, what his brother had called the "blood trade." The Chinese, after all, were fighting and killing American and British soldiers in Korea; therefore, it made no sense that British shippers, especially, were so flagrantly arming and provisioning the battlefield enemy. Up until now, for reasons of Allied diplomacy, the U.S. had held back from confronting them.

Calling the shots from his Senate basement office, Bobby, along with his colleagues, was able to discover that Britain—whose own troops were among the U.N. forces fighting along the 38th Parallel—was actually sending strategic war materials to the enemy. He documented that, since 1950, there had been $2 billion in trade by non-Communist countries with Red China. The final report revealed a total of 162 foreign ships delivering cargo—including oil, essential to the North Korean army—to China in the first three and a half months of 1953.

In late March, McCarthy, at a press conference with Bobby standing alongside him, announced the subcommittee's findings. Liberal columnist Doris Fleeson called the report "that rara avis, a documented and sober story produced by the McCarthy subcommittee." Going on, she praised the thorough work done by Robert Kennedy. "It received much more credence . . . than anything else to which Senator McCarthy's name is attached."

Yet his boss's detractors chimed in as well, which brought forth a frustrated response from his assistant counsel. According to *The Boston Post*, Bobby was "alarmed and shocked at the manner in which the McCarthy haters hopped all over" the uncovering of mainly British trade with Communist China. "I really don't know," Bobby told the newspaper. "I'd supposed that it just didn't make sense to anybody in this country that the major allies, whom we're aiding financially, should trade with the Communists who are killing GIs."

But the article went on to make a point of separating the junior Massachusetts senator's brother from the Cohn-Schine pair and their recent antics. "Kennedy," it read, "contrary to general belief, apparently, has not taken part in any of the McCarthy committee's probes into subversives in the State Department, the Voice of America, and other government agencies. What he has done is work on ways to shut off strategic materials of war to countries in the Russian Zone, including North Korea. He'll continue to do so."

Bobby, who felt nothing but contempt for the self-promoting shenanigans of Cohn, was more accepting when it came to the same behavior by McCarthy himself. He kept a warmth for the senator, and a respect for his goals, also honoring his status as a family friend. It appealed to Bobby, moreover, that Joe McCarthy was battling the forces of the establishment.

But he worried that the ongoing fallout from Cohn's schemes— as well as the committee's loosely researched accusations—were going to ruin his boss. "Most of the investigations," he later said, "were instituted on the basis of some preconception by the chief counsel or his staff members and not on the basis of information that had been developed. Cohn and Schine claimed they knew from the outset what was wrong; and they weren't going to allow the facts to interfere. Therefore no real spade work that might have destroyed some of their pet theories was ever undertaken."

If Bobby could see the truth, McCarthy couldn't. His assistant counsel had to accept that nothing was going to change.

Stubborn as ever, Joe Kennedy was still hoping to convince Bobby to run for office. Writing to a friend, he mentioned "confidentially" that his second son was "giving serious consideration" to establishing residence in Connecticut. In that way he'd be able to launch his political career out of range from Jack's in Massachusetts.

His success as a legislative aide seems to have lessened his resistance to a political life. He began to explore seriously a run of his own. It didn't go unnoticed.

"At one point, Bobby Kennedy almost ran against me for Congress," Tip O'Neill wrote in his memoirs, *Man of the House*. "There was a rumor that he'd been thinking of running against Tom Dodd in Connecticut. When Dodd heard about it, he confronted Kennedy and asked if the story was true. 'No,' said Bobby, 'but I am looking for a seat, and I may run up in Tip O'Neill's district.'

"I stormed into Jack's office in the Senate. 'Listen,' I said, 'Tom Dodd says that Bobby may run against me. I've always been good friends with you and your father. If Bobby runs, you'll never be able to outspend me. I can raise a quarter of a million dollars. And if you people spend more than that there'll be a backlash. And what about loyalty? I'm telling you, Jack, if Bobby runs against me, it will be the dirtiest campaign you ever saw.'"

The next morning Jack Kennedy phoned him. "I talked with my old man," he said, "and these are his exact words: 'Bobby will not be a candidate in Tip O'Neill's district, and that's all there is to it. Tip is a friend of the family.'"

That summer, with his work on the arms trade concluded, Bobby gave notice he'd be leaving his job. He'd already made clear his strong feelings about the path to "disaster" he saw McCarthy on, including his refusal to jettison Cohn.

Please accept my resignation as assistant counsel and deputy staff director of the Senate Permanent Subcommittee on Investigations, effective as of the close of business July 31, 1953.

With the filing in the Senate of the subcommittee report on trade with the Soviet bloc, the task to which I have devoted my time since coming with the subcommittee has been completed.

I am submitting my resignation at this time as it is my intention to enter the private practice of law at an early date.

Senators on the permanent subcommittee were quick with their praise for Bobby's work. Henry "Scoop" Jackson, a Democratic senator from the state of Washington, emphasized his objectivity and careful documentation: "I was particularly impressed with the thorough, impartial and fair way in which you handled all matters coming to your attention. In all your investigations you were most diligent in adhering to the facts." The implicit—anti-Cohn—message was clear.

It had been a summer of two Kennedy weddings, beginning in May with Eunice's to Sargent Shriver, then working for her father. Joe McCarthy's wedding gift was a silver jewel box engraved "From the one who lost out." The second was Jack's in early September to Jacqueline Bouvier. One of the year's major social events, it took place in Newport, Rhode Island, with six hundred guests attending and Archbishop Richard Cushing performing the ceremony. Bobby Kennedy was best man as his brother had been for him.

There was another marriage to come. Two weeks after Jack's, Joseph McCarthy wed his staff researcher Jean Kerr at Washington's St. Matthew's Cathedral. Eunice Shriver was one of the bridesmaids. Roy Cohn was an usher. Joe Kennedy and his sons Jack and Bobby all attended, as did his daughter Pat. Richard Nixon was there, too, although President Eisenhower made excuses. Outside the cathedral two thousand McCarthy supporters waited to cheer the couple.

McCarthy's honeymoon in the British Virgin Islands was soon cut short. He was called back to Washington to review new evidence his staff had collected on Communist infiltration of the United States Army. This information supported his current agenda. He'd recently been accusing the army of "coddling Communists," of failing to remove security risks, and, also, of harassing Roy Cohn's friend Schine, who'd been drafted that summer.

Despite his own reservations about Schine, McCarthy put in a call on his behalf to Secretary of the Army Robert Stevens—who'd been a guest at his wedding—with a special plea prompted by Cohn's distress. "I'd like to ask you a personal favor. For God's sake, don't assign him back on my committee. He's a good boy, but there's nothing indispensable about him. If he could get off weekends—that's one of the few things I've seen Roy completely unreasonable about. He thinks Dave should be a general and work from the penthouse of the Waldorf!"

McCarthy's standing in the Gallup Poll was at its highest ever. Sixty-two percent of Republicans approved his combative stance against the army; only 19 percent disapproved. He even held a modest edge among Democrats: 39 to 38. When it came to Catholics, 58 percent backed him; only 23 percent disapproved.

The subcommittee's investigation now centered on the Army Signal Corps installation at Fort Monmouth, New Jersey, where McCarthy had zeroed in on Dr. Irving Peress. Just promoted to major in the Army Dental Corps, he'd been identified by subcommittee research as a Communist. In November McCarthy was angered to learn Peress had been given an honorable discharge. His battle with the army had begun.

For his part, Bobby Kennedy, who'd resigned from the subcommittee, was at loose ends. Facing no financial need to make a living, he still needed a job, and a purpose. Beckoned by his father, he went to work for the commission headed by former president Herbert

Hoover—to promote efficiency and economy in the federal government—on which Joe Kennedy sat as a member.

"He had a lot of frustration in his Hoover Commission job" is how Lem Billings saw this period. "He'd decided to dedicate himself to the government, and he hadn't found his niche, and he didn't know where he was going to find it. This made him, at the time, an unhappy, angry young man."

It was then, said Billings, when "many people formed their ideas about him—people who didn't know him, who met him in Washington at parties and sometimes found him antagonistic and argumentative. It was because he was frustrated inside. He was filled with so many things he wanted to do, but he felt he wasn't accomplishing anything. He was getting nowhere. He just didn't see his future."

Suddenly, a door opened. The Democratic senators on McCarthy's subcommittee had lost patience with the chairman's highhandedness. They especially resented his exclusive control over the hiring of counsel. To force a change, the Democratic members boycotted the current round of hearings, threatening to remain away until McCarthy agreed to share power over staff appointments.

In January 1954, McCarthy agreed to give the Democratic senators a minority counsel, a clerk, and a voice in planning the subcommittee agenda. Arkansas's John McClellan, the senior Democrat, used his new authority to hire Bobby Kennedy as Democratic counsel. In Roy Cohn's view, Kennedy's chief reason for now returning to the committee was to get *him*.

Bobby's father, who never wavered in his support for McCarthy, was proud of his younger son's new ferocity, a pride that no doubt included any open warring with the formidable Cohn. "Put your mind at rest about that," he reassured a friend, former secretary of defense Robert Lovett, who was worried about the "tough company" Bobby was keeping. "Bobby's just as tough as a bootheel."

With all his hostility to Cohn and objections to the chairman's tactics, Bobby had become close to Joe McCarthy personally. "You can't believe it," remembered Ethel Kennedy, swept up by the memories. "We'd go over there for drinks, Joe's house." Looking at her daughter Kathleen—sitting there with us—she told her, "You were a year old. You loved him and he loved you. We'd go over, and we'd be carrying you, and the minute they'd open the door, Joe would take you away. I was very happy holding you, but he'd say, 'No, Kathleen's mine.'"

The conflict the zealous senator had begun with the U.S. Army was heating up. For him now, the rallying cry was: Who Promoted Peress? Angering him further was the fact that it had been Peress's distinguished commanding officer, Brigadier General Ralph Zwicker, who'd just approved the dentist's honorable discharge. "General, you are not fit to wear the uniform," Joe McCarthy said with contempt in a closed hearing. "You're shielding Communist conspirators."

With that outburst from McCarthy, a line had been crossed for Army Secretary Stevens. Zwicker was a highly respected field officer who'd come out of World War II with two Silver Stars, three Bronze Stars, a Purple Heart, and France's Croix de Guerre. Stevens wasn't going to let McCarthy browbeat such a man.

"Just go ahead and try, Robert," McCarthy now threatened when the army secretary dared resist letting Zwicker testify before his subcommittee. "I'm going to kick the brains out of anyone who protects Communists. Just go ahead. I will guarantee that you will live to regret it."

Secretary Stevens now counterattacked. He released a printed list detailing each attempt Roy Cohn had made at intimidating the army in order to gain special treatment for the recently inducted David Schine. Cohn's insistence that his protégé be given a direct commission as an officer was just one of the preposterous benefits he'd demanded.

To Bobby, the Senate Caucus Room had become a chamber of bad feelings. "Every night when I come home from work I feel my neck to see if my head is still attached," he joked.

Ken O'Donnell saw his friend's conflict. "He thought," reported O'Donnell, "that there were unfair aspects to the criticism of the senator. If Bobby had a weakness, that was it—whenever somebody was in real trouble or was being unfairly treated, then he was for him."

But he was also aware of Bobby's anger "at the way they were treating witnesses. He was incensed at the Cohn-Schine investigations, and thought they'd lost all sense of direction."

One example of the subcommittee's obsessive yet careless pursuit of its targets was the McCarthy panel's handling that March of Annie Lee Moss. A teletype operator in the Army Signal Corps, this forty-nine-year-old African American widow was being portrayed as a known Communist who now had access to coded intelligence messages.

Part of the evidence being used against her involved a man named Rob Hall who'd been known to regularly deliver her a copy of the *Daily Worker*. Bobby realized something was amiss when a reporter tipped him off that the fellow bringing around the newspaper was African American. Robert Hall, the known Communist activist and editor at the *Daily Worker*, was white.

The following is from the Senate Permanent Subcommittee

on Investigations hearing on March 11, 1954. First, Annie Moss is asked a question by Roy Cohn.

"Isn't it a fact that you regularly received the *Daily Worker* . . . through Rob Hall, one of the leading Communists in the District of Columbia?"

But Bobby now had a question for Cohn himself.

"When you spoke about the union organizer, you spoke about Rob Hall, and I think we all felt that he was a colored gentleman."

Cohn: I was not talking about a union organizer, Bob. I was talking about a Communist organizer.

Kennedy: Evidently, it was a different Rob Hall.

Cohn: I don't know that it was. Our information is that it was the same Rob Hall.

Committee chairman John McClellan: If one is black and the other is white, there is a difference.

Cohn: I think that might be something we should look into and get some information on.

Kennedy: I think so, too.

That same month CBS's Edward R. Murrow offered a special presentation of his *See It Now* program, entitled "A Report on Senator Joseph R. McCarthy." Invoking the credibility he'd earned as an American broadcaster in wartime London—with bombs falling around him—he made a patriotic case *against* McCarthy. He'd become, he said, a liability to our side in the Cold War.

"We proclaim ourselves, as indeed we are, the defenders of freedom, wherever it continues to exist in the world, but we cannot defend freedom abroad by deserting it at home. The actions of the junior Senator from Wisconsin have caused alarm and dismay among our allies abroad, and given considerable comfort to our enemies."

McCarthy loyalists were defiant. A week after Murrow's CBS report had aired, the Wisconsin senator spoke to 1,200 men at a St. Patrick's Day dinner in Chicago, reminding his audience that the saint they honored "drove the snakes out of Ireland and the snakes didn't like his methods either."

"Traitors," he told the admiring crowd, "are not gentlemen."

The ongoing conflict between McCarthy and Secretary Stevens had now reached the point of reckoning. Serious charges had been laid against the army in its handling of the Peress case. But what about the investigating subcommittee's own conduct in regard to Schine? Its chairman now stood accused of abusing his power on behalf of a subordinate. That charge also hung in the air.

With McCarthy attacking the army and the army firing back, the consensus formed that both those disputes needed to be resolved, and done so publicly. It was decided that the subcommittee itself would be the proper tribunal, but that McCarthy must remove himself from the chair. The Army-McCarthy hearings began that April. With Democratic leader Lyndon Johnson pushing hard, the decision was made to have them televised live. Detesting McCarthy, the Texan sensed the wind was about to shift.

The American Broadcasting Company decided to cover the proceedings in the Senate Caucus Room gavel to gavel. For thirty-six days ABC's daily coverage became a national obsession. The hearings addressed both McCarthy's charges against the army and the army's against him, specifically whether he or his staff had pressured the army to give special treatment and privileges to Schine. McCarthy would be both accuser and accused.

Though Bobby Kennedy was the senator's first choice to be chief counsel for the hearing, Senator McClellan objected.

I still remember how that period seemed to me, even though I was only eight. I'd arrive home from school to find our new black-and-white Admiral TV tuned to those hearings. Something unusual was happening. Looking back, I realize my very Irish mom didn't want to miss a minute of it. She wasn't rooting for the army.

The hearings began in late April. Two moments stand out. Weeks into the proceedings, Senator McCarthy made the mistake of going after Fred Fisher, a young law associate of Joseph Welch, the army's counsel. The charge against Welch's colleague was his membership in the National Lawyers Guild, a group tagged by the U.S. attorney general as a Communist front.

Shaking his head in exasperated disbelief, Welch was now on the attack: "Until this moment, Senator, I think I never really gauged your cruelty or your recklessness." When McCarthy persisted, Welch broke in with a simple plea, "Let us not assassinate this lad further, Senator. You have done enough. Have you no sense of decency sir, at long last? Have you left no sense of decency?" If the skilled trial lawyer had rehearsed his performance, as some believed he had, it took nothing from the drama and the moral power of his indictment.

At this, the Caucus Room audience burst into applause. That loud clapping signaled a change in the national atmosphere: Joe McCarthy was headed downward.

Two days later, it was the hostility between Bobby Kennedy and Roy Cohn that seized attention. With Kennedy assisting him, Scoop Jackson began to interrogate Cohn about his friend Schine's qualifications. His questioning focused on a scheme Schine had devised for the U.S. government to promote democracy worldwide.

One part of the "Schine Plan" was to approach fraternal organizations such as Elks Lodges for help. Jackson, enjoying himself, asked whether there were any Elks Clubs in Pakistan, for example. The unlikelihood of this drew an appreciative roar from the crowd.

"What's wrong with that?" Senator McCarthy jumped in, coming to Cohn's rescue. It's better, he declared, than "putting out the thirty-thousand-odd books written by Communist authors that we found in our investigations." He was referring to the purge Cohn and Schine had conducted the year before in Europe.

But as Jackson kept asking questions about Schine's pet project, his broad smile remained. This drove Cohn beyond his boiling point. When the chair called a recess, he darted for Kennedy, where he jabbed a file in front of his face. "Tell Jackson we're going to get him on Monday," Cohn warned. "We've got letters he wrote to the White House on behalf of two known Communists."

"Tell him yourself," Kennedy shot back. "Don't threaten me. You've got a fucking nerve threatening me."

The taunting was now turning physical. Seeing Cohn cock his arm, bystanders stepped in and stopped him. Bobby had gotten to his rival and knew it.

Ken O'Donnell, watching the hearings in the Bellevue Hotel bar—a time-honored political hangout by the Boston State House—was startled by the response of the crowd. "Remember, it was a group there watching—Boston Irish politicians, some truck drivers, and hardworking guys—most tinged with anti-Semitism. So Cohn wasn't the type of fellow you'd think they'd like. Yet every single person in that bar cheered and yelled and hoped he'd belt Bobby one."

My dad, whose parents were English and Northern-Irish Protestant, had a more measured view of McCarthy than Mom. Just as

Jack Kennedy had, he thought he was onto something—yet was now convinced he'd gone too far. He was hardly alone in this estimate. Polls showed the senator's national approval had dropped 15 points from 50 percent down to 35.

Despite Bobby's continued personal feelings for McCarthy, it now fell to him to draft the Democratic report on the Army-McCarthy hearings. It would become the basic record of senatorial misconduct for later use by the entire Senate in its proceedings against McCarthy. Clearly action needed to be taken. After weeks of insults, taunts, threats, and other examples of juvenile behavior, the Senate looked like anything but "the world's greatest deliberative body."

What Bobby wrote indicted McCarthy for "attacking the character and impugning the loyalty" of Secretary Stevens and others. He focused on Roy Cohn's hectoring of the army on Schine's behalf. On this score, however, he did not exonerate Cohn's boss. "The Senator cannot escape responsibility for the misconduct of Cohn. The Senate should take action to correct this situation."

The ball was now rolling. In August a Select Committee divided evenly between Republicans and Democrats was asked to recommend the appropriate sanctions. The Senate was now moving to resolve the McCarthy situation by a vote to censure. For Jack Kennedy, this presented political danger. While McCarthy's popularity around the country had been battered, he remained an admired champion in Kennedy's backyard, with an entrenched appeal that more than matched Jack's own. "Hell," he told Arthur Schlesinger in 1953, "half my voters in Massachusetts look on McCarthy as a hero."

The mail coming into his office was overwhelmingly pro-McCarthy. But Jack Kennedy needed to reply with the most careful and ambiguous of phrases. "I am giving attention to this situation, and I am hopeful that the outcome will be the one most desirable for the good of the Senate and the country."

"To understand my situation," he told a reporter some years later, "you must remember that my father was a friend of Joe's, as was my sister Eunice, and my brother Bobby had worked for him. So I had all those family pressures." The Kennedys' long personal involvement with McCarthy, he later told biographer James MacGregor Burns, was "really the guts of the matter."

Having read this far, readers should have picked up on my strong surmise that, for Jack, it was more than that. I've always thought that he—though maybe not as much as his brother—had a soft spot for Joe McCarthy. I think Jack loved the tumult in the man, the rebellious spirit that led him, finally, too far.

Apart from his own unresolved feelings toward McCarthy, Jack was trapped on a fence between two very different sets of Massachusetts voters. There were those who saw the Wisconsin senator as their hero and others who marked him as a historic villain. Years later, when Jack had positioned himself as a liberal, he'd say he hadn't known any of those whom McCarthy terrorized. But what he failed to say is that he'd never made the slightest effort to do so.

With Jack there was always the issue of his bad health lying in the background. During this highly charged period of political turmoil leading into the fall of 1954, the attempts Jack had been making to maintain the pace expected of him began to fail. Having relied on crutches for most of the 1952 race, he now faced the prospect of a wheelchair. By the summer of 1954, the disease and the steroids prescribed for him since his first episode of Addison's disease seven years earlier had placed him in dire straits. He'd dropped in weight from 180 pounds to 140. His back pain was so severe he waited in the Capitol between votes rather than try walking across Constitution Avenue to the Senate Office Building. His Addison's disease made surgery all the more dangerous. Since his body couldn't produce the necessary adrenaline, it reduced its vital ability to fight off infection.

Despite such fears, he agreed to undergo an experimental operation at the New York Hospital for Special Surgery. There, an infection sent him into a coma. Bobby remained at his side, watching over him, as once again he was now, for the third time, given the last rites of the Catholic Church. Only after many hours had passed, with the outlook grim, did it look like his older brother was going to live.

Ted Sorensen, Kennedy's legislative assistant, was afraid to ask the hospitalized senator where he stood on the upcoming McCarthy censure vote. There existed a long-standing procedure whereby Jack could "pair" with an absent senator holding the opposing position, this way putting himself on the public record. People would know where he stood. But as Sorensen later confirmed, he was afraid to even suggest this step, fearing "the wrath of the senator's brother and father more than the senator's."

On December 2, 1954, the Senate vote to "condemn" McCarthy for conduct "contrary to Senate traditions"—with Jack Kennedy still hospitalized up in New York—was 67 to 22.

Not long after the Senate vote, Bobby went out with a few journalist buddies. "Why do you reporters . . . feel the way you do?" he asked them. "Okay, Joe's methods may be a little rough but, after all, his goal was to expose Communists in government—a worthy goal. So why are you . . . so critical of his methods?"

But over the years he'd known and observed McCarthy, seeing, he realized, that he'd created most of his problems himself. "His whole method of operation was complicated because he'd get a guilty feeling and be hurt after he'd blasted somebody," Bobby wrote five years later. "He wanted so desperately to be liked. . . . He was sensitive and yet insensitive. He didn't anticipate the results of what he was doing. He was very thoughtful of his friends and yet could be so cruel to others."

A husband and now the father of three—Robert F. Kennedy, Jr., had been born that January—Bobby was now having to come to grips with life's complexities. While he'd never forgo his penchant for dividing the world, as Ethel would say, between "white hats and black hats," heroes and villains, he was learning vital lessons: your sympathies and your sense of justice are not always in congruence; those you root for are not necessarily the good guys.

Jack and Bobby.

CHAPTER NINE

HAIL MARY

"Well, I guess you could call it a Hail Mary.
You throw it up and pray."

—ROGER STAUBACH

With the coming of the new year, Senator Joe McCarthy—who'd been censured in December before the Congress adjourned—lost control of the Subcommittee on Investigations. The Republicans, minus the magic name of Dwight Eisenhower at the top of the ticket, were no longer on top in either the House or the Senate.

John McClellan, Democrat from Arkansas, was now the subcommittee chairman, with Bobby Kennedy his chief counsel. As the months passed, however, Bobby's thoughts began shifting to his brother's ambitions and how he might help achieve them.

In late September 1955, on vacation in Denver, President Eisenhower suffered a heart attack in the early hours of the morning. Speculation quickly arose over whether he'd be able to serve a second term. One man, betting against a full recovery, saw an opportunity opening for his son.

Joseph Kennedy, believing Ike would have to forgo reelection, now offered a deal to Lyndon Johnson, the new Senate majority leader. If Johnson agreed to run for the 1956 Democratic nomination, Kennedy would pick up the bill. There was a single condition. If the Texan *won* the Democratic nomination, he was to name Senator John F. Kennedy his vice presidential running mate.

Whether it was the crassness of the offer itself—with its assumption Johnson's political plans might be for sale—or the majority leader's fear of losing, Joe's scheme was rejected out of hand. Always cagey, Johnson may merely have been playing it safe. But it wasn't the way it was taken. Bobby Kennedy, for one—not inclined to be sympathetic to the man—counted it as another affront to the Kennedy family.

When the Democrats met in Chicago in the summer of 1956, they ended up again nominating Governor Adlai Stevenson of Illinois. He'd won despite early strong competition from Tennessee senator Estes Kefauver. The real question left to be decided at the convention was who would be the Democratic vice presidential nominee. Well apart from his father's amateurish proposition to the Senate majority leader, Jack Kennedy had mounted a quiet push to sell himself to Stevenson. The strategy was to make his Roman Catholicism not a liability but a bonus.

Statistics compiled on Catholic voting patterns were key. These showed that the number of Catholics casting ballots for Roosevelt in the early years of the New Deal had begun to trail off in the 1940s, and then even more so by 1952. Having John F. Kennedy on the ticket, the argument went, might well bring those voters back to the Democratic coalition.

Kennedy aide Ted Sorensen gathered the data and wrote a report. It was then passed to John Bailey, the Connecticut party chairman and ally, to sign and spread around. Widely circulated as "The Bailey Memorandum," its purpose was to get Stevenson to see the light and select the junior senator from Massachusetts as his running mate.

With the convention about to get under way, Jack Kennedy went to Tip O'Neill, calling upon the man who'd succeeded him for a favor—a large one. He asked O'Neill to cede to him one of the delegate's credentials he'd been allotted. As a Member of Congress, O'Neill was given four delegates to name. When approached by Jack, he'd already awarded three of his four, and intended to keep the last for himself. Kennedy now wanted it. It was as blunt as that.

Jack said he wanted it for Bobby. Calling his brother the "smartest politician" he knew, he pointed out that "lightning may strike . . . and I could end up on the ticket with Stevenson." He wanted his brother to have full access to the delegates on the floor.

For O'Neill, the forfeiture of his credential could be accepted as necessary political business. But he didn't like it. Not one bit. Here was a perk he fully deserved and had put in time achieving, and now he was being asked to hand it over to a young guy he couldn't even stand who'd once made noises about possibly bumping him from his congressional seat. "To me, he was a self-important upstart and know-it-all," Tip would write, still simmering decades later. "I was simply a street-corner pol." Once again, Jack escaped blame while Bobby was never forgiven.

As Jack Kennedy arrived in Chicago, he already had the benefit of public recognition outside the political arena. His second book, *Profiles in Courage*, published earlier in the year, stayed on the *New York Times* bestseller list for over thirty weeks.

Based on that success, he was asked to narrate a twenty-minute documentary that would open the convention and be broadcast to the television audience. *Pursuit of Happiness* was a history of the U.S. focusing on Democratic presidencies from Thomas Jefferson through Harry Truman. Producer Dore Schary, a major Hollywood figure, was impressed with Jack's performance. "All of us who were in contact with him immediately fell in love with him because he was so quick and charming and so cooperative, and obviously so bright and skilled."

From the first words he spoke—"Ladies and Gentlemen, I am Senator John F. Kennedy. To some, the Democratic Party represents a philosophy, a way of life and a point of view"—his personal appeal was unmistakable. He'd been handed a perfect vehicle with which to enter into the country's consciousness. When he was introduced on the podium afterward, he was greeted by wild enthusiasm from the floor. As a result of this triumph, Stevenson asked Jack to be the one to formally place his name in nomination. On getting the offer, Jack expressed his concern that this was really a consolation prize, removing him from vice presidential contention. The nominee assured him it was not. But Stevenson's denial masked his own indecision. He couldn't bring himself to make the choice. With time running out, he flinched.

With the convention ending the next day, Stevenson declared late Thursday night that "the selection of the vice presidential nominee should be made through the free processes of the convention." Thus, he said, "the Democratic Party's candidate for this office may join me before the nation, not as one man's selection, but as one chosen by our great party, even as I have been chosen."

This, of course, left it to the assembled delegates to do what their chosen leader had been unable to—determine who might best help him beat the likable Ike. Stevenson's public justification for passing the buck—according to the political spin from his headquarters—was to remind voters, aware of Eisenhower's alarming heart attack, just how important choosing a vice president is. The very idea of Richard Nixon sitting in the Oval Office, he was convinced, would be sufficient to stampede voters to any Democratic candidate.

It was clear who would be the early front-runner in this unexpected convention balloting. Tennessean Estes Kefauver, representing his state since 1939, had run vigorously in the 1952 convention, come awfully close—and kept running ever since. Kefauver continued to benefit from his series of televised hearings on organized crime in 1950. A well-recognized figure nationally, he was ready to claim the number-two spot on the ticket.

It was at this moment that Jack and Bobby decided to go for it. With the clock ticking, they were about to take the risk of the game-winning touchdown. "Call Dad and tell him I'm going for it," Jack told Bobby. Carrying news to their difficult, too often unpredictable father had become his job. So he picked up the phone.

Joseph Kennedy was fond of telling his family, "Things don't happen, they're made to happen." Only months before he'd been the one conniving to snag the VP nomination for his son; now Jack and Bobby were doing it, but with him a continent away, in the South of France. Jack could hear his father's reaction to the news from across the room. He was calling him an "idiot" to be doing this. *Idiot!*

"Whew!" Bobby said, putting down the receiver. "Is he mad!"

Up in the Kennedy hotel suite, the first necessity was a plan to enlist delegates to their side. But despite frantic attempts to identify those they knew, they were coming up short. It was quite obvious they were in over their heads, at least at the start.

Bobby knew several senators from his work on what was now the McClellan Committee. Finding the Arkansas senator himself, he went straight to the point. "What can you do to help?" he asked the lawmaker he'd been serving as right-hand man.

The encounter was an education in itself. McClellan first let him know he thought his brother would make an attractive addition to the Democratic ticket. Now encouraged, Bobby pushed him further asking how much assistance could he be in gathering together other delegates for Jack?

The Arkansas senator, who liked and admired Bobby personally, now had to be candid, and also a bit embarrassed. United States senators, despite their stature on the national stage, possessed little or no political clout at party conventions, he told him. Governor Orval Faubus was the one actually wielding power over his state's delegation. McClellan was lucky to be a delegate himself, he confessed. All that he had to offer, as it turned out, was counsel.

His advice: if you want to win a delegation at the next political convention, go to that state and "find out who has the power . . . and stop reading the newspapers."

The learning curve in those early morning hours, as Bobby tried working the system as he saw it, unfortunately kept producing setbacks. The good news was that every bit of education he absorbed he wouldn't need to learn again. I once heard historian Arthur Schlesinger say, "Politics is essentially a learning profession." These hours in the summer of 1956 were teaching him its basic dynamic.

The truth is, the mere act of announcing for office creates a reality not present beforehand. Suddenly the new candidate sees himself as a force, one requiring those previously allied, hostile, or neutral, to choose. Each must decide whether to support the new candidate or not, responding publicly with positions of either loyalty or enmity. You become a figure, and potential rivals have to deal with you.

During those few hours, the scene there in the International Amphitheatre changed. Jack Kennedy had now made himself a wild card in the proceedings, as well as a player on the national political stage.

The Kennedys' effort was facing powerful resistance in Chicago from Democratic Party liberals. Coming across the progressive Michigan governor, G. Mennen "Soapy" Williams, Bobby grabbed his arm. "Why are you against my brother?" he scolded him. Stunned, Williams pulled himself free and headed off. They assumed this was triggered by the family's association with Joseph McCarthy.

The convention vote for vice president took place that Friday in early afternoon. The first ballot had Kefauver in the lead with 483½ delegates; Kennedy in second with 304; Senator Albert Gore, Sr., of Tennessee with 178; New York City mayor Robert Wagner with 162½; Minnesota senator Hubert Humphrey with 134½.

On the second ballot, the Southerners were out in force to stop Kefauver because of his support for civil rights, which they took as regional betrayal. They began heading to Kennedy.

Ted Sorensen recalled the moment. "The second ballot was underway and a Kennedy trend had set in. The south was anxious to stop Kefauver. Kennedy was picking up the Gore and Southern favorite-son votes. He was getting Wagner votes, too. Bob Kennedy and his lieutenants were all over the floor shouting to delegations to come with Kennedy."

Despite Bobby's baleful treatment of him, Lyndon Johnson had jumped onto the bandwagon. "Texas proudly casts its vote for the fighting senator who wears the scars of battle, that fearless senator, the next vice president of the United States, John Kennedy of Massachusetts." Kennedy was now beating Kefauver 504 to 395. It certainly looked as if he was headed to a 684 majority. Bobby was on the convention floor holding up his fingers in a Churchillian "V" sign.

Unknown to him, a pattern of resistance to Jack was beginning to emerge on two fronts. Both were owing to the candidate's religion. Sorensen had gone to the Minnesota delegation to plead for the backing of Congressman Eugene McCarthy. "Forget it!" came his dismissive reply. "All we have are farmers and Protestants."

Then, there were the anti-Catholic politicians, who were now, on the second ballot, looking to stop the Kennedy momentum. Oklahoma governor J. Howard Edmondson phrased his own feeling on the matter this way: "He's not our kind of folks." The speaker of the house, Texan Sam Rayburn, was not so tactful. "If we have to take a Catholic, I hope we don't have to take that little pissant Kennedy."

Since Rayburn was chairing the convention, he soon had the opportunity to act on his own clear bias and help steer the decision. With South Carolina, Illinois, and Alabama seeking recognition from the podium to shift their delegates to Kennedy, he instead recognized Edmondson, eager now to throw his state's Gore votes to Kefauver. That settled, Rayburn next called on Gore, who threw his remaining votes also to Kefauver.

"Let's go!" Jack Kennedy ordered Sorensen the moment he realized what was happening, and began pushing his way toward the podium through hundreds of milling delegates. It was a master class in how to make pure gold from a bad break.

His superb timing now added to his eloquence. Looking down and surveying the convention floor, he had every delegate's attention fixed upon him. Stepping back gallantly from his own quest, he asked that the vote for Estes Kefauver be made unanimous. The gesture was spontaneous, gracious, memorable—and calculating.

And it had the expected effect. The crowd loudly welcomed his call for party unity. The question now was where he stood. Their Hail Mary play, after all, had fallen short. "He was very depressed when he lost to Kefauver," Jean recalled. Joe Kennedy's children had been taught never to be content with losing.

It was then that they heard from their always unpredictable father. "It's the best thing that ever happened to you," came the vigorous voice from the Riviera. Less than a year before, when he'd made the approach to Johnson, the senior Kennedy had imagined his son on a winning ticket. But that was then. The outlook now was for a Democratic loss in 1956. Not only was his son now free from the coming wreckage but, even better, an attractive alternative for next time.

But for Bobby, the eleventh-hour defeat was still tough to accept, and it left him seething. He'd imagined it would be a fair fight—and it turned out to be anything but. Behind the scenes, he suspected, strings had been pulled.

The milling delegates at a political convention may look like a stadium crowd at a sports event. But the individuals filling these seats aren't there randomly. Each delegate is present either at the behest of a political boss or else owing to a candidate's success in a primary. Conventions in those days, before primaries became dominant in selecting presidential nominees, were more fluid. Delegations, often led by governors or party leaders, were free to make decisions in the moment. Once Stevenson threw the choice for his running mate to the convention floor, it became a live contest, with all the unpredictability that goes with it.

At the 1956 conventions the expected candidates—Kefauver, Gore, Wagner, Humphrey—were suddenly joined by a new face, who'd made his national debut in their midst. Recognizing the excitement he'd generated on the first night, Jack saw his chance. His prediction to Tip O'Neill that "lightning" could strike in Chicago had been correct. Seizing the moment, and charging through all the time pressure and chaos, the Kennedys and their team managed for a thrilling half day to capture much of it in a bottle.

But Bobby saw that at the climactic moment of the vice president fight, the contest had been tilted by those running it. Rayburn and the governors, who controlled the levers, had used them to stop the upstart Kennedy.

Leaving Chicago Bobby started to go back over what he'd seen and learned. He understood the extent to which his brother would need his skills to put it all together. The lessons were these: first, they had to create from scratch a state-by-state national organization; second, they'd have to achieve backroom clout, enough to muscle the bosses when necessary and keep them in line; and, third, they'd have to overcome the religious issue which had reared its head in the final hour. That meant winning every open contest on the way to the convention. The Kennedys could not afford to lose a single primary.

For my family, our awareness of the situation in Chicago came that Friday afternoon, as the convention was ending. We were on our way home from the store in our '54 Chevy Impala. On the radio, the states' delegates were being called upon to declare their choices. "Kefauver" was a familiar name by then, "Kennedy" an unknown. My mother, once she later realized what had happened, couldn't help but see it as an echo of Al Smith's rejection back in 1928.

Two days after Chicago, Jack Kennedy headed to the South of France. Pausing to stop to visit his father, he proceeded to meet up with his younger brother Ted, old Harvard pal Torby Macdonald, and a bevy of more pleasurable company awaiting them on a yacht. He hadn't altered these plans despite the fact that Jacqueline was seven months pregnant. When she delivered a stillborn daughter on August 23—Arabella, as her mother would call her—the child's father was still on the Côte d'Azur, relaxing after the strains of the convention six days earlier.

It was Bobby who raced through the night from Hyannis Port to Newport where his sister-in-law was staying at her mother's. And it was he who made the choice, then, to keep his fun-loving brother in the dark about the sad trauma his wife was enduring.

Proud, now, of his ability to take decisive action, he judged it unwise to summon Jack back quickly under such circumstances. Despite the fact that he knew Jackie had had a miscarriage the year before and now had to be suffering greatly, he felt it best for her to begin healing in the presence of her own mother and family. Bobby decided that the last thing his fragile sister-in-law and her delinquent husband needed was an angry confrontation.

It was Bobby to whom the task fell of telling his sister-in-law she'd lost her baby. It was also he who arranged for the infant's burial. He was not the only party concerned about the situation. When Jack's close Senate buddy George Smathers read in the papers what had happened and that Jack was still in Europe, he sent word that he either come back to his wife now or forfeit both his marriage and his political career. "If you want to run for president, you'd better get your ass back to your wife's bedside, or else every wife in the country would be against it."

It wasn't until the day after Arabella's interment that Jackie finally heard her husband's voice on the telephone. He was in the Mediterranean port town of Genoa. "I'm now committed to being a total politician," Jack had recently sworn, having decided to focus on the difficult path leading to the largest prize of all. Smathers had reminded him he needed to think, too, about being a total husband.

That fall, with the Senate adjourned, Bobby set off to join the Stevenson campaign. Sacrificing weeks with his family, he would be serving, in reality, as a double agent. For Stevenson's purposes, he was along to help the Protestant, divorced candidate connect with devout Roman Catholics. Bobby would play a liaison role in such rituals as introducing Stevenson to local bishops. For purposes of the Kennedy Party, it was to discover for himself the dos and don'ts of a national effort committed to winning.

Mainly, the experience with Stevenson would teach him how not to run for president. "I came out of our first conversation with a very high opinion of him," he would say of the two-time nominee. "Then I spent six weeks with him on the campaign and he destroyed it all."

For one thing, Bobby, who took pride in being able to make decisions, saw that Stevenson couldn't. "You wouldn't believe it," he told Kenny O'Donnell when the campaign swung through Boston. "This is the most disastrous operation you ever saw." But the nominee's other big problem, as Bobby could see, was his failure to connect with real people. His critique was the same as my own dad's of Adlai. "He talked over the heads of people." Bobby's example was classic: he'd seen the governor deliver an elaborate speech on world affairs to a group of twenty-five coal miners standing on the railroad tracks in West Virginia.

Kennedy thought Stevenson quite simply spent too much time writing speeches and not enough campaigning for votes. To him, Stevenson's belief in his oratorical ability caused him to miss the human aspect of a campaign. Bobby had watched his brother do it right, starting in 1946, traveling the state and meeting with crowds, introducing himself personally to voters who'd shown up. It was why, in 1952, Jack had kept sticking those pins into the Massachusetts map on his wall.

Riding along with Stevenson also did little to lessen the younger Kennedy's contempt for liberals.

"The subject of Nixon came up, and I was strongly against making the campaign built around an attack on him." Bobby recognized that the true believers surrounding Stevenson were deluding themselves. They thought that the country's undecided voters shared their hostility for the Republican vice president. Bobby knew better, that the Nixon haters and the reliable Stevenson voters were one and the same—and that they constituted a minority of the electorate.

The result of such close-up observation of the Democratic candidate had the effect of changing Bobby's vote. He'd concluded that Stevenson wasn't up to the job of president. He cast his ballot for Eisenhower and Nixon.

And America agreed with him that November, overwhelmingly awarding Eisenhower a second term. The question now was who would succeed him.

Here's Ted Kennedy's account. "After the traditional Thanksgiving dinner in Hyannis Port in November 1956, Jack and Joe, Sr., left the table and repaired to the study near the living room for a private talk. When they emerged, grinning, arms around each other's shoulders, the rest of us learned that Jack had decided to run for president in 1960."

As now was inevitable, Bobby would have two jobs, one on the inside, the other on the outside. The first involved, as before, his making sure their father was a help, not a hindrance. The convention had proven again the worth of that talent he'd first displayed in the uphill race against Lodge, acting as a bridge between his father and his brother.

His other role, too, was by now familiar: Bobby was to be the enforcer, the *heavy*, making his presence felt in situations where Jack needed to remain at a distance.

Rose Kennedy, watching her sons commit to this all-consuming enterprise, saw what role each would play. Jack would be the candidate, Bobby the one responsible for getting him elected. "It was understood," she said, "that when Jack ran, Bobby would be his campaign manager."

The Kennedy brothers on the Senate Rackets Committee.

CHAPTER TEN

IRISH COP

"I thought Teamster meant mob."

—Kathleen Kennedy Townsend

Bobby Kennedy learned politics from the ground up. From his first volunteer effort in the Italian wards of East Cambridge—when he'd won over the neighborhood playing softball with the kids—to his taking charge of Jack's 1952 campaign, he'd been immersed in its day-to-day demands. Now, with the challenge and disappointment of Chicago behind him, he was returning to the Senate's Permanent Subcommittee on Investigations.

One conversation in Chicago, connected to his work in Washington, left a strong mark. It had happened on the floor as the balloting had ended. A respected investigative reporter—Clark Mollenhoff of *The Des Moines Register* and *Tribune*—had gotten in his face, taunting him about a key factor in Kefauver's success. "He did his investigations five years ago," Mollenhoff reminded him, "and it got him enough clout to beat your brother's butt."

He was referring to the Kefauver Committee's televised hearings on organized crime that had made the Tennessean a household name across the country. That celebrity had carried him to the vice presidential nomination over Jack.

Mollenhoff said that Bobby could do *exactly* what Estes Kefauver had made his name doing—taking on the mob. But now he was talking about the widening corruption in organized labor. This meant taking on prominent labor leaders closely allied to Democratic politicians as well as dangerous hoodlums. To pursue such criminals, they both knew, was a risky enterprise.

Mollenhoff told Kennedy about Pulitzer Prize–winning reporter Ed Guthman of *The Seattle Times*, who'd been engaged for eight years in an investigation of Teamsters president Dave Beck. Guthman, he explained, needed help from a partner like Bobby Kennedy, one with the law behind him. Having an ally with the power of subpoena would make all the difference.

Guthman wanted a man who held such a weapon and the conviction to use it. He had to be certain that the person joining him in the hunt would not back off under pressure.

Bobby listened and agreed to consider the mission. Next, Mollenhoff phoned Guthman, telling him the news. "A young lawyer from the subcommittee would like to come out and see you, and I hope you'll help him." His listener—unimpressed on hearing that it was Jack Kennedy's younger brother—had a single question: "Can you trust him?"

Both reporters had had too much experience with politicians afraid to take on organized labor. After grabbing a few headlines, they'd move on, leaving the reporter dangling and his sources in trouble. Both had seen good men pay dearly for sticking their necks out.

Mollenhoff was the perfect man to vouch for Kennedy. He, too, was digging into the activities of the Teamsters, specifically those of a Detroit official named Jimmy Hoffa. Having been sold on Kennedy's commitment, Guthman agreed to welcome him when he came west.

As the year was ending, Bobby informed his father that he intended to use the Permanent Subcommittee on Investigations to bring to justice crooked labor leaders like Beck. Hearing this, Joseph Kennedy, now fixed on the idea of a 1960 presidential run for his eldest living son, was strongly opposed. Bobby, he angrily insisted, was being reckless. Pursuing such figures as Beck was politically dangerous and could hurt Jack with labor. This fight between father and son was, according to Jean, "the worst ever."

Two days after Christmas, Bobby met with his boss, Senator McClellan, and won the case for action. But for Democrats to target the labor unions required legislative finesse. McClellan's panel needed to avoid trampling on the Labor Committee's turf. To accommodate that, it was agreed to create a new panel, its members drawn equally from the two committees. That January, the Select Committee on Improper Activities in the Labor or Management Field—soon to be known as the "Rackets Committee"—was formed with McClellan as chairman and Bobby Kennedy its chief counsel.

Among the Republicans were Barry Goldwater of Arizona and Bobby's old boss, Joe McCarthy. The Democrats included Kennedy of Massachusetts. Jack had agreed to serve as a member, but only because Bobby pressed him. "Bobby wanted me on that committee," he said, because without him, his brother argued, it would have been too heavily conservative and anti-labor. There was also the factor of Kefauver's crime-busting fame and its enduring electoral value.

Whether or not Jack came on board, Bobby's role as chief counsel meant the Kennedy name would always be identified with the inquiry. "If the investigation flops," Bobby told Ken O'Donnell, whom he'd named his administrative assistant, "it will hurt Jack in 1958 and in 1960, too. A lot of people think he's the Kennedy running the investigation, not me. As far as the public is concerned, one Kennedy is the same as another Kennedy."

Kennedy declared two rules for committee procedure, each of them learned the hard way watching Joe McCarthy as chairman. The first was to go for the facts and not just headlines; the second was about showing respect for those being investigated. He would never call a witness until the committee staff had thoroughly checked out his testimony ahead of time. Unless he was personally satisfied as to the credibility of the charges, he would never put a witness in front of the cameras.

What Bobby most wanted to avoid was the sheer recklessness of the committee under his former boss, who'd made "McCarthyism" a term of infamy. "If we allowed witnesses to come before the Committee with no real idea of what testimony to expect from them, without first interviewing them, studying and checking their information we should have had utter chaos and confusion, plus many inequities," he wrote later.

He'd been an eyewitness to the human cost of this. "The most important advantage of checking and rechecking testimony is that it lessens tremendously the possibility of damaging an innocent person's reputation. It is usually possible to find a witness who will testify to almost anything about a person who has been active in public life or who has taken a stand on issues: such a man is bound to have made enemies. . . . You cannot put a man—or a woman—

on the stand, allow him to hurl accusations indiscriminately and, when the testimony is found to be untrue, disown him and accept no responsibility."

Ed Guthman, who'd convinced him of the enormity of the cause, could see that Kennedy both understood the need to expose Beck's abuse of power yet was drawn to the even larger mission of saving a basic and very important American institution. The Teamsters were the largest union in the country, with a million and a half members in its rank and file. In the panel's investigation of its president, Bobby—Guthman realized—was "more concerned with what the corruption, dishonesty and arbitrary use of power were doing to the democratic process and individual morality than he was with the specifics of the crimes that were being uncovered."

Two weeks after the Rackets Committee was formed, Bobby received a call from a New York lawyer with a story he thought he needed to hear. This attorney said he had been contacted by Teamster vice president Jimmy Hoffa and handed $1,000 as a down payment for infiltrating the new panel as a spy.

When informed of the tip-off by Bobby, McClellan let FBI director J. Edgar Hoover know. Go ahead and put this fellow on the committee's payroll, Hoover instructed him. Any Hoffa payment to his spy would then be a criminal act, the bribery of a government employee.

A week later, Kennedy, armed with that knowledge, met face-to-face with Hoffa at a dinner arranged by a Teamsters PR man. It was mutual hostility at first sight, starting with the handshake. "Here's a fella thinks he's doing me a favor by talking to me," Hoffa said to their host after Bobby had left. To him, Joe Kennedy's son was nothing but a "spoiled jerk."

The repulsion was shared. "Bob, who had an underlying distaste for the kind of people his father used to buy, recognized the devil in

Hoffa," New York columnist Murray Kempton would write, "something absolutely insatiable and wildly vindictive. He recognized in Hoffa a general fanaticism for evil that could be thought of as the opposite side of his own fanaticism for good, and therefore involved direct combat."

Three weeks later, an FBI sting operation caught on camera—right in public at Washington's Dupont Circle—Hoffa's mole handing over to him a manila envelope. In return, the Rackets Committee spy accepted $2,000 in cash. The trap had been set and sprung: Hoffa was under arrest.

Ed Guthman, still covering the Teamsters corruption story, recalls getting the word. "It was Ethel Kennedy who roused us out of our beds at midnight so that we didn't miss being at the United States Courthouse for our papers when Hoffa was arraigned."

The scene at the courthouse captured the growing antagonism between Kennedy and Hoffa. "He stared at me for three minutes with complete hatred in his eyes," Bobby recalled. Hoffa then made clear it was going to be a long war. "Listen, Bobby, you run your business, and I'll run mine. You go home and go to bed. I'll take care of things. Let's don't have any problems."

Two days later, a reporter queried Bobby on the story to date and what might lie ahead. Throwing out possibilities, he asked what if Hoffa, now caught red-handed, somehow escaped justice. "I'll jump off the Capitol," Kennedy answered.

Later that month, and awaiting Hoffa's trial in federal court, the Rackets Committee turned its attention to Dave Beck. Senator McClellan opened the hearings by saying the panel had evidence that the union president had "misappropriated" $320,000 in union funds. Beck now took advantage of his Fifth Amendment right against self-incrimination.

"I'm only doing it on the advice of my chief counsel, Senator Duff," he told the committee, "who occupies or did occupy a position of honor in the United States Government comparable to what you now occupy." Beck had hired former Pennsylvania senator James Duff, defeated for reelection the previous year, to defend him before the committee.

In the end, what hurt Beck more than the big theft was a smaller one. The Teamsters rank and file reacted negatively to the revelation that the labor boss had raised $76,000 in contributions for a union man's widow, only to then pocket $12,000 of it for himself.

Ed Guthman, who'd brought Bobby to the investigation of Beck, was impressed with what he'd seen. He saw Kennedy as dedicated to bringing down big shots who exploited the average worker. He also liked him personally. "Bob kept his word that he would protect our sources within the union. I appreciated that, and respected the skill and tenacity with which he and his investigators went about their work."

Since his censure, Joe McCarthy was now a spent force on Capitol Hill and in obvious decline. While Bobby regarded the once highly combative figure as now the most cooperative Republican on the Rackets Committee, the tragedy of the man was clear. "Drunk the last three times he's been to the hearing," he noted in his diary.

Lem Billings recalls Bobby taking him along on a visit to the McCarthys at home. Jean, the senator's young wife, did most of the talking while Joe himself appeared to be in a stupor. "It was typical of Bobby," Billings said, "to go and see somebody who was in trouble."

That May, Bobby's former boss died at Bethesda Naval Hospital due to inflammation of the liver. Senator Joseph McCarthy, who'd dominated the national press from early 1950 through 1954, had drunk himself to death. Kennedy received the news over the car radio at National Airport. "I was in the car with Daddy," his daughter Kathleen, six years old at that time, told me. "I remember that he drove around three times—it was sad." Later, in his diary Bobby wrote: "It was all very difficult for me as I feel that I have lost an important part of my life, even though it was in the past."

The flag-draped coffin containing the body of Senator McCarthy was carried up the steps of the U.S. Capitol for services in the Senate Chamber following a funeral mass at St. Matthew's Cathedral. Seventy senators were in attendance. The burial took place the next day at St. Mary's Church in Appleton, Wisconsin. Arriving there to pay his respects, Bobby asked a reporter he knew for a ride to the church, at the same time *requesting* that he not report on his being there.

Decades later, just before his own death, Edward Kennedy wrote of his brother's steadfast loyalty to McCarthy: "He was castigated repeatedly for this, but he probably could not have made himself behave otherwise. Loyalty was one of my brother's greatest virtues, and he would not toss over a friend just because he had fallen out of favor with the world."

That June, Jimmy Hoffa went to trial in federal court for payments to the spy he'd placed on the Rackets Committee. Representing him was a rising Washington trial attorney, Edward Bennett Williams, who'd been defense lawyer for Joseph McCarthy in the hearings leading to his censure.

Kennedy, who'd had several lunches with the Holy Cross grad—now faced Williams as a prosecution witness. Given the film footage it held of the defendant handing an envelope to his plant on the committee staff, he had every reason to be confident of the government's case.

Knowing he faced the damning evidence, the streetwise Williams saw the need for audacity. His chance of winning the case depended on the attitude of the jury, two thirds of whom were African American, to the defendant. Would they look at Hoffa in terms of the power he wielded or in terms of whom he represented? As a boss or as a champion of labor?

Williams's bold stroke was to arrange for former heavyweight champion Joe Louis, a national hero for decades, to stop by the courtroom. There, in full view of those about to decide Hoffa's fate, Louis offered a warm greeting of support to the defendant. It was a moment most of the spectators there that day would never forget. What had moved Louis to make such a dramatic gesture? A record company hired Louis in a "public relations" capacity soon after his appearance at the Hoffa trial. It had just received a $2 million loan from the Teamsters pension fund.

But with all the goodwill generated by Louis's public support of Hoffa, Williams needed a clear explanation for the facts at hand. He still had to explain why his client was passing all that cash to a federal employee. The defense he conjured was tantamount to a magic trick. Yes, that was a manila envelope filled with money. Yes, it was being passed—right there on camera. The rabbit Williams now pulled from the hat was an imaginative and a narrowly plausible explanation.

The dramatic evidence the jurors had watched was evidence not of a crime, Williams declared, but rather a fee. What the scene had shown was a client—Hoffa—simply paying his own attorney for services rendered. The gambit was just enough for reasonable doubt. And it worked.

Kennedy, getting news of the acquittal, was devastated.

Ed Williams, meanwhile, was already enjoying his rout of the righteous Senate counsel. He recalled for all in earshot what young

Kennedy had promised to do if he lost the case. "I'm going to send Bobby Kennedy a parachute for when he jumps off the Capitol dome."

Williams, as a criminal lawyer, thought Bobby naive. "He divided everyone up. There are the white hats and the black hats. If you weren't for him, then you were against him. There was no middle ground."

Kennedy friend and biographer Arthur Schlesinger agreed. He believed Kennedy, for whom contests such as the Hoffa trial offered a moral battlefield, was frustrated by the constraints of the courtroom. The assumptions Bobby made about the Hoffas of the world, he thought, were "driven by a conviction of righteousness, a fanaticism of virtue, a certitude about guilt that vaulted over gaps in evidence." What he failed to take into account was that justice isn't always served, that the "white hats" don't always win.

Two months later, Kennedy called Hoffa before the Rackets Committee. His acquittal, in the face of powerful evidence for conviction, had by now covered him with an aura of invincibility. And Hoffa knew it. "Don't you know I could have you killed?" he brutally confronted one potential witness. "Don't you know I could have you pushed out this window? I've got friends who would shoot you in your tracks someday while you're just walking down the street. If I did it, no jury would even convict me. I have a special way with juries."

Now having the union official on the stand before him, Bobby wasted no time establishing his criminality.

Kennedy: Since you've been with the Teamsters union, you've been arrested a number of times, haven't you?

Hoffa: That is correct.

Kennedy: How many times, approximately, do you think?

Hoffa: Well, I don't know, Bob. I haven't counted them up.

Unlike Dave Beck, whom he hoped to replace, Jimmy Hoffa wanted to show how tough he was. For him, claiming the Fifth Amendment right not to give evidence that might tend to self-incriminate was a sign of weakness. Instead, he again and again clung to a failure of memory, all the while cloaking his passivity in a villainous demeanor.

Hoffa, Bobby would recall, "was glaring at me across the counsel table with a deep, strange penetrating expression of intense hatred. . . . There were times when his face seemed completely transfixed with this stare of absolute evilness."

Rather than avoid eye contact, Bobby had no trouble returning the dirty look. Hoffa, catching his eye, switched to winking at him. "It would drive the bastard crazy," the labor boss said.

Chairman McClellan had given Kennedy a free hand to run the hearings. Again and again, the Teamster official would reply to Bobby's questions saying he didn't remember. It continued like this for four days. "We've proceeded to the point where the witness has no memory," McClellan said. "And he can't be helpful even when his memory is refreshed." Finally, the chairman had had it. For him, the questioning of Hoffa had become "useless and a waste of the committee's time." Realizing they weren't getting anywhere, he dismissed the witness.

Ed Guthman, still covering the hearings for *The Seattle Times*, could see what was driving Kennedy's and McClellan's persistence, as well as their frustration. The man testifying in front of them— leader of the country's largest, most powerful labor union, with vast funds under his control—was repeating his MO. He seemed once again about to escape justice.

For Guthman, however, the difference lay in Hoffa's pursuers. They weren't ready to quit. "With McClellan and Bob, pressure from Beck and Hoffa had the opposite effect. The more evidence of improper financial transactions, gangland connections and oppressive use of power that they found, the harder they investigated and the more determined they became to see that law violations were prosecuted and that new laws were enacted to curb the expanding power of corrupt union leaders."

The effect of Hoffa's acquittal—in his 1957 criminal trial—was to enhance his stature among his million and a half members. After all, hadn't he beaten the law? That October, he was elected to replace the discredited Dave Beck as the general president of the International Brotherhood of Teamsters.

Despite Hoffa's continued rise, Bobby's crusade earned him the admiration of the man who'd brought him into the fight. "You have carried a candle that has been a beacon to hundreds of reporters and editors, thousands of politicians and labor leaders, and literally millions of the rank-and-file labor union members and their families," Clark Mollenhoff wrote Bobby soon after the union election. "You may go ahead to higher office than committee counsel, but it is doubtful if anything you do will have greater force for good government and clean labor than what you have done this year."

The following months proved even harder for Bobby on the Hoffa front. "This year seems to have been tougher than last," he wrote in 1958. "I feel like we're in a major fight. We have to keep going, keep the pressure on or we'll go under."

Called yet again before the Rackets Committee, Hoffa showed himself once more as an exasperating and exhausting witness. At one session lasting into the evening, he gloated at the obvious fatigue on Bobby's face. "Look at him, look at him!" Hoffa raged openly to the committee. "He's too tired. He just doesn't want to go on."

Yet, weary as he was, Bobby wasn't about to abandon the fight. His battle with the crooked and dangerous labor boss brought out in him a spirit he'd lacked before. While it wasn't the first time he'd faced public combat, in previous contests—the challenge to Lodge; the McCarthy period—he'd seen too much of the dirtiness on both sides. The drive to take down Jimmy Hoffa was different. It refreshed the altar boy in him, and, unlike any other role before, even as tough as it'd become, it suited him perfectly. "He wasn't frustrated during that period," Lem Billings recognized. "This is when he blossomed. He wasn't the angry young man anymore, and he was much more pleasant to be around because he hadn't this terrible feeling that he wasn't contributing. For the first time in his life, he was happy."

He could see it himself: "My first love," Bobby said with no little irony, "is Jimmy Hoffa." But the further irony was now Hoffa's own, self-inflicted plight, damned by the company he'd deliberately chosen to keep. Asked whether he thought Hoffa might be capable of reform, of cutting off his underworld connections, Bobby's reply was knowing and dark. He can't do it, was his answer. They won't let him. "He wouldn't live."

In April 1959, the Kennedy team held its first strategy session for the upcoming presidential campaign. Though he was to have the major role in running the operation, Bobby gave priority for the moment to a project of his own. Staying at Hickory Hill, his stately home in Northern Virginia, he worked on *The Enemy Within*, a memoir detailing his efforts on the Rackets Committee. The publishers trumpeted it as "a crusading lawyer's personal story of a dramatic struggle with the ruthless enemies of clean unions and honest management."

In its pages the reader looks back with him at the frightening alternate universe of the rogue figures he'd been battling. Of Dave

Beck, who'd crumbled before his eyes, he wrote: "Now he was dead, although still standing. All that was needed was someone to push him over and make him lie down as dead men should." Bobby accused Jimmy Hoffa of continuing to operate "a conspiracy of evil."

You also meet here in Bobby's narrative such hard men as John Dioguardi, known as "Johnny Dio," the garment industry racketeer charged in the acid-blinding of labor columnist Victor Riesel; Frank Kierdorf, the arsonist who on his last job turned himself into a human torch, whose dying words to the police officer trying to gain a confession were "go fuck yourself"; and, finally, Momo Salvatore "Sam" Giancana, the Mafia hitman and Al Capone's Chicago successor, known for hanging his victims on meathooks.

In the end, though, Hoffa remained the most despicable figure for Bobby. "Every man has his price," the union boss frequently announced, bragging of his ability to control the very institutions society had built to bring down such outlaws as him. Often adding, "I have every politician in town in my office." His pervasive influence was more than Kennedy could bear. It was what drove him, for three years, to fight the malignancy Hoffa represented in our national body.

"The tyrant, the bully, the corrupter and corrupted are figures of shame. The labor leaders who became thieves, who cheated those whose trust they had accepted brought dishonor on a vital and largely honest labor movement. The businessmen who succumbed to the temptation to make a deal in order to gain an advantage over their competitors perverted the moral concepts of a free American system," he concluded in *The Enemy Within*.

There's that word again: "moral." It was the all-important one for Bobby Kennedy. In the campaign that followed, the Kennedy brothers would be lionized for the quest in which chief counsel

Bobby had taken the lead to push corruption out of the American labor movement. It had, he wrote, brought into public view the values Bobby Kennedy held dearest. They were the concluding words of Bobby's book: the "toughness and idealism that guided our nation in the past," a "spirit of adventure, a will to fight what is evil, and a desire to serve."

Bobby on the floor of the 1960 Democratic
National Convention in Los Angeles.

CHAPTER ELEVEN

ENFORCER

"... and keep me out of it."
—JACK KENNEDY

"How do you expect to run a successful campaign if you don't get started?" Bobby Kennedy demanded of his brother, now launched on his bid for the Democratic presidential nomination. "A day lost now can't be picked up on the other end. It's ridiculous that more work hasn't been done already."

After hearing that rebuke late in 1959, Jack's quiet aside to Red Fay was equally telling: "How would you like looking forward to that voice blasting into your ear for the next six months?"

One of the candidate's strengths was his instinct for spotting the talents of others, and understanding how best to use them. It wasn't his brother's company he now sought, but his competence. Bobby understood. "It doesn't matter if they like me or not," Bobby would say. "Jack can be nice to them. . . . Somebody has to be able to tell them 'no.'" Jack Kennedy trusted Bobby to say "no" more emphatically and to speak for him more authoritatively than anyone else.

This included confrontations Jack wished to avoid. To win the Democratic Party's nomination was the first step, but to gain that meant shoving all possible rivals off the course. Most urgently, he needed first to know who they were.

An important assignment now fell to Bobby. He couldn't be blamed for not welcoming it. Lyndon Johnson, the man most likely to emerge as the greatest threat to Jack's presidential ambitions, had been denying any interest in it.

But was he telling the truth? A master of the political balance sheet—who owed what to whom—Johnson preferred to control information rather than dispense it. And because of their history of mutual antipathy—not to mention Johnson's contempt for Joseph P. Kennedy—sending Bobby down to Texas to conduct reconnaissance didn't seem the most obvious choice.

As Senate majority leader since early 1955, Johnson had both taken and made every advantage he could to strengthen his power. It helped that President Eisenhower focused his strengths mainly on national defense and foreign policy, leaving domestic matters to Johnson and House Speaker Sam Rayburn.

Not surprisingly, Bobby Kennedy was a contrarian when it came to Johnson's reputation as a shrewd, forceful leader. To him, Johnson merely happened to be in the right place at the right time, benefiting from the confluence of a large Democratic Senate majority and a Republican president less interested in at-home issues.

But the Kennedy effort badly needed to know what Johnson was up to in 1960. Bobby, on Jack's orders, arranged to visit the Texan at his ranch. For him, it would be setting off for alien territory—the spread near Stonewall, Texas, where Johnson had been born and would always call home. It became even more alien when he was dragooned into a deer hunt. Knocked to the ground by the recoil from his shotgun, Bobby had to endure a gloating rebuke from his host. "You've got to learn to handle a gun like a man!" Johnson told him. For someone who'd played varsity football and taken on Jimmy Hoffa, that couldn't have sat well.

Leaving Texas, the visitor felt that he'd accomplished his mission, carrying with him Johnson's firm commitment on several scores: that he wouldn't be a candidate in 1960, that he wouldn't help any other candidate, and that he would do nothing to hurt Jack's run. Bobby would never forget the fervor with which Johnson delivered those three promises.

When the Kennedy for President effort kicked into gear in late 1959, its command center was in an office building near the U.S. Capitol. Now at the helm, Bobby was acknowledged as the leader. It linked to another base already operating in Jack's suite in the Old Senate Office Building, where Ted Sorensen was in charge. Observing those early days, Dave Hackett could see the possibilities of conflict between the two power centers.

After all, Sorensen had spent three years traveling across the country with Jack. He'd heard him speak hundreds of times, gauging the reactions. Working together, they'd refined his message. But when it came to launching the national enterprise, the relationship changed. Even Sorensen, whom Jack called his "intellectual blood bank," knew Bobby's greater skills as an organizer and enforcer. Most important, he knew that Jack's trust in Bobby's judgment could not be matched. As Dave Hackett put it, there was "absolutely no question who the campaign manager was and where the candidate went for advice. I think anybody who felt they were talking to Bob were talking to the senator. Ultimately, decisions were made by *him*."

One critical task, delegated by Bobby to Hackett, involved putting together as much information as could be gathered on those men and women likely to be Democratic delegates at the July convention in Los Angeles. It was the basic principle taken away from the Chicago vice presidential tumult four years earlier: the importance of identifying the true political power in each of the states. "What we basically did," said Hackett, "was go state by state to, first, figure out how the delegates were selected and by whom. Then, second, to figure out who the most influential people in the state were and how that influence might affect delegates." In the end, he and the campaign wound up with a working file of fifty thousand three-by-five cards on potential delegates.

Another subsidiary but also crucial aspect of Hackett's record keeping was Bobby's insistence that his trusted old friend maintain a "loyalty index." That meant adding to those records a one-to-ten scale estimate of the potential delegates' steadfastness, the precise depth of their Jack Kennedy commitment.

Hackett tried to leave as little to chance as he could. "To get a ten," he explained, "we'd require that at least two people designated him as a ten. We'd never rely on one person's judgment." Jack and Bobby, after all, had seen how, when it came to the decisive stand-up-and-be-counted moment, Estes Kefauver had parlayed his long-standing personal connections into victory. The Kennedy system had reduced the intangibles of human behavior to hard arithmetic.

Another rule from which the Kennedy for President campaign now was benefiting was a precept Jack had picked up running for Congress the first time. He'd seen then the importance of beginning to campaign as early as possible. This was why he'd been traveling throughout the country accompanied by Sorensen, introducing himself and making local connections, whenever he could get away.

Ohio governor Michael DiSalle was one of the big-state politicians the brothers had counted upon as an early backer. But given his continuing public silence, they began to doubt his commitment. DiSalle, though privately claiming he supported Jack, now informed them he wasn't yet ready to endorse him. His explanation was that if he, a Catholic, was the first national figure to support Jack's candidacy, it wouldn't have the same value as it would were he from a different background.

The Kennedy brothers knew if they had any hope of convincing powerful party leaders to start jumping on their bandwagon, they needed to win early and keep winning. This meant taking the New Hampshire primary first, then following it up with a victory outside New England. The options were Wisconsin or Ohio.

The problem was, it needed to be one or the other, in terms of the campaign's focus. If they split their effort, the effect would necessarily be weaker—and they couldn't be sure of winning both. Added to this, there was the religion issue. If Jack took Ohio, it could well be dismissed as simply a Catholic winning in a largely ethnic state. However, if he beat rival Senator Hubert Humphrey in his neighboring Wisconsin, a farm state and largely Protestant, that would send a powerful message.

By the end of the year, Wisconsin, not Ohio, was the one targeted. This meant wrapping up Ohio by other means. They couldn't afford forfeiting the larger state's wealth of convention delegates. The only way to get them was to convince Governor DiSalle to climb down off the fence. They needed him to announce publicly and soon that he intended to deliver Ohio's delegation to Kennedy.

The stakes were made higher by the fact that Jack had already laid claim to DiSalle's state as a sign of muscle. Challenged by a reporter earlier on how he planned to demonstrate his not being "just another pretty boy from Boston and Harvard," he'd raised the stakes with this retort. "Well, for openers, I'm going to fucking well take Ohio!"

The task of backing up his brother's words fell to Bobby—even though he was reluctant. According to Ken O'Donnell, Bobby wasn't given much choice. " 'You're mean and tough,' Jack told him. 'And can say more miserable things to Mike than I can. And if you get too obnoxious, then I'll disown you and disavow what you said. I'll just say to him, "he's a young kid and doesn't know any better." '"

To which Bobby replied, "Thanks a lot." But he went. And, in the end, Bobby prevailed. But he'd made no friend of Governor DiSalle, who regarded his techniques of persuasion as anything but diplomatic. One witness to the backroom conversation between the two men reported that Bobby's side of it sounded practically like "mob threats." The candidate's brother/campaign manager had informed DiSalle he needed to be the first major governor to come out for John F. Kennedy . . . or else.

On January 2, 1960, in the Senate Caucus Room, John F. Kennedy declared himself a candidate for president. On January 5, Ohio's Michael DiSalle came out in support.

Since that public endorsement meant the Ohio delegation was theirs, the Kennedy campaign's attention now turned to Wisconsin. The first to arrive there, Bobby made quick work of a reporter's open skepticism as to the possibility of a Roman Catholic being elected president of a largely Protestant country. "Did they ask my brother Joe whether he was a Catholic before he was shot down?"

Still, he wasn't taking any chances. His first act upon arrival in Milwaukee was a purely pragmatic one. He moved their state headquarters away from the Catholic cathedral just across the street.

There were, naturally, more pressing issues. These included the fact that Humphrey supporters were spreading word about the candidate's father's financial support for Richard Nixon's 1950 Senate run as well as making sure voters were aware of Jack's own friendly connection to the late Wisconsin senator Joseph McCarthy.

"First, I'm some kind of witch hunter!" Jack exploded to his speechwriter, Richard Goodwin. "Because I was in the hospital when the censure vote on McCarthy was taken. Then it's the money Dad gave Nixon ten years ago. Hell, he's a businessman. He gave to everybody. Then it's Bobby out buying votes. Do you know how many votes there are in Wisconsin? I know we're rich, but not *that* rich. He talks about me, about my family, about my friends, the only thing he won't discuss are the issues. Son of a bitch."

What lay behind his anger was the essential truth of his rival's charges. And the further truth was that what defined Hubert Humphrey was very different from what defined Jack Kennedy. One of the two was a party-line liberal, the other was not. From the beginning of his political career, Jack had offered himself as a different kind of Democrat, and one who valued his independence from all doctrinaire positions. This meant he had every right, as he saw it, to choose his friends as well as his political stances. In truth, his maverick instincts were the ones he cherished most.

Soon, the religion issue claimed center stage. In a political ad that ran in over 250 local papers, Kennedy was attacked for benefiting from the state's open primary rule. Under Wisconsin law, Republicans as well as Democrats were able to cast ballots in the Kennedy-Humphrey contest. The ad pointed to numbers showing Catholic Republicans lining up behind Kennedy. Was it fair, it asked righteously, that such voters from the other party should decide "who the Democratic nominee for president shall be?"

The story behind the ad, however, wasn't to be found in the data on Catholic Republican crossovers but in who'd paid for it. It hadn't been the Humphrey campaign. Wisconsin's attorney general would later determine that the money for the anti-Kennedy ad could be traced back to Teamsters connections. Jimmy Hoffa was still out to get Bobby Kennedy.

In the end, on the 5th of April, Jack Kennedy won the Wisconsin primary. But along the way his campaign had, like Humphrey's, wooed voters with material that wasn't what it seemed to be. One gambit had been devised by an intriguing figure, Paul Corbin, whom I came to know in a later campaign. He was the one distributing anti-Catholic literature where it would do the most good: Catholic neighborhoods.

It was a dirty trick. With its denunciation of the Catholic Kennedy, aimed supposedly at Protestant voters, it had the effect of tempting wavering Catholics—including those Republican ones—to overcome their doubts and cast their vote for their fellow communicant now under assault for his religion.

I know firsthand how it would have worked, remembering my mom's anger when a group of zealous canvassers knocked at our door to warn us of the imminent danger of a Catholic in the White House. Always sensitive to the Protestant rejection, it confirmed Mom's worst suspicions: here was the specter of Al Smith all over again.

On election night in Wisconsin, CBS's Walter Cronkite queried Jack about the role the "Catholic" vote had played in his victory. Bobby saw this as a deal-breaker. Cronkite's producer had agreed, he said, to lay off the religion issue. By not doing so, Cronkite was seen by Bobby as breaking a deal made with the Kennedy campaign—not to bring up religion.

Afterward, according to Cronkite, "Bobby stormed through the studio saying, 'You violated an agreement! We had an agreement that no question be asked about Catholicism and the Catholic vote. I'm going to see you never get another interview.'"

The casting of the Wisconsin victory in religious terms, with the margin of Jack's win attributed to crossover Catholic Republicans, had the effect of tainting his success. What should have been a triumph pure and simple—a senator from Massachusetts had just beaten a Midwesterner on his home turf—wound up a disappointment. If not exactly a setback, it was very definitely a spur to redoubled effort in the state that came next.

This was West Virginia, where the vanquishing of Hubert Humphrey would now need to be decisive. But in a surprise to the Kennedys, the old issues of religion surfaced from the start. In an early meeting with volunteers in Charleston, Bobby quizzed them. "What are our problems?" he wanted to know. The reply was Jack's religion. Bobby was more shocked than anyone. Hadn't the campaign's numbers shown him leading Humphrey in West Virginia by 70 to 30 percent?

Not anymore. Once that extra biographical detail—Jack's religion—was added, a new poll showed him getting just 40 percent of the vote to Humphrey's 60 percent. Rose Kennedy recalled the way the younger son had bluntly broken the news to his older brother. "The people who voted for you in that other poll—the 70–30 one—have just found out that you're a Catholic."

Bobby decided to meet the religious issue in West Virginia head-on, with Jack coming out openly about his religion to the strong Protestant majority of West Virginia voters. When asked reasonable questions about his religion, he'd answer them plainly. He also appealed to the voters' patriotism. "Nobody asked me if I was a Catholic when I joined the United States Navy," he told audiences of voters.

At the same time, Hubert Humphrey was devoting his energies to reminding voters where their natural religious loyalties lay. His campaign theme song suddenly became the Southern gospel classic, "Give Me That Old Time Religion."

Both Kennedys said and believed the campaign there should focus on economic issues. Jack, observed Arthur Schlesinger, "was genuinely appalled by what he saw . . . hungry, hollow-eyed children, dispirited families living on cornmeal and surplus lard, gray, dismal towns, despair about the future." Watching Bobby when he went out to meet coal miners leaving their shifts, Pierre Salinger, the ex-reporter Bobby had brought with him from the Rackets Committee, remembered how Bobby's hands were blackened by dust after he'd shaken theirs. He'd greet them simply, saying only "My name is Bob Kennedy. My brother is running for president. I want your help."

The Kennedys had come to resent Humphrey's continuing candidacy. They believed he was staying in the race merely to prevent Jack Kennedy from an early victory. It seemed to them that the Minnesotan was keeping the door to the White House open just wide enough for his Senate leader Lyndon Johnson eventually to squeeze through. They decided to lower the boom.

"From an anonymous source in Minnesota," Goodwin recalled, "the Kennedy camp received copies of correspondence between Humphrey and his draft board, letters revealing that Hubert had tried on several occasions to postpone his military service. It was decided that the material should be made public by Franklin Roosevelt, Jr."

The surrogate did as asked. "There's another candidate in your primary," the junior Roosevelt told one crowd. "He's a good Democrat. But I don't know where he was in World War II."

Jack denied any responsibility for what, in fact, had been a well-choreographed insinuation. "Any discussion of the war record of Senator Hubert Humphrey was done without my knowledge and consent," he stated. "And I strongly disapprove of the injection of this issue into the campaign." Without defending Humphrey's deferments, he reminded the voters there were more important issues in the campaign.

In fact, Humphrey had been rejected for military service because of medical reasons. Later, FDR Jr. would explain his having been pressured by Bobby, whom he described as being obsessed with winning at all costs, to raise the issue. From Humphrey's perspective, any and all Kennedy denials were meaningless. They "never shut FDR Jr. up, as they easily could have," he pointed out.

Watching events from Washington, Senate majority leader Lyndon Johnson easily guessed who'd armed Roosevelt with the smear against Humphrey. "That's Bobby," he asserted.

Then, too, there were other grievances Humphrey was smarting under, most significantly the amount of cash being spread around by the Kennedy campaign. "I don't think elections should be bought," he openly complained. "I can't afford to run through with a checkbook and a little black bag. Bobby said if they had to spend a half million to win here they would do it. Kennedy is the spoiled candidate, and he and that young, emotional, juvenile Bobby are spending with wild abandon."

He summed up his growing sense of victimization at the hands of the Kennedy brothers with what amounted to a playground gibe: "Anyone who gets in the way of papa's pet is going to be destroyed."

It was becoming a tense and not very pretty fight, with Bobby staying on top of both the front and backroom tactics. He made the decisions where to spend the money and to whom it went. Gone were the old volunteer days in Massachusetts. It was Bobby, Roosevelt recalled, who made the choices as to "which local county slate we should get Jack on. He'd go into a county, analyze it, talk to everybody he could talk to going directly to the point, and his judgment turned out to be exactly right."

Still, Bobby worried from the start that his brother was going to lose West Virginia. If that turned out to be the case, they needed an insurance policy. They needed another primary they could count on. The answer was Maryland, scheduled for the week after West Virginia's. There, Governor J. Millard Tawes had hoped to run as a favorite son, win the state's primary, and then arrive at the convention with Maryland's delegates at his personal disposal, to award to the candidate of his choice.

But Bobby had another idea. Once again, he made it happen. After a session closeted alone with him, Governor Tawes emerged agreeing to what the Kennedy forces wanted: not to run as a favorite son but to give his blessing to Jack in the Maryland primary. If Jack lost West Virginia, he was now primed for an uncontested victory a week later.

On the night of the West Virginia primary, Jack Kennedy wanted to be elsewhere. No candidate likes to be present at a loss, thereby giving photographers and camera crews the opportunity to catch them in the eye of defeat. Instead, he spent the evening back in Washington, waiting nervously for the news as the polls closed. "He'd get up every twenty minutes to call Bobby in West Virginia," his friend Ben Bradlee, then a reporter for *Newsweek* magazine, remembered.

But the news was good: a big win.

In Charleston, where it had been raining all day, the other side of Robert Kennedy now came into play. He headed off onto the wet streets to offer his respects to the race's loser. Joseph Rauh, a Humphrey supporter, has painted a vivid portrait of his arrival at their headquarters. "I said to myself, 'Oh, my God, it's Bobby,' really the devil as far as our camp was concerned. . . . He was the one all our people were so bitter about."

Rauh watched, amazed, as the winner's brother and campaign manager made his way toward the defeated Humphrey and his wife. "Everybody walked backwards, and there was a path from the door to the other side of the room where Hubert and Muriel were standing. I'll never forget that walk if I live to be a hundred."

Bobby's generous gesture was of the moment and received as such. It couldn't make up for the "ruthlessness and toughness" he'd displayed throughout the contest. That aspect of him, said Humphrey, "I had trouble either accepting or forgetting."

Bobby, Jack, and Lyndon Johnson at the Biltmore Hotel, 1960.

CHAPTER TWELVE

THE ENEMY WITHIN

"Friend is sometimes a word devoid of meaning; enemy, never."
—Victor Hugo

Jack and Bobby's partnership served their mutual goal, to see the older of them achieve the presidency of their country. Yet the division of labor between the two brothers could easily be confounding.

Jack was a charmer, with a lightness about him, and a 150-watt smile. This affable affect masked an innate coldness. Bobby's emotions ran hot—in anger or in empathy. With regard to the running of the campaign, Jack never lost sight of the road ahead and how the ever-shifting strategies needed to close the distance between himself and victory. For Bobby, the politics was day-to-day, and personal. He kept track of who was loyal and who was not; who was friend, who was enemy.

This difference in their outlooks would reveal itself sharply in their view of one man: Lyndon Johnson. If they complemented each other as they jointly moved forward through the months of 1960, they clashed in their assessment of the Texan's potential value to their effort. Bobby didn't trust him, never had, and didn't see the current moment as the time to start. Jack, though, was pragmatic, maintaining his belief that Johnson might prove to be of use.

Dealing with this larger-than-life operator seemed to Jack simply elemental in the political menagerie. He called him a "riverboat gambler," appreciating his "pluses" while remembering never to lose sight of his "minuses." To Bobby, on the other hand, Johnson was a figure of ill will from the start. The idea of ever needing him—even tolerating him—for any purpose was abhorrent to him.

In short, it was a matter of either appreciating what Lyndon Baines Johnson could do for them or disdaining him for who he was. Unlike Bobby, his brother was willing to do what was necessary, stepping past any history of bad blood. It was a matter of geography. As a New Englander and Roman Catholic, Jack needed a ticket balancer. The Texan was the ideal candidate to be his running mate: Southern, Protestant, and battle-hardened.

The Democratic National Convention was now looming on the horizon.

On July 4, exactly one week before the Democrats were set to convene at the Los Angeles Memorial Sports Arena, a press conference was staged in the host city. Two Johnson surrogates—aide John Connally, then an ambitious young figure in Texas politics, and former party official India Edwards—stood before a crowd of newsmen to divulge vital information about the front-running candidate that they believed American voters needed to know. They revealed that forty-three-year-old Jack Kennedy suffered from Addison's disease. This fact, they said, would jeopardize his ability to serve adequately as the country's leader.

Springing into action, Bobby Kennedy held his own press conference to contain the damage. Speaking with a family member's authority, he told reporters that his brother didn't suffer from what is "classically defined as Addison's Disease." He was quibbling, though reporters couldn't know it. The story faded as quickly as it had appeared.

The next day, what wasn't supposed to have happened did. Lyndon Johnson declared his candidacy for president. Joining the race this late, the Texan's best hope was to keep his Massachusetts colleague from gaining a majority of delegates on the first ballot. This way, he could keep the nomination open. Yet by tossing his hat in the ring, Johnson was now brazenly breaking the second of three promises he'd made to Bobby Kennedy during his ranch visit. He'd told him that he wouldn't be a candidate and that he wouldn't do anything to hurt Jack's run.

Questioning a candidate's mortality showed a desperation, and a bitterness, that couldn't be masked. The true message behind the Addison's revelation he'd orchestrated was clear: if he couldn't have the nomination, Johnson didn't want Jack to have it. The fact, which he refused to face, was that Jack Kennedy had sewn up the nomination back in West Virginia. With his brother at his side, he'd won every primary he'd entered—and that's what mattered now.

The Kennedys came west armed with what they believed to be reliable delegate counts the campaign had been collecting for months. Such political intel was the name of the game. Back then, only a fraction of those arriving in Los Angeles had been selected in the primaries, the rest were under the influence of state leaders. The cultivation of these make-or-break allies had obviously been the organization's top priority, with the complex tallying process accomplished under the oversight of Bobby and Dave Hackett.

Meanwhile, as more and more Democrats poured into Los Angeles, speculation on who might wind up filling the ticket's second spot became part of the pre-opening buzz. The likely Democratic nominee's brother had a favorite. On the Saturday before the convention, Bobby told *Seattle Times* reporter Ed Guthman he was pushing for Scoop Jackson.

The Washington State lawmaker had served alongside Bobby, its chief counsel, on the Permanent Subcommittee on Investigations. "He's my choice," the campaign manager declared, "and Jack likes him. But between now and Thursday he is going to have to convince some of the midwestern and eastern leaders that he can help the ticket the most. We've told him that. I hope he can do it."

Jack Kennedy, meanwhile, still had come to no conclusion about who might best serve his vice presidential needs. A variety of factors figured, but in the end his focus was on a single goal. And that was how to amass the winning amount of electoral votes in November's general election.

Examining the data, the importance of the Democrats holding the Southern states was vital. In the previous two presidential elections, both lost by the Democrats, not just Texas but also Louisiana, Florida, Virginia, and Tennessee had gone to Eisenhower-Nixon.

Members of Jack's circle of Washington buddies were on the case. Among these friends were *Washington Post* publisher Phil Graham and nationally syndicated columnist Joe Alsop. Each now began pointing out to him the wisdom of choosing none other than Lyndon Johnson. It was the worldly Alsop, in fact, who not only stressed the political logic of picking Johnson . . . but also the dangers of *not* doing so.

The convention—with all its many time-honored rituals—began Monday. On Tuesday, the eve of the presidential balloting, Tip O'Neill delivered a message to fellow Bostonian John Kennedy. It was from Speaker of the House Sam Rayburn, Lyndon Johnson's

Texas mentor. He was relaying the information that if Kennedy offered him the vice presidential nomination, Johnson would take it.

Meanwhile Johnson was continuing to stir up anti-Kennedy sentiment. He now went after Joseph P. Kennedy's reputation as a World War II "appeaser," hoping to attach the sins of the father to the sons.

Jack and Bobby had spent their public lives trying to overcome this legacy. Now, before the convention cameras, Lyndon Johnson was taunting them with their paternal history: "I wasn't any Chamberlain umbrella man," Johnson declared vehemently to a group of delegates, referring to the trademark umbrella of the British prime minister at Munich. "I didn't think Hitler was right."

Following that, he'd made it his business to draw attention once again to Jack's failure to cast a vote in the Joe McCarthy censure. He was saying that the front-runner was neither a loyal Democrat nor even a decent American.

This enraged Bobby. Spotting a Johnson aide not long after, he erupted venomously. "You've got your nerve! Lyndon Johnson has compared my father to the Nazis and John Connally lied in saying my brother is dying. You people are running a stinking damned campaign and you're gonna get yours when the time comes!"

And if the blatant anti-Kennedy attacks weren't enough, Johnson had one further trick up his sleeve. In his ongoing effort to prevent a first-ballot win for Jack, he plunged into a backroom effort on behalf of the already twice nominated (and twice defeated) Adlai Stevenson. On Wednesday, Johnson ally Eugene McCarthy went forth to do the honors, delivering the most eloquent speech of the convention for Stevenson. "Do not reject this man who made us all proud to be Democrats."

With that move—everyone was aware who was pulling the

strings—the Texan had broken his third promise to Bobby, that he wouldn't back another candidate.

Just fourteen at the time, I remember the excitement in the broadcast booths at the prospect of an eleventh-hour Stevenson win, a repeat of what had occurred in Chicago eight years earlier. But the smart observers caught the problem: the excitement for the two-time nominee was primarily up in the galleries, packed with his liberal California supporters. Down on the floor, the delegates were quietly committed to Kennedy. It was Stevenson's last hurrah.

Bobby was now in total command. "I want the cold facts," he demanded of his delegate counters. "There's no point in fooling ourselves. I want to hear the votes we're guaranteed to get on the first ballot." The information system he'd set in place, not to mention his own prodigious efforts to keep the troops in line, was producing exactly the hoped-for results.

Jack needed 761 delegates to win the nomination. They'd arrived with 600 already in pocket. The rest would have to be squeezed by the time of the balloting on Wednesday. Late that night, after the decisive roll call had confirmed what most had expected, Jack Kennedy was officially declared the Democratic presidential candidate. Bobby's numbers proved on the mark.

As good as the Kennedy effort was on the math side, there was still a problem brewing on the human front: the question of whom Jack would select as his running mate.

Soon after receiving the nomination, Jack sent a message to Missouri's senator Stuart Symington—with an invitation to join him on the ticket. But that pairing was not to be. An event occurred much later that night that would set the drama's key figures on a different course. Lyndon Johnson now dispatched a note expressing his support to Jack Kennedy. He'd made an insistent point that it be hand-delivered, with no possibility—*none*—of its not quickly reaching the candidate.

Whatever Jack thought of this, we know what he did. Contacting Johnson at 8 a.m., he arranged for them to meet at ten in the Texan's room two floors down. There he asked Johnson if he'd like to be his running mate. Johnson said he would.

In the hours that followed, events become murkier.

However he'd expected Johnson to answer, Jack Kennedy had indeed put the vice presidency out there on the table, and Lyndon had grabbed it.

But then there arose Robert Kennedy's fury when he heard the news. In addition to his own feelings, there were objective problems. At the top of the list were the reform-minded labor leaders with whom Bobby had formed a mutually respectful relationship during his Rackets Committee days. There were also the party's liberals. Hadn't Jack spent the past four years trying to convince that Democratic voting bloc he was one of them?

A group of union representatives, arriving now in the Kennedy suite, were livid. Ken O'Donnell said he'd never seen Bobby "so savagely attacked in his life. They felt bruised and betrayed by the choice of LBJ."

Jack, looking to break the tension over what he'd done by choosing Johnson, now reassured his brother. "I'm forty-three years old," he said. "I'm not going to die in office."

Still, the stored-up hatred for the Texan felt by Bobby Kennedy couldn't be appeased. Inviting him to be part of the Kennedy campaign felt to him as if a foreign organ was being implanted in the political body the two brothers had formed over the years.

Shaken by his brother's fierce resistance, Jack now agreed he'd been wrong to make the offer. The challenge was how to take it back without giving dangerous offense to Johnson.

The difficult task—as was so regularly the case with their unpleasant jobs—fell to Bobby. Arriving at the Johnson suite, he was met by Rayburn and Connally, both assuming he was there to confirm the deal and make arrangements for the announcement.

They'd guessed wrong. "Johnson can't accept this nomination," Bobby bluntly informed them. "It was a mistake." Then he cited labor's objections to Johnson. They were in an uproar, he said, which meant there'd be a fight on the convention floor if Jack put Johnson on the ticket. Cutting to the chase, he suggested a consolation prize—that the Senate leader, instead, take the role of national party chairman.

"Shit" was Rayburn's response to hearing this.

With the hours passing, and not managing to come face-to-face with Johnson himself, Bobby kept trying to get past his gatekeepers. At last, after several visits to the Johnson suite, he managed to get to him. He began by warning the majority leader of the amount of delegate opposition the Kennedy effort was likely to encounter if they went ahead and selected him.

The Johnson people, clearly upset that Bobby had gotten past them to see LBJ, now demanded a reckoning. An immediate one. This could come from only one source, Jack Kennedy. When the presidential nominee was reached, he settled it, but not with the decision Bobby had sought. "Bobby's been out of touch and doesn't know what's happening," was at the heart of what he said. Then Bobby himself was handed the phone. Though he'd been preparing last-minute arguments, he'd recognized his own cause was lost.

"It's too late now," he told Jack and hung up.

The exhausted nominee, torn by the arguments and uncertainties, was still adjusting to the fact of his decision. "Don't worry, Jack," his father told him after the announcement was made. "In two weeks they'll be saying it's the smartest thing you ever did."

But their dad's scorecard wasn't Bobby's. He didn't believe the ends—assembling a winning ticket in November—excused getting in bed with Lyndon Johnson. In his mind, his brother had now chosen a liar for a running mate, a man who'd publicly claimed Jack was dying, who'd derided the family's patriotism, despite it having given one son to their country and nearly a second. How could Bobby Kennedy *live* with this?

"Yesterday was the best day of my life," he told Jack's friend Charlie Bartlett late on Thursday. "Today is the worst day."

Teddy, Bobby, and Pat in Hyannis Port the night
of the 1960 presidential election.

CHAPTER THIRTEEN

VICTORY

"Kick him in the balls."

—BOBBY'S ADVICE TO JACK, SEPTEMBER 26, 1960

Jack Kennedy now faced the daunting challenge of the general election. Richard Nixon, having won the Republican nomination handily, selected Kennedy's old rival Henry Cabot Lodge as his running mate. Right through to election day the polls would show the two tickets historically close.

With the November 8 election drawing closer, the Democratic candidate accepted an invitation to address the Greater Houston Ministerial Association, a Protestant ministers group. It was the chance to face down the religious issues directly. It was, in Ted Kennedy's words, an appearance that "even the normally fearless Bobby had advised against."

It turned out to be Kennedy's most effective speech to date. Another family member, Jacqueline Kennedy, expressed a different opinion. She saw no reason why her husband was having to defend his religious commitment. "I think it so unfair of people to be against Jack because he's a Catholic," she quipped to a family friend. "He's such a poor Catholic. Now, if it were *Bobby*, I could understand it."

What she didn't grasp was how her brother-in-law was finding ways to turn the Kennedys' religion to political advantage. One was to barnstorm through New York's Catskill mountain resorts explaining to Jewish audiences that an attack on one religion could easily lead to assaults against others.

And even as both Kennedys reminded non-Catholics of the quintessential American notion of religious tolerance, they appealed to the ethnic and religious tribalism of Irish, Italian, and Polish voters. When Jack arrived that fall to campaign in Milwaukee, a newspaper photograph showed popular congressman Clem Zablocki draping the candidate in his own overcoat on an especially chilly day. As Zablocki at the time portrayed the gesture he'd made for his fellow Democrat: "Not only do we keep you warm; we provide you votes."

The Kennedy and Nixon campaigns had agreed to four nationally televised debates, the first to be held on September 26. Never before had such a face-to-face between candidates occurred with the country watching.

Arriving at the CBS studio, Jack refused director Don Hewitt's offer of makeup before going on the air. More than an instinctive "no, thanks," it was a cagey move. Ted Kennedy explained it this way: "Jack, who'd needled Hubert Humphrey for wearing TV makeup in Wisconsin, said he wouldn't go into the makeup room unless Nixon went first. Nixon said he would not go in unless Kennedy was seen going in as well."

Nixon, who'd just spent two weeks in the hospital for an infected leg—it had kept him off the campaign trail—looked it. But Bobby, spotting a chance for mischief, reassured a Nixon aide that there was nothing to worry about. In fact, it was just the opposite. The Republican candidate looked "terrific!"

Nixon now felt trapped by the thought his rival would mock him just as he'd teased Humphrey for unmanly primping the previous spring. He now made the unfortunate decision to cover his darkening five o'clock shadow with a product called Lazy Shave, a kind of powder concealer.

Meanwhile, Jack was being devious. Bill Wilson, the media expert Bobby had brought into the campaign, walked me through the goings-on that historic night. "I was in the green room," Wilson recalled. "Bobby was there. Anyway, I said, 'Okay, we've got to close it down. Jack needs about ten minutes before he goes on to get quiet, and I've got to put some makeup on him.'" Ironically, the candidate with the healthy tan was taking cosmetic help while the one with the sickroom pallor was not.

Before departing the candidate's holding room, Bobby added a bit of spirit to the night's main event: "Kick him in the balls," he cheered on his brother.

The Kennedy plan now was to let Nixon head out onto the set and sit there, all by himself, until the very last moment. It was the purest psychological warfare. Even with just sixty seconds to go, the seat waiting for Jack was still empty. As it was down to about fifteen seconds, he strolled out. When the debate began, its seventy million viewers saw Jack Kennedy, with his legs crossed and his hands folded on this lap, appearing poised, elegant. Next to him, Nixon seemed not just ill but ill at ease, unshaven, his legs awkwardly apart.

Kennedy used the largest audience of the campaign to make his sharpest critique of the status quo. Even under the still-popular

Eisenhower, the 1950s were ending with a slow economy and growing fear. Playing on both, the Democratic challenger began his pitch. "This is a great country, but I think it could be a greater country. And this is a powerful country, but I think it could be a more powerful country." He went on to inventory what he saw as America's failure to keep up its post–World War II momentum.

Among the many disappointing facts he marshaled—economic growth, widening poverty, inferior education, among other shortcomings—he made specific mention of corruption in the Teamsters. "I'm not satisfied when I see men like Jimmy Hoffa—in charge of the largest union in the United States—still free." He was pointing not just to the man's criminality but his and his brother's three-year campaign to bring him down.

In that first Kennedy-Nixon national face-to-face, the Democrat was seen as the clear victor.

The second presidential debate came eleven days later. The first had been broadcast from the CBS bureau in Chicago. This time around it would be televised from the NBC studios in Washington. It's where we did *Hardball* for twenty years.

Veteran television journalist John Harter, then a young NBC page, remembers watching Bobby and Jack Kennedy enter the building on Nebraska Avenue NW. He saw Jack right away start to complain about the cold temperature once he'd stepped into the studio. "What the hell is this?" Jack demanded, according to Bill Wilson, once he passed through the heavy doors into the frigid studio. Bobby instantly realized what was afoot. The frozen air told him the Nixon team was trying to prevent its candidate from sweating as heavily as he had in the first debate. Angrily—though it was just the sort of trick Bobby might have tried himself—he raced to the studio's control room, demanding to know what was going on.

But Wilson, unlike Bobby, guessed where the setting might actually be changed. Dashing down to the building's basement, he met with a surprise. "There was a guy standing stationed there. He said he'd been told not to let anybody change anything. I said, 'Get out of my way or I'm going to call the police!' He immediately left, and I switched the air conditioning back down."

The night before, in Cincinnati, the Democratic candidate had given a major speech on what he called "the glaring failure of American foreign policy." Just as the Republicans had accused the Democrats of "losing" China under Truman, the out-of-power Democrats were now doing the same with Cuba. By the autumn of 1960, the island nation had become a major election issue, a hot trigger of the Cold War.

Just ninety miles from Florida, Cuba had long been a North American playground, a haven for prostitution and gambling. All that, however, had changed on New Year's Eve 1958 when dictator Fulgencio Batista—with whom the U.S. had enjoyed a cozy relationship—fled the country, leaving it to the rebel forces of Fidel Castro advancing from the mountains. Initially, the United States had greeted the bearded, army-fatigues-clad Castro as a hero—his admirers then had included teenagers like me—a leader who'd bring freedom to Cuba. When he visited New York that spring, he arrived as a democratic leader, promising a free press and elections to a country now freed of its despotic regime.

The first sign of betrayal came when the new Cuban leader began executing hundreds of former Batista supporters by firing squad. Next came the mass expropriations of farmland and foreign-owned businesses, along with his growing ties to Moscow and Castro's own declaration that he was a Communist. Within months, Americans realized they had a Soviet ally less than a hundred miles away.

Fidel Castro's Cuba was a point of special vulnerability for the current vice president and Republican hopeful. Long a firebrand anti-Communist, Nixon found himself having to defend the embarrassing failure that had come on his and President Eisenhower's watch. He could not even mention whatever thin hope he held for the current administration to bring down the despised Castro regime. That knowledge was top secret.

Nixon knew that the CIA had been training a Cuban exile force to attack the island. What angered him now was that Jack Kennedy also knew it. Already suspicious that the CIA, then a popular destination for Ivy Leaguers, was favoring the Harvard guy, he became infuriated when a Kennedy press release, sent out on the eve of the final debate, claimed: "We must attempt to strengthen the non-Batista democratic anti-Castro forces in exile and in Cuba itself who offer eventual hope of overthrowing Castro. Thus far, these fighters for freedom have had no support from our government."

As far as he was concerned, his opponent was taking advantage of his required silence on the Cuban invasion operation to make him, Richard Nixon, look weak. But what he didn't know was that Kennedy had a source of his own. Alabama governor John Patterson, one of his strong backers—a courageous position given the Bible Belt opposition to the Catholic candidate—had given him a heads-up. Patterson had been let in on the invasion plans when the CIA had sought recruits for the operation in his state's National Guard. He had also been told the plan had the full support of President Eisenhower.

Harris Wofford's first encounter with Bobby Kennedy in 1957 wasn't auspicious. At the time, he was a legal assistant on the U.S. Commission on Civil Rights and planning a trip to the Soviet Union. Friends suggested that he drop in on Bobby, who'd traveled there two years earlier. He found himself kept waiting while Bobby ate his lunch, talked on the phone, and continued working on the papers in front of him. What he wound up getting for his time was a warning about Soviet surveillance of tourists, with an anti-Communist diatribe thrown in, and a swift goodbye.

Now a law professor at Notre Dame, Wofford came to the campaign with impressive credentials. In May 1960, Jack Kennedy having asked his brother-in-law Sargent Shriver to set up a civil rights unit in the campaign, Bobby called upon Wofford to lead it.

"We're in trouble with Negroes," Bobby, in his role as campaign manager, told the new recruit. "We really don't know much about this whole thing. We've been dealing outside the field of the main Negro leadership and have to start from scratch." He was admitting that neither his brother nor he had taken up civil rights as a personal cause.

In October, the American Baptist minister Dr. Martin Luther King, Jr., along with a group of student protesters, was arrested in Atlanta. They'd been participating in a sit-in at the Magnolia Room, the segregated restaurant of the landmark downtown Rich's Department Store. The first such "sit-in" had taken place the previous February at a Woolworth's lunch counter in Greensboro, North Carolina.

Coretta Scott King, who married the civil rights leader in 1953, described the reality African Americans then had to face throughout the South: "There was hardly a place outside our own neighborhoods where a Negro could even get a soda except by going to the side door of a drugstore and having it handed out."

While the other protesters were soon released, King, who the year before had been charged with a traffic violation, now had that probation revoked and his conviction reinstated. Sentenced to six months in prison at hard labor, King heard the judge refuse to allow him to post bail. "We must prepare ourselves," King told his father and fellow minister, "for the fact that I am going to have to serve this time."

Coretta King wept in public, she would say, "for the first time since the Movement began in 1955." Five months pregnant, she was afraid her baby would come with her husband still imprisoned. She became further horrified when her husband was awoken in the night and driven from the city jail to a cell two hundred miles into rural Georgia. Reaching her friend Harris Wofford, now working in the Kennedy campaign, she desperately begged for his help. "They are going to kill him," she repeated. "I know they are going to kill him."

Wofford began to toss ideas around with his good friend, newspaper publisher and civil rights activist Louis Martin. What they were looking for was a possible gesture in support of King that Wofford, with his connections, could help accomplish. What they came up with was the possibility of the Democratic candidate Jack Kennedy making a compassionate phone call to Coretta King.

Shriver, excited by the plan Wofford presented to him, was in Chicago where Jack was on the campaign trail. He knew he needed to talk to him alone, at a moment when he could make the appeal on a personal basis. Shriver didn't want the campaign advisers weighing only the political pluses and minuses.

"Why don't you telephone Mrs. King and give her your sympathy?" Shriver said to Jack once the coast was clear. "Negroes don't expect everything will change tomorrow, no matter who's elected. But they do want to know whether you care. If you telephone Mrs. King, they'll know you understand and will help. You'll reach their hearts and give support to a pregnant woman now afraid her husband will be killed."

"That's a good idea," the candidate replied unhesitatingly. "Why not? Do you have her number? Get her on the phone."

Mrs. King would later recount Kennedy's words to her: "I want to express my concern about your husband. I know this must be very hard on you. I understand you're expecting a baby, and I just wanted you to know that I was thinking about you and Dr. King. If there is anything I can do to help, please feel free to call me."

When Pierre Salinger learned of the call and informed Bobby, Jack's campaign manager was at first disbelieving, then furious. "Bob wants to see you bomb-throwers right away," was the summons Wofford and Martin heard when called in to account for their actions. He was waiting for them, and had no trouble expressing his displeasure. "Do you know," he asked the two men responsible, "that three Southern governors told us that if Jack supported Jimmy Hoffa, Nikita Khrushchev or Martin Luther King, they'd throw their states to Nixon?" Adding, "Do you know that the election may be razor close and you've probably lost it for us?"

In the hours that followed, Bobby experienced a change of heart as he had more time to think about it while on a plane to New York. What bothered him was the abuse of power. He said later that he couldn't believe that a judge would deny bail in a case like King's, which involved a misdemeanor. "It just burned me, all the way up here on the plane," Bob told reporter John Seigenthaler afterward. "The more I thought about the injustice of it, the more I thought what a son of a bitch that judge was."

At three o'clock in the morning, he was on the phone to Louis Martin. He'd done something Martin deserved to know about. And because of his role in getting the Kennedys involved, he wanted him to hear it from him directly. "I wanted you to know," Bobby told him, "that I called that judge in Georgia today." He'd managed to win King's release.

"You are now an honorary brother," Martin, an African American, told him.

What Bobby didn't say was how it all happened. Jack had phoned Georgia governor Ernest Vandiver, a fellow Democrat, and asked for his help. He agreed but explained the need to protect himself, which meant the need to call on intermediaries. Only then would it be safe for Bobby to contact the judge.

Dr. King expressed his gratitude with careful seriousness. "I am deeply indebted to Senator Kennedy, who served as a great force in making my release possible. There are moments when the politically expedient can be morally wise. I hold Senator Kennedy in very high esteem. I am convinced he will seek to exercise the power of his office to fully implement the civil rights plank of his party's platform."

Jack Kennedy's conversation with Mrs. King may well have been the single most important episode of the campaign. It is now a touchstone moment of twentieth-century American political lore.

Within hours, Wofford and Martin put together a pamphlet to showcase the role the Kennedys had played in Reverend King's release from prison. The "blue bomb," as it soon became known—it was printed on light blue paper—included strong praise for Jack's intervention from Coretta King, Martin Luther King, Sr., along with other major civil rights leaders. Kennedy's willingness to jump in and help contrasted with Nixon's stepping away from requests for help. It gave rise to the unforgettable banner running across the top of the flyer: " 'No Comment Nixon' Versus a Candidate with a Heart, Senator Kennedy." With two million copies sent to black churches across the country, it proved a game changer. Even as the Kennedy-Johnson ticket held on to the Democratic "Solid South," the African American vote in the North and Midwest contributed to its triumphs in the big electoral states.

Throughout the weeks since Jack had become the Democratic candidate, he and Bobby had rarely been in the same place at the same time. Once, however, they found themselves together on the campaign trail.

"Hi, Johnny. How are you?" Bobby greeted him.

"I'm tired," Jack said.

"What the hell are *you* tired for?" Bobby wanted to know. "*I'm* doing all the work."

And if that claim wasn't the exact truth, it was true enough. As November 8 grew closer and closer, the candidate could see the toll it was taking on his chief lieutenant. "He's living on nerves," Jack said.

But he also made clear his appreciation. "I don't have to think about organization. I just show up. He's the hardest worker. He's the greatest organizer. Bobby's easily the best man I've ever seen."

The trouble was, whatever they'd like to have believed, the race wasn't over.

Jack himself couldn't see the problem. He and the people traveling with him, experiencing the large enthusiastic crowds in the major cities like New York, Philadelphia, and Chicago, believed they were now well in the lead. It seemed to them they were pulling further and further away from Nixon, to whom for a while, back in the early fall, they'd seemed uncomfortably close.

But Bobby suspected, as he assessed the information coming in, that the religion issue had not been put to rest. "Nixon was gaining," Richard Goodwin started to realize. "Another week and he'd have won. Kennedy felt that, too. You could tell. He didn't say it, but you could tell."

Another factor worrying Jack was the appearances the ever-popular Eisenhower had started to make on behalf of the vice president who hoped to succeed him. "Last week, Dick Nixon hit the panic button and started Ike speaking," Jack complained to navy pal Red Fay. "He spoke in Philadelphia on Friday night and is going to make about four or five speeches between now and the election. With every word he utters, I can feel the votes leaving me. It's like standing on a mound of sand with the tide running out. I'm telling you he's knocking our block off. If the election was tomorrow I'd win easily, but six days from now it's up for grabs."

Finally, it was election night. Bobby's house in Hyannis Port became an oceanside headquarters. Bobby set it all up in preparation for the countdown once the returns started to come in. "Each state has certain bellwether counties, and those were what we were monitoring. There was little you could do at this point but wait," Ken O'Donnell remembered.

The first big sign of trouble was Ohio. "Bobby found me and pulled me aside. He said, 'Kenny, it looks like we're gone in Ohio.' I said, 'Let's wait until Cleveland comes in and we'll make it up there.' Bobby shook his head and gave me this wan smile. 'No, you don't understand. These figures include Cleveland.' I couldn't believe it could be over so quickly."

O'Donnell went on: "We called the Senator, and he came over. Ohio continued to dribble in, but we were obviously going to lose it. Bobby and I were devastated, and we felt it might all be over. The Senator was calm as could be, though, and said, 'Let's just wait.'"

NBC's John Chancellor now began reporting that the count was tightening, that Nixon was catching up to his Democratic rival. O'Donnell recalled how Kennedy reacted on hearing this. "I don't mind him closing the gap," he said, watching the screen, "as much as I mind him smiling while he was doing it."

"I think, around eleven or twelve o'clock there was sort of . . . not a shock," said Dave Hackett, "but everybody being a little bit surprised at the turn it began to take."

The candidate, to break the tension, now described the call he'd just had from his running mate. One thing Johnson had said to him was reassuring, that even if it had appeared a tough fight at the start in Texas, he thought it'd turn out all right in the end. Next, Jack reported, had come a pure LBJ kicker: "I see *we* carried Pennsylvania, but what happened to *you* in Ohio?"

The long watch continued until dawn. Jack went off to bed. Bobby couldn't, still at his post watching the numbers. He could see during the predawn hours what was happening. Having expected to win comfortably, the verdict was now resting with a few yet to be decided states. The election was going to be close.

With the sun having risen, the Kennedys were learning just *how* close. It would end up Kennedy: 34,220,984; Nixon: 34,108,157. Whatever effect religion had, along with all the other variables—helping with Roman Catholics in the larger states, hurting in others—there had been small room for mistakes, either actively or by omission. They had run the very campaign that was necessary.

That Christmas, the president-elect and his wife presented Bobby with a special leather-bound copy of *The Enemy Within*, which had made the bestseller list during the campaign. "For Bobby—The Brother Within—who made the easy difficult," Jack wrote in it. But Jacqueline's inscription was heartfelt, unalloyed with the usual Kennedy irony. "To Bobby—who made the impossible possible and changed all our lives."

President-elect Kennedy declaring the appointment
of his brother as U.S. Attorney General.

CHAPTER FOURTEEN

FREEDOM FIGHTER

"At last, Bobby's moral center seemed to stir."

—Harry Belafonte

"We're going to do what we thought Eisenhower was going to do in 1952 and never did—bring a new spirit to the government," Bobby Kennedy said just after the election.

He went on to explain what he meant: "Not necessarily young men, but *new* men, who believe in a cause, who believe their jobs go on forever, not just from 9 to 5; who believe they have a responsibility to the United States, not just to an administration, and who can really get things done."

The big question was the obvious one. With a large debt to his own efforts, his brother was soon to be installed in the White House. What sort of place was Bobby imagining for himself in the Kennedy administration? "I wouldn't take an appointment to Jack's Senate seat," he explained in a morning-after *Newsweek* interview.

Nor would he, he said, look to assume any sort of chief of staff type role. "I'd want my own position with my own authority. But there you run into the relationship problem again. Jack and I discussed the whole thing briefly this week, but I really haven't worked out the problems in my own mind."

Meanwhile, Bobby's friends were finding their way into the White House. One of the earliest to land there was Ken O'Donnell, his Harvard teammate. Jack gave him the coveted role of Oval Office gatekeeper, with the understated title of "appointment Secretary." Over O'Donnell's opposition, the president-elect then appointed Pierre Salinger, another of Bobby's finds, to the front-line post of White House press secretary. Jack made clear to Salinger that it was Bobby's appointment.

It wasn't long before Bobby and Ethel's house at Hickory Hill turned into a busy way station both for the new administration's job vacancies and those seeking to fill them. According to Red Fay, the supplicants were "understandably reluctant to call the president-elect, with all his new responsibilities and obligations." And so they turned to Robert Kennedy. "The phones—all four lines—rang continuously. It was not unusual to see all four buttons on the phone light up, pick up the phone and discover that a future Cabinet officer or ambassador had been patiently waiting, sometimes for ten or fifteen minutes, to get Bob's ear."

Fay himself hadn't been forgotten by his friend Jack, who slotted him to be under secretary of the navy. Then came a hurdle. The president-elect had accepted the demand of Robert McNamara, newly named defense secretary, for carte blanche in picking his subcabinet officials. Fay's selection meant McNamara would have to be talked into making an exception. It was Bobby who made the successful appeal.

Bringing Arthur Schlesinger to Washington for a one-of-a-kind position was Bobby's idea. Officially, he'd be an aide to the president, though unofficially regarded as the White House historian-in-residence. Many, however, would refer to him as its "*intellectual*-in-residence."

Here's Schlesinger, explaining: Bobby had "suggested to me the possibility of coming to the White House as some sort of roving reporter and troubleshooter. The proposed assignment could not have appealed to me more, and I said that I would of course be delighted to come. He said that he would bring this up with Jack." The two had met when they'd found themselves seated together on a stormy plane ride to Pittsburgh during the Stevenson campaign. The man of action, the other of deliberation, became fast, if unlikely, friends.

Bobby also took on the tricky job of refereeing the disputes arising among his brother's top aides. He delegated the day-to-day issues that came up to the supervision of a neutral figure, Fred Dutton, former chief of staff for Governor Edmund G. "Pat" Brown of California. As a special assistant to the president, Dutton was expected to deal with friction between the "Irish mafia" led by Ken O'Donnell and the more cerebral group presided over by Ted Sorensen.

Jack Kennedy simply hadn't given much thought to such personnel matters. "For the last four years I spent so much time getting to know people who could help me get elected president," he admitted, "that I didn't have time to get to know people who could help me, after I was elected, to be a good president."

Soon after the election, the new president had leaked to *The New York Times* that he was considering naming his brother attorney general. It was an obvious trial balloon, to see how it might fly with opinion leaders. But part of the trouble lay with Bobby. "I said I didn't want to be attorney general," he later recorded, citing as his reasons both the nepotism factor and that he'd already been chasing after bad guys for three years on the Rackets Committee. "I didn't want to spend the rest of my life doing that."

Nonetheless, Joseph Kennedy was of a single mind. It didn't matter to him what his sons thought. They "listened as he explained why Jack needed someone in the cabinet in whom he had complete trust," the senior Kennedy's biographer David Nasaw has written. "The Kennedys would always be outsiders, unable to fully trust anyone but family members. Jack needed all the protection he could get; only Bobby was going to put his welfare first."

Finally, Jack dispatched Clark Clifford—an urbane political adviser now at the head of the Kennedy transition team—to try to counter Joseph Kennedy's conviction regarding where Bobby belonged in the new administration. "I do want to leave you with one thought," the senior Kennedy said, after listening to Clifford, who was as much a pillar of the Washington establishment as Kennedy himself was not, make his case. "Bobby is *going* to be Attorney General. All of us worked our tails off for Jack, and now that we have succeeded, I'm going to see to it that Bobby gets the same chance that we gave Jack."

Whether pulled or pushed, Bobby wrote a letter in mid-December to syndicated columnist Drew Pearson: "I made up my mind today, and Jack and I take the plunge tomorrow. For many reasons, I believe it was the only thing I could do—I shall do my best and hope that it turns out well."

"I need to know that, when problems arise, I'm going to have somebody who's going to tell me the unvarnished truth, no matter what," is how Jack explained it. "And Bobby will do that."

Despite the criticism from editorial writers and columnists, one person, surprisingly, proved himself stalwart in backing the appointment: Lyndon Johnson. The new president had asked him to help his brother's confirmation get through the Senate. And so Johnson, terming it a "real crusade," took seriously the trust Jack was placing in him. "It's the first thing he's asked me to do, and it's very personal with him," he told an aide.

Johnson also understood how much the one brother relied on the other. He'd learned it the hard way. But he also knew who was the boss. "If I learned anything last year, it's that Jack Kennedy's a lot tougher, and maybe a lot smarter, than I thought he was. Bobby Kennedy won't get to go to the bathroom unless Jack Kennedy feels like taking a pee."

John F. Kennedy assumed office "with all flags flying," as Chuck Spalding would often say of his friend. At home in Philadelphia, I watched my mother respond to exactly that notion as she proudly watched the ceremony take place.

On that icy clear January day when the world witnessed him taking the oath, what we all saw was a striking young leader, debonair and confident, and accompanied by his beautiful younger wife. The first couple seemed perfectly emblematic of "the new frontier" that he said beckoned us. His inaugural call to "ask not what your country can do for you; ask what you can do for your country" reached us at a place above politics.

Three months later, on April 12, Richard Bissell, deputy director of the Central Intelligence Agency, briefed Bobby on an upcoming U.S.-backed invasion of Cuba. This operation was the Cold War power play that, had it been carried out before the November election, Nixon hoped would bring him victory.

The secret action that Bissell now described was originally conceived by the CIA as a loud detonator, the chain reaction from which would result in an overthrow of the newly established Castro regime. It was based on the following intelligence estimate: "The great mass of Cuban people believe that the hour of decision is at hand. . . . It is generally believed that the Cuban Army has been successfully penetrated by opposition groups and that it will not fight in the event of a showdown."

Four days later, on Sunday the 16th, two World War II bombers with Cuban Air Force markings made emergency landings in Miami and Key West. They had just attacked the island's airfields. U.S. Immigration took them into custody, then issued a statement that the pilots were defectors from the Cuban military. Adlai Stevenson, who'd been appointed U.S. ambassador to the United Nations, issued a statement confirming the official position. Speaking for the Kennedy administration to the world body, he said the aircraft were Castro's "own planes that took off from Castro's own airfields."

None of this was true.

The next day, Monday, just hours after midnight, Brigade 2506—1,400 anti-Castro Cuban exiles trained, equipped, transported, and given limited air cover by the CIA—landed on the island's south side near an inlet known as Bahía de Cochinos, or Bay of Pigs. From the outset, the invasion faced strong resistance from government troops who met them on the beach.

"I don't think it's going as well as it should," the president told Bobby, then giving a speech to a convention of newspaper editors in Williamsburg, Virginia. "Come back here."

As the day went on, the situation on the ground at the Bay of Pigs grew more and more dire. "I think we've made a terrible mistake," Bobby told Ed Guthman, now his press secretary. "The worst thing is that we're caught in a lie." That cover story, that the pilots had been Castro defectors, was now as incredible as bogus reports that the invaders were succeeding.

When Guthman inquired what was to be done now, Bobby told him, "You can start praying for those poor fellows on the beach."

Two days later, with the invasion force utterly crushed, President Kennedy went before the country to accept, personally, full blame for the debacle. "There's an old saying that victory has a hundred fathers and defeat is an orphan," he said in a press conference. "I'm the responsible officer of the government."

Away from the cameras and microphones, he held a stronger view of whom to blame. "Those sons-of-bitches with the fruit salad just sat there nodding, saying it would work. I've got to do something about those CIA bastards. How could I have been so stupid?"

It was now clear that the CIA had both deceived him and underestimated his willingness to stand up to them. They'd assumed Kennedy would send in U.S. forces to carry the day. This is what they promised the exiles, what they led themselves to believe as well. They thought that President Kennedy, at the critical moment, would buckle under the fear of defeat and approve a U.S. military attack on Cuba. But he didn't.

It was this miscalculation that allowed Bissell and company to support a force of 1,400 civilians to land on a deserted beach where they'd have to face the arriving Cuban army. The rationale had always been that at the critical moment the United States would commit its armed forces and secure the victory.

Grasping all this too late, Jack Kennedy recognized that the CIA, in dealing with him, hadn't understood for whom they were working. They'd kept information from him in order to better control him. It was a big mistake—for which he was now suffering.

As the full dimensions of the failed Cuban enterprise sank in, Bobby saw his brother trapped between advisers who'd deceived him and the enemy in Moscow and Havana, who now regarded him as a paper tiger. For Bobby, Castro, whom he saw as the villain behind Jack's humiliation, had become not just a national threat but a personal enemy. Seeing him begin to make Cuba a base for hemispheric subversion, Bobby didn't doubt that Castro was on the way to forging stronger and stronger Soviet ties. In fact, looking ahead, he predicted that the Cuban leader would be willing to accept the presence of Russian nuclear missiles pointed at the United States.

In other words, Castro had to be overthrown.

"There can be no long-term living with Castro as a neighbor." This conclusion came in a report compiled by Robert Kennedy and the others who'd been appointed by the president to a panel charged with performing an autopsy on the Bay of Pigs disaster. But participating in that intensive month-long study was only part of the attorney general's newly broadened portfolio. As he described it, "I then became involved on every major and all the international questions."

It involved an assignment close to his heart: to find the way to win release of the many hundreds of men now imprisoned in Cuba who had trusted America to help them free their island.

On May 4, thirteen "Freedom Riders"—seven black, six white—left Washington, D.C. Boarding two buses, their mission—launched by the student-led Congress of Racial Equality, or CORE—was to travel into the Deep South. The purpose of the journey was to test a 1960 Supreme Court decision, *Boynton v. Virginia*, which had forbidden racial segregation of interstate transportation.

"During those days," recalled civil rights leader John Lewis, himself one of the original Freedom Riders, "it was impossible for a person of color to get on a bus in the South without being forced to go to the back of the bus or go to a waiting room marked 'Colored Waiting' or use a restroom facility marked 'Colored Men.' We wanted to bring down those signs."

Hostilities first erupted in South Carolina, with Lewis one of those attacked. But the worst violence didn't begin until the buses crossed into Alabama. There, on Sunday, May 14, outside the city of Anniston, one of the buses had its tires slashed and then was firebombed, with the fleeing passengers beaten with baseball bats. The other bus reached Birmingham, where Klansmen viciously beat passengers with iron pipes, bicycle chains, and bats.

When Bobby Kennedy had first heard of the Freedom Rider plan, he'd immediately contacted Harris Wofford, their liaison with civil rights leaders. "Stop them!" he urged him. "Get your friends off those buses!"

All he could see was the likely embarrassment abroad. Just a month later President Kennedy was about to meet with Soviet leader Nikita Khrushchev for the first time at a two-day summit in Vienna. Bobby didn't want this already sensitive occasion to be overshadowed by headlines of racial protest at home.

The new attorney general disapproved, in fact, of such acts of civil disobedience. He believed the correct path for achieving equal rights ran through the courts and the ballot box. Entertainer and lifelong social activist Harry Belafonte has offered this take on the Kennedy brothers' attitude. "To them, the Freedom Riders were as much to blame as the angry mobs." He said, "The last thing the White House needed was news footage of American Negroes being beaten by white policemen—perfect propaganda for the Soviet Union to make its case that the land of the free was anything but free."

Bobby also felt a genuine concern for the safety of a second group of Freedom Riders, which was now poised to launch itself into danger. He sent John Seigenthaler, now his administrative assistant, to his home city of Nashville, from where this second group of activists were departing. His mission was to talk them out of it. Unsuccessful in that effort, he then dispatched Seigenthaler to see if Alabama governor John Patterson, who'd backed Jack Kennedy during the campaign, would be willing to help.

Bobby's purpose was to keep people from getting hurt. When Patterson refused to deploy his state troopers, Seigenthaler threatened him with armed federal intervention. And "that's the last thing you want!" he warned. Hearing this, Patterson banged the table. "If Marshalls or troops come into Alabama, blood'll run in the streets!" Then, grudgingly, he agreed to protect the Freedom Riders with an escort of state police and National Guardsmen but only as far as Montgomery.

At the city limits, however, they departed the scene.

Seigenthaler and Assistant Attorney General John Doar were now together in a car following the bus from Nashville as it made its way into the Alabama capital. When they reached the Montgomery station, they could hear the screams and knew there was trouble. "I just leaped out of the car," said Seigenthaler. At this point two men grabbed him and spun him around.

"Get back!" he shouted. "I'm with the federal government!" Then he tried to turn away, but was hit on the head with a pipe. Seigenthaler lay on the ground for almost half an hour before the police took him to a hospital.

The next night, 1,500 people packed into Montgomery's First Baptist Church to honor the Freedom Riders and hear Martin Luther King, Jr., speak. Surrounding the house of worship were now several thousand angry white demonstrators. Keeping them at bay outside were fifty U.S. marshals, summoned there by the attorney general in Washington.

King, who'd rushed there on hearing the news of the attack, had to calm those in the church once the tear gas used on the mob outside begin to seep through the doors and windows.

"Troops are on the way in from Montgomery now," King reported. "They have requested that all of us stay in here for the time being, that nobody will leave. And may I make another personal request on behalf I think of all of us, that we must be sure that we adhere absolutely to nonviolence. Now it's very easy for us to get angry and bitter and even violent in a moment like this. But I think this is a testing point. Now, we had to go out a few minutes ago and counsel with some of our own people who were getting to the point of returning to violence. And we don't want to do that. We can't do that. We have won the moral victory."

Governor Patterson finally sent in the National Guard to relieve the marshals. And at dawn, the Justice Department negotiated safe passage out of the church for those being held hostage there. The Freedom Riders continued on to Jackson.

"Robert Kennedy became educated in a real hurry," John Lewis recalled. "And I can tell you the thing that sealed it for him, perhaps more than anything else—after John Seigenthaler was beaten, someone he knew." Seigenthaler himself would say, "I think everything he thought the administration of justice and law enforcement was supposed to be about had been violated . . . and that it was an outrage, a stain on law enforcement that we let that happen."

Observed Harry Belafonte, a friend to both King and Kennedy, "At last, Bobby's moral center seemed to stir."

On a Voice of America broadcast six days after the rioting at the Montgomery bus station, Attorney General Robert F. Kennedy spoke of his family's own history, about how "the Irish were not wanted when his grandfather arrived in Boston." And he reminded listeners: "Now an Irish Catholic is president of the United States. There is no question about it—in the next forty years, a Negro can achieve the same position my brother did."

James Meredith registers at the University of Mississippi, October 1962.

CHAPTER FIFTEEN

GENERAL

"He would have taken a bolt of lightning for Jack.
All he cared about was his brother's presidency."

—JOHN SEIGENTHALER

As he settled into his new office in the Justice Department—six blocks up Pennsylvania Avenue from the White House—Robert Kennedy was having to choose his priorities as the country's chief law enforcement officer. He soon discovered he still liked "chasing bad guys."

Surprisingly, J. Edgar Hoover, longtime director of the Federal Bureau of Investigation, was less interested than he in pursuing organized crime. While he relished the FBI's reputation as tommy-gun-toting "G-Men," Hoover deployed the greatest number of his special agents shadowing the country's dwindling number of Communists. He feared that agents would be corrupted by their dealings with the criminal syndicates. Stubbornly, he denied even the existence of a "mafia."

As Hoover's superior, Bobby was about to change all that. One of his first acts was to order a list of the country's top organized crime figures along with strategies for apprehending them. Although the FBI made extensive use of wiretapping and bugging, Kennedy wanted more of it, and more training, all with newer technology.

He also recognized the crime-busting potential of tax records. That was, after all, the route by which the government had brought down notorious mobster Al Capone three decades earlier. His first step was contacting Mortimer Caplin, under whom he'd studied tax law at the University of Virginia. He wanted to know if his former professor believed in the use of tax returns as a legitimate means of establishing criminal activity. Getting the answer he wanted, he went forward with his plans.

"One of the things I'm going to do as attorney general is to take on organized crime in this country," Bobby told Caplin, whom President Kennedy now named director of the IRS. Accepting the position, and referring to his new boss's goal, Caplin said he couldn't emphasize too strongly the importance he attached "to the success of the Service's contribution to this overall program."

Jimmy Hoffa remained high on Kennedy's target list. "From the moment he was named attorney general, Bobby was determined to prosecute Hoffa," recalled Nicholas Katzenbach, who was running Justice's Office of Legal Counsel. "He was convinced from his work on the McClellan Committee that Hoffa was evil, corrupt and capable of corrupting our political institutions." The same was true of Chicago gangster Sam Giancana, the heir to Capone, whom Kennedy saw as "unstable as an animal," who'd "kill people for kicks."

But Bobby also found himself engaged by the issue of preventing young criminals from turning into hardened ones. At his first press conference as attorney general, he alluded to the growing problem of juvenile delinquency—a very real social issue, though one J. Edgar Hoover insisted on belittling as "muddle-headed" sentimentalism—and soon made it a department priority. In May 1961, President Kennedy brought into being the President's Committee on Juvenile Delinquency and Youth Crime, with his brother its chairman and Dave Hackett its director.

There was, as Hackett would say, a clear sense of shared identity for Bobby with the street kids for whom he hoped to make a difference. Poverty and race were the main underlying causes for their behavior, but Bobby found ways to identify with them. "It goes back to the very early days," Hackett recalled. "Part of it was he was slight and small and was way down in a huge family. I think he was a misfit in school, and I think he was a misfit all the way through his whole career, in a way, in the best sense of the word."

Bobby himself probably put it best with the answer he gave to his friend the reporter Jack Newfield, who'd asked him what he thought he might have been if not born a Kennedy. "Perhaps a juvenile delinquent or a revolutionary."

Now, professionally, he was both boss and mentor. "I started in the Department as a young lawyer in 1950," Bobby would tell younger Justice attorneys, understanding the value of such a frank—and wry—approach. "The salary was only $4000 a year, but I worked hard. I was ambitious. I studied. I applied myself. And then my brother was elected president of the United States." That way of meeting the nepotism issue head-on fell into the category he liked to refer to as "hanging a lantern on your problem."

When it came to the men and women working for him at Justice, it was important that they trust his leadership, believing he'd always support them as needed, that he wouldn't buckle to pressure and leave a Justice Department attorney hanging, his case thrown aside because of politics. From the outset, Bobby was endeavoring to build a team, loyal to him, loyal to each other.

One of his regular routines was to tour the floors of the Justice Department, introducing himself, but also stopping to listen. "Maybe at one o'clock in the afternoon he'd come into my office," said John Seigenthaler, "and say, 'Let's go see what's going on.'"

The two of them would then head off. Stopping in an office, he'd stick out his hand. "I'm Bob Kennedy. What are you working on?" Even though, according to Seigenthaler, he'd ask for only five minutes of the staff lawyer's time, he wound up always staying longer, to learn more.

The lawyers working for him had, many of them, been junior officers during World War II, and this meant they were likely to have picked up aptitudes that served them well now. These included improvisation and working together, skills not often mutually compatible. Katzenbach, a navigator in the Army Air Corps, had been captured when his B-25 bomber was shot down; then, as a prisoner of war, he twice escaped only to be recaptured. John Doar and John Seigenthaler, who'd shown courage during the riot at the Montgomery bus station, had also been in the Air Corps.

Those men working for Kennedy learned from the start not to stand on ceremony, and not to stand around waiting for orders. "In the next three and a half years," Guthman wrote, "I don't recall Bob saying very often that he was going to have a meeting and that he would like me to attend, or that he was going somewhere and wanted me to accompany him. He expected us to anticipate his needs and act accordingly."

What struck me personally, early in the 1970s when I first met Paul Corbin—a loyalist close to the new AG—was his reference to him as "Bob." I would learn it was the name Kennedy's loyalists used regularly, eschewing the family nickname entirely.

One early observation Kennedy made on his excursions through the building was the lack of minority attorneys at Justice. "Did you see any Negroes?" he asked Seigenthaler one day. It was then that he learned there were only eight African Americans working at Justice, each in a custodial job. Pursuing the matter further and being told that applications from men and women of color were nonexistent, he refused to accept the excuse. Instead, he began sending letters to law schools saying that the Justice Department was open to hiring black graduates.

"We're not seeking to give Negroes preference," he wrote. "But we're not getting any applications, and we want these young people to know that they will not be excluded because of their race. Will you please make a special effort to let Negroes know? Because we fear that over a long period they have been excluded."

During that first December of Jack's presidency, an event took place that changed everything, entirely altering the world he, his mother, and his brothers and sisters knew. Joseph P. Kennedy suffered a debilitating stroke, one that left him unable to express himself. Bobby received word in his office at Justice. By afternoon he was flying with Jack to the family home in Palm Beach.

Capable now only of muttering "no," their once famously powerful—overbearing, manipulative, and ever critical—father was reduced to being a man trapped entirely inside himself, his rage at his fate daily visible on his paralyzed face.

The January 26, 1962, issue of *Life* magazine featured Attorney General Kennedy on its cover. Billing him as "The No. 2 Man in Washington," the piece's author, Paul O'Neill, began the article with the knowing observation that his subject disliked being called "Bobby." The only person in government with the acknowledged right to do this, readers learned, was his brother, the president. Otherwise, "he wears that diminutive as restively as a hair shirt."

The article described the way the attorney general had revamped

White House operations following the Bay of Pigs. It credited his decisive summoning of federal marshals and later the National Guard to the Montgomery church where Martin Luther King, the Freedom Riders, and their supporters were surrounded and held captive. It emphasized the importance of his seat on the National Security Council. Robert Kennedy, wrote O'Neill, is "wondrously qualified for the multiple roles in which he has so confidently cast himself."

What stands out most is O'Neill's spotlight on Bob Kennedy's personal characteristics. Among those he cites are his "contempt for liars," his role in the Kennedy family as "chief of the clan" since his father's stroke, and his "idealism in the extreme."

Such feelings led him to a kinship with those wanting to commit themselves to this country. Once coming across a naturalization ceremony in a Brooklyn courthouse, Bobby asked if he might say a few words. As he often did, he invoked the experience of his forebears. "When my grandparents came to Boston not so many years ago, they found signs outside employment offices which read, IRISH NEED NOT APPLY—but I want you to remember that my brother has been elected president of the United States."

O'Neill found himself fascinated by the contradictions in Bobby. "He seems to be genuinely horrified," he wrote, "to learn that some helpless fellow human has been pushed around by a price fixer, a crooked politician or a conniving labor leader—although his impulse to smite the wrongdoer usually precedes his impulse to bemoan the victim."

That spring, the issue of price-fixing commanded the attention of both Kennedy brothers, and, this time, labor was the victim not the transgressor. Early in April, the United Steelworkers union's leaders signed an agreement with the major producers. Forgoing a wage increase, they accepted a new contract offering only a modest upgrade in fringe benefits—estimated at 10 cents an hour. The

Steelworkers did so because they were relying on President Kennedy's personal assurances that management—the top brass at U.S. Steel had sought his support in the matter—was committed to fighting inflation.

Four days after signing the new labor contract, Roger Blough, U.S. Steel's CEO, requested a meeting with the president. There he handed him a press release announcing the company's intention to raise its prices 3.5 percent. "You've made a terrible mistake," Jack told Blough, his anger barely contained. "You've double-crossed me."

The news grew worse. Within twenty-four hours, five other steel companies made public the exact same price hike. Learning this, the president was swift in his response. At a press conference, he used his own already celebrated inaugural words to heap contempt on Blough et al. "Some time ago, I asked each American to consider what he would do for his country. And I asked the steel companies. In the last twenty-four hours, we had their answer."

But the Kennedys had more than shame with which to strike at the steelmakers. They had hard evidence of illegal collusion. Just before U.S. Steel declared its price hike, a wire service story had quoted Edmund Martin, president of rival Bethlehem Steel, questioning an increase on economic grounds. "There shouldn't be any price rise," he had said; the market wouldn't support it.

So why, then, did Bethlehem and its other competitors suddenly fall into line with U.S. Steel? To make his case for price-fixing, the attorney general needed to see for himself the exact language Martin had used in that meeting. To accomplish that, he would have to have the notes of reporters who'd been there. Such documentation would be persuasive evidence the steel industry chiefs had been colluding, that Bethlehem was simply following the leader.

The orders to the FBI agents went out after midnight. They began knocking on reporters' doors at 3 a.m., looking for notebooks.

"The attorney general asked us to call you," one agent told a *Wall Street Journal* reporter.

By the time Bobby arrived at work that morning, those predawn appearances had already raised a ruckus. But he quickly understood where the buck stopped. "I get some credit when FBI agents do something good," he said. "I'll take the heat when they goof."

Later, at a private party, the Kennedy brothers lampooned the aggressive tactics they'd put into play when they'd forced the steel companies to reverse themselves. "Why is it that all the telephone calls of all the steel executives in all the country are being tapped?" Jack quoted Thomas Patton, head of Republic Steel. "And I told him that I thought he was being totally unfair to the attorney general, and that I'm sure it wasn't true."

He went on: "And he asked me, 'Why is it that all the income tax returns of all the steel executives in all the country are being scrutinized?' And I told him that, too, was totally unfair, that the attorney general wouldn't do such a thing. And then I called the attorney general and asked him why he was tapping the telephones of all the steel executives and examining the tax returns of all the steel executives . . . and the attorney general told me that that was totally untrue and unfair."

Now came Jack's punch line: "And, of course, Patton was right." It was followed by Bobby's: "They were mean to my brother," he explained, interrupting the president. "They can't do that to my brother."

Chicago mobster Sam Giancana was well known to the FBI—and also to Bobby Kennedy, who'd been tracking him since his days on the Rackets Committee. As attorney general he'd maintained the heat, keeping him under continual surveillance. This was despite the fact that his father had enlisted the mobster's help in the 1960 election. It was such behavior on the son's part that enraged Giancana.

In late February 1962, in duplicate memos sent to the attorney general and presidential aide Ken O'Donnell, J. Edgar Hoover informed the two men of troubling information. The bureau had hard evidence that Judith Campbell, a young woman close to Giancana, was involved in an ongoing relationship with the president. Two years earlier, she'd been introduced to Jack by Frank Sinatra. Since his earliest days as a young crooner, Sinatra had been known both to hang out with and be indebted to underworld figures.

Confronted by this irrefutable government evidence—coming from an agency that at least on paper was subject to his control—Bobby immediately took action on two fronts. Overcoming his longtime practice of staying out of his brother's sexual affairs, he knew he now had no choice.

First, taking care to use trusted emissaries, he passed on to the president the fact that the FBI was sitting on phone records he needed to know about. Specifically, Hoover had logs of seventy calls between the White House and Campbell, who he said was enjoying a relationship with Giancana. Still, learning that the FBI had the goods on him was not enough for Jack. It took the director's visit to the Oval Office the next month, when he handed the president a memo detailing Campbell's ties to both him and the murderous gangster, to end it.

The president had scheduled an upcoming weekend visit to Sinatra at his Palm Springs estate. His brother now talked him out of it. "Johnny, you just can't associate with this guy," he informed him. The trip was canceled. And so was their friendship.

It had been in the early months of the new presidency, back in May of 1961, that Bobby had received word from Hoover of how the CIA had, during the previous administration, approached Giancana for help in ridding Cuba of Castro. The agency assumed that the mob—ever since the revolutionary leader had shut down its highly profitable gambling interests on the island—had good reason to want Castro disposed of. So, Hoover knew, did Bobby. He'd signed a report, after all, declaring there could be "no long-term living with Castro as a neighbor." Hoover figured he'd be a ready listener to hear about this "dirty business" involving Giancana.

Even with the ending of JFK's affair with Judith Campbell, Bobby could see that the Giancana-Kennedy connection still held menace. Having succeeded in severing Jack's ties to both Giancana's mistress and Frank Sinatra, he now wanted a clear statement from the CIA. Did the United States continue to be involved in a kill-Fidel plot? In May of 1962, at his request, he received an official briefing in which he was told that the Bay of Pigs fiasco had marked the end of that conspiracy involving Giancana. "I trust that if you ever try to do business with organized crime again—with gangsters—you'll let the attorney general know," Bobby said.

Keeping his brother free from scandal was his priority. Yet Bobby left no one in doubt, least of all his CIA contacts, that he wanted Fidel Castro gone.

On the evening of President Kennedy's inauguration, an air force veteran named James Meredith had applied to the University of Mississippi. Knowing that Ole Miss did not permit African Americans to attend, he followed up with an eloquent two-page letter to the Justice Department. In it, he stated his desire to enroll at Ole Miss, explaining at the same time he realized it would be a goal he'd be unable to accomplish on his own. The "delaying tactics" used by the state, Meredith explained, would mean that he'd neither be accepted nor rejected, but simply kept at bay.

"What do I want from you?" he asked the attorney general. Then, answering his own question, he expressed his belief that "the power and influence of the federal government should be used where necessary to ensure compliance with the laws as interpreted by the proper authority." In conclusion, Meredith said, "I simply ask that the federal agencies use the power and prestige of their positions to insure the full rights of citizenship for our people."

Over the next year and a half, legal battles were fought. The final result saw the Supreme Court upholding an appeals court ruling in Meredith's favor. Despite this, Mississippi governor Ross Barnett remained staunchly resistant. "I won't agree to let that boy go to Ole Miss," he told the U.S. attorney general.

Both Kennedys hoped to avoid the use of federal troops in the matter. President Eisenhower bringing them in to integrate Arkansas's Little Rock High School in 1957 had left a bad history in its trail. They didn't want to repeat it. Unfortunately, an eruption of ugly violence—one necessitating outside intervention—seemed all too likely, given the inflamed emotions now gripping the Ole Miss campus.

The daily headlines mirrored the differing regional perspectives on the crisis: "U.S. Is Prepared to Send Troops," announced *The New York Times* on September 26, while the local *Jackson Daily News* reported, "Thousands Said Ready to Fight."

Barnett now proposed an elaborate plan in which a large detachment of U.S Army troops would be deployed to escort Meredith onto campus. There, Meredith would be greeted by the governor himself, backed up by a line of unarmed highway patrolmen. Those would be supported, in turn, by a line of unarmed sheriff's deputies; and behind them would be a third line of students and citizens. Barnett would next read a proclamation barring Meredith, which would signal the soldiers to draw their weapons. The scene had Governor Barnett, facing overwhelming odds and the danger of bloody clashes, to give up, calling nobly for law and order.

Bob Kennedy refused to play any part in this Theater of the Lost Cause which Barnett had concocted. Fearing the strong possibility of a disastrous mishap—the all-too-likely chance a hothead might start shooting—Bobby rejected the governor's scenario outright. In fact, he already had had a great many futile discussions with the governor, all attempts to find a face-saving way for him to admit Meredith.

Finally, the decision was made to whisk Meredith onto campus that Sunday and register him the next day. But when Meredith made it onto campus, accompanied by U.S. marshals, a mob quickly began to grow in size and menace. The scene grew worse and worse.

Representing the Justice Department at Ole Miss were Nicholas Katzenbach and Ed Guthman, the latter describing to his boss a scene he said was "like the Alamo." More than a third of the marshals—160 in all—wound up injured, with twenty-eight hit by gunfire. Two civilians, including a French journalist, were killed in the mayhem.

At ten o'clock that night, Katzenbach reported to Kennedy the army needed to be called in, that it might even be too late. He worried that the five hundred beleaguered marshals couldn't hold off the rioting protesters until reinforcements arrived from Memphis, eighty miles away. The attorney general, understandably alarmed at what his assistant AG was telling him and concerned about Meredith himself, told Katzenbach to issue the order: "Shoot anybody that puts a hand on him."

Later, Bobby paid tribute to the courage of James Meredith in what he called "the mightiest internal struggle of our time." He saluted as well the "500 United States Marshals, most of them from the Southern states, who remained true to their orders and instructions and stood with great bravery to prevent interference with federal court orders." Meredith later saluted Kennedy's leadership in the dangerous episode. "It seemed to me very clear that Bobby Kennedy was the main man. . . . Bobby sent the marshals. He could have sent just two. His decisions kept me alive."

Not until that night in Oxford did either Kennedy brother grasp the depth of opposition to racial integration in the Deep South.

Bobby and Jack in the Oval Office.

CHAPTER SIXTEEN

TWO GREAT MEN

"Every time they have a conference, don't tell me about who is the top advisor. It isn't McNamara, the chiefs of staff, or anybody else like that. Bobby is first in, last out. And Bobby is the boy he listens to."

—LYNDON JOHNSON

Bobby Kennedy was haunted by the Bay of Pigs. The least mention of "Cuba" would gnaw away at his sense of humiliation over the way the U.S. had been, in the eyes of the world, beaten.

Moscow, for its part, very much wanted its strategic outpost in the Western Hemisphere to remain Communist. Yet the Russians could only assume that the Bay of Pigs might soon be followed by an all-out U.S. invasion. There was pride, too, in the alliance. "Cuba means a great deal to the old Bolsheviks like Khrushchev," a Kremlin official told Secretary of State Dean Rusk. "This is the first time a country has gone Communist peacefully." Unlike in Eastern Europe, the Red Army didn't move in and take over.

Bobby Kennedy's feelings directly countered those of the Russian leader. He'd long hated Communism, now loathed having a Communist country as a near neighbor, and, above all, hated that the enemy looked strong when his brother so clearly had not. He also was one of those predicting that it was only a matter of time before the Soviets brought in nuclear missiles to the island nation. For all these reasons, he accepted the leadership of a special interagency task force focused on the problem. "It was almost as simple as, goddammit, we lost the first round, let's win the second," National Security Council adviser McGeorge Bundy said.

Code-named Operation Mongoose—after the snake-killing animal—it would carry out anti-Castro acts of sabotage, paramilitary plots, and a wide range of black bag schemes, all of which repeatedly failed. The Communist leader remained in unchallenged command of his country. Unmistakable with his cigar, trademark fatigues, and patrol cap, he cut a figure that seemed to mock the superpower determined to remove him.

Bobby was also drawn at that time to a different sort of below-the-radar mission. This was one aimed at establishing a back channel for communicating with Moscow. Within weeks of the Bay of Pigs, journalist friends, including Charlie Bartlett, had put him in contact with an information officer at the Soviet embassy, Georgi Bolshakov.

At their first meeting, the pair spent four hours strolling the streets of Washington. Those were the weeks of 1961 before the president's Vienna summit with Khrushchev. Bobby's goal then was to transmit a single message to the Kremlin: don't be misguided by the American president's restraint in the Bay of Pigs. Don't underestimate his toughness. If pushed, especially on West Berlin where the Soviets were again pressing the U.S. to evacuate, he will fight.

Through the ensuing months, the liaison between the U.S. president's brother and Bolshakov, a man known for his closeness to Khrushchev, achieved some useful if limited purposes. Mainly it allowed each leader to avoid irritating the other for no good purpose. It won a commitment from the Soviet leader to take no action that would influence the 1962 congressional elections. Both the White House and the Kremlin recognized that any instance of Soviet aggression could only play into the hands of the more hawkish Republicans.

As the fall election campaign heated up, however, Republican New York senator Kenneth Keating began charging that nuclear bases were now under construction in Cuba, saying that he had information to prove it. The political firepower was enormous. It told voters that the Soviets were converting Cuba into a strategic base just off American shores.

In early October, Attorney General Kennedy received Bolshakov at the Justice Department. Gone was their usual casualness. Bobby's extreme anger was masked by a cold, all-business demeanor. Knowing the headlines and facing him across his desk, however, the Russian repeated the earlier Moscow commitment—made by Khrushchev in a letter to the president—that these weapons were purely of a defensive nature, surface-to-air missiles "intended for protecting the interests of the Cuban revolution."

On October 15, a U-2 spy plane—a reconnaissance aircraft built for high altitudes—discovered three ballistic missile launch sites near San Cristóbal, which analysts determined were of medium range. That meant they were capable of reaching targets 1,100 miles away, which would include such cities as Washington, D.C.

Early the next morning, a Tuesday, National Security Adviser McGeorge Bundy entered the family quarters of the White House, carrying the photographs. The president was in his bedroom, still in his pajamas reading the newspapers, as he received the startling news. Quickly, he drew up a list for Bundy of those he wanted summoned to an emergency meeting in the West Wing.

Next, he reached Bobby at the Justice Department.

The attorney general was meeting that morning with the new CIA deputy director, Richard Helms, on a different matter. Asked to confirm what he had just heard from the president, Helms did just that. Bobby's response: "Shit."

When Jack reached Bundy's office, he found Bobby there waiting for him.

"Ken Keating will probably be the next president," Jack wryly commented after they'd studied the three large photographs taken from the U-2. Yet there was no clear answer to the question of how long it would take, now that they were in place, for the Russians to have them ready to launch. Given the estimate of two weeks, the president realized he had sufficient time to consider his options.

The initial recommendation from the Joint Chiefs of Staff was to deliver an air strike. Either that, they advised, or an all-out invasion. The Kennedys understood the danger that posed, that the Soviets could take any attack the United States might make on Cuba as a pretext to match it in Europe. This could mean Russian tanks advancing into U.S.-occupied West Berlin. Khrushchev had recently warned Jack that any Cuban incursion would bring a retaliatory move in Germany. Nonetheless, the danger of American inaction was equally a risk.

To help steer him through the crisis, President Kennedy now set up a working group within the larger National Security Council, seen as too large and therefore too leak-prone. The Executive Committee of the NSC—ExComm, as it became known—would deliberate and suggest strategies to force the missiles' removal while avoiding a nuclear showdown with the USSR.

When he returned to his office, Bobby alerted Ed Guthman to the situation. "We kidded ourselves," he admitted. "And the Russians have lied through their teeth."

Furious at the Russians' deceitfulness, Bobby, in the first Ex-Comm meeting, proposed a quick air strike, to "get into it and get it over with and take our losses." That position, Defense Secretary Robert McNamara noted, made him the toughest hawk among them, "both in his head and in his heart."

The most senior adviser seated around the ExComm table was Dean Acheson, an old cold warrior who'd served as President Truman's secretary of state. Like Bobby, he made a strong case for an immediate surprise attack. The alternative, he argued, would be to repeat the mistakes of the Western powers in the years before World War II. In his mind, allowing such clear provocation to go unchallenged would be tantamount to appeasement, another "Munich." This, of course, was a sensitive topic with both Kennedys, but they could see its truth.

Yet as the days passed, both Kennedys found themselves espousing more of a dove's view, coming to the belief that a naval blockade presented a wiser strategic course. In their minds, the ExComm advisers pushing for swift retaliatory aggression were taking too short a view. They weren't considering the possible Soviet countermove, which, catastrophically, could force a nuclear standoff over West Berlin. There was no way the U.S. and its occupying allies, Britain and France, could withstand a Soviet move on the Western enclave with conventional weapons. An attack would escalate within hours.

By Thursday, the president feared that the Joint Chiefs and other hawks were gaining the upper hand. Pressure was growing in the ExComm to go all the way, to hit the missile sites with a full invasion to follow. "This thing is falling apart," Jack confided to his brother. "You have to pull it together." Contributing to the urgency were new photographs arriving Friday that revealed the arrival of intermediate-range missiles able to travel three thousand miles, able to target nearly every major city in the United States.

The clock was ticking. At the ExComm meeting that same day, Bobby now made the case against a surprise air attack, citing the break it would make with American principles. A State Department staffer taking notes recorded his argument: "For 175 years we had not been that kind of country. A sneak attack was not in our tradition. Thousands of Cubans would be killed without warning, and a lot of Russians too." He favored action, to make known unmistakably the seriousness of the United States' determination to get the missiles out of Cuba, but he thought the action should allow the Soviets some room for maneuver, to pull back from their overextended position in Cuba.

On Monday evening, a full week after first seeing those missile site pictures, President Kennedy addressed the country on television. The U.S. would proceed with a blockade, he announced, which meant any ships en route to Cuba would be stopped, searched, and turned back if found to contain any nuclear material. The main question, of course, was whether the Soviets would honor what the American leader chose to call a "quarantine." In the same speech, he warned that any nuclear missile fired at the United States from Cuba would trigger an all-out U.S. nuclear attack on Russia. He was talking about the near possibility of a Third World War—a nuclear one.

At the Kennedy house across the Potomac River, the mood, as it was throughout the country, was both somber and frightened. "I remember going into Joe and Bobby's room," Ethel recalled to me. "All the children were around their beds, saying their prayers. And then Bobby was saying they might have to evacuate Washington. And I said, 'we're not going anywhere without you.'"

Her husband, still in search of other avenues of negotiation, now made cautious contact with Georgi Bolshakov through an intermediary. The deal he suggested to the Russians was this: the United States agrees to remove its offensive nuclear missiles, currently pointed as they were at Soviet targets, from Turkey. In exchange, the missiles would be taken out of Cuba.

On Friday, October 25, a teletype message arrived in the White House Situation Room. Sent by Khrushchev, it offered a deal in which Russia would remove its Cuban missile sites if the United States promised not to invade the island. But the relief was short-lived.

On Saturday a second message arrived from the Kremlin, this one dictating a further condition. For the Russians to remove their missiles from Cuba, the U.S. would have to do the same in Turkey. Had Bobby's overture to Bolshakov played a role in that second, tougher Kremlin proposal? The fact is, this proposed Turkey-for-Cuba trade-off was being floated by others in contact with the president.

Now, confronted by the two letters from Moscow, the decision was made to answer the first. Bob Kennedy and Ted Sorensen did the actual drafting to the earlier, more conciliatory approach from Khrushchev. If the missiles were taken away from Cuban soil, their response said, the U.S. would commit itself not to invade. In this reply, there was no mention of U.S. missiles in Turkey.

More was to come, however. The president asked his brother to meet that evening with Ambassador Anatoly Dobrynin and inform him that, as part of the arrangement, the United States would remove its Turkey missiles within five months. Most critically, Bobby was to make powerfully clear that none of this was to be made public.

After their meeting, Dobrynin cabled his Kremlin superiors, telling them that the attorney general didn't know how long his brother could hold back the hawks: "I should say that during our meeting R. Kennedy was very upset. I've never seen him like this before," adding, "The generals are itching for a fight."

The next day, Soviet radio broadcast the official Kremlin statement that the missiles installed there were to be removed from Cuba. "In order to save the world, we must retreat," it gravely declared.

British prime minister Harold Macmillan, watching the perilous situation hour by hour from Downing Street, was one statesman to give a historic verdict on the Kennedys' handling of it. "Looking back on it, the way that Bobby and his brother played this hand was absolutely masterly," he said in an interview later. "What they did that week convinced me that they were both great men." Macmillan never learned of the role played by the Turkish missiles.

The attorney general, for his part, still had a Cuban crusade of his own. For the rest of the year he applied himself steadily to the difficult task of winning the release of those 1,113 members of Brigade 2506 captured at the Bay of Pigs. To oversee the negotiation, he brought in James B. Donovan, a New York lawyer who'd been general counsel to the Office of Strategic Services during World War II and an assistant prosecutor at the Nuremberg Trials. It was Donovan who'd managed the exchange of Soviet spy Rudolf Abel for U-2 pilot Francis Gary Powers, who'd been shot down over Soviet airspace in May 1960.

Donovan convinced Castro that the ransom he was demanding— the sum first stood at $62 million, but was negotiated down to $53 million—could not, for political reasons, be raised in cash. Cold War feelings wouldn't permit it. Instead, the payment for the prisoners, he explained, would have to be transmitted as baby food and medical supplies. Bobby himself approached the companies who wound up contributing.

At the last minute, when the Cuban dictator suddenly asked

for an extra $3 million in cash before turning over the men, the attorney general managed, personally, to raise it in twenty-four hours. Driving him was his awareness of the exiles' grim fate back in their native land. Fearing execution when captured, they'd been held in filthy cells, inadequately fed, and contemptuously cared for. And yet, they continued throughout their imprisonment to refuse to cooperate with the dictator's demands that they speak out against the United States and voice their support for Castro's regime.

In *Thirteen Days*, his behind-the-scenes account of the Kennedy White House's handling of the Cuban Missile Crisis, Bobby would write that its lesson lay in "the importance of placing ourselves in the other country's shoes." He meant the necessity, in such a confrontation, to weigh carefully each step being taken, always thinking ahead, never backing the adversary into a corner that could prove ultimately dangerous to both sides.

The president had, above all, wanted "not to humiliate the Soviet Union, not to have them feel they would have to escalate their response because their security or national interest so committed them."

The edge-of-the-seat memoir comes to an end when Ambassador Dobrynin visits Bobby's office. It was Sunday morning. The Soviet diplomat wanted to bring the news that the missiles were to be withdrawn.

Though the State Department had already learned of the decision through official channels, this was a personal call. Once he'd conveyed the news about the missiles' removal, Dobrynin had a further message from Moscow to pass on. Mr. Khrushchev, he said, "wanted to send his best wishes" to the president and his brother.

Three children unite against fire hoses in Birmingham, Alabama, 1963.

CHAPTER SEVENTEEN

CIVIL RIGHTS

*"What I didn't fully appreciate, and most critics did not
understand, was the relationship between the President and
Bobby—that it was remarkably close even for brothers."*

—Edwin Guthman

In early 1963, to mark the Kennedy administration's halfway point,
Ben Bradlee sat down with President Kennedy for a *Newsweek*
cover story he was writing on Bobby. "Never mind the brother bit,"
he told his friend Jack. What Bradlee was looking for was a fair and
frank assessment of the attorney general's on-the-job performance.

Nevertheless, it couldn't be helped: the president quickly revealed strong personal feelings on the subject. Praising Bobby's
"high moral standards" and "strict personal ethics," he described him
as "a puritan, absolutely incorruptible."

Next, he spoke of the "terrific executive energy" he possessed. As
Jack explained it, anybody can have ideas, the problem was actually

making them happen. Bobby, he declared, was "the best organizer I've ever seen." And not just when it came to running his department, but in his off-hours, too. Making reference to that trademark of Kennedy life, touch football, the president commented, "it was always Bobby's team that won, because he had it organized the best, the best plays."

Saluting loyalty—"It wasn't the easiest thing for him to go to Joe McCarthy's funeral"—as another of Bobby's virtues, Jack also cited his conscience. He spoke of his brother's dogged crusade to win release of the men taken prisoner at the Bay of Pigs. "And it's got nothing to do with publicity or politics," the president added. "In Palm Beach now, I bet there isn't one of the Cuban exile leaders who hasn't been invited to his house and to be with his family."

The president's estimate of his brother was not out of line with the conventional wisdom. Prominent columnists that year began offering confident predictions that, following a John Kennedy second term, Robert would look to succeed him in office. "No Kennedy likes to wait too long," wrote one in the *New York Herald Tribune*.

Two men found such assumptions unsettling. The first was Jack himself—who likely considered such dynastic speculation bad politics. The other was the Texan waiting next in line. By 1963, the First Brother had grown to become an obsession with Lyndon Johnson, an inside threat to his obtaining the prize he'd signed on for. According to biographer Robert Caro, he'd accepted the 1960 vice presidential nod because it was his best chance, possibly his only one, of being the Democrats' choice in 1968.

Now it looked as if the president's brother was setting his sights on the same goal. Bobby, not discouraging the buzz, only offered that he had no plans "at this time." Still, rumors kept reaching Johnson from the press corps that there was already a well-organized move to ready Robert Kennedy for the presidency by 1968, shoving aside the patient vice president.

By early 1963, there were the inevitable discussions about opponents Jack might face in the next year's presidential election. Both brothers were rooting for the GOP to select Senator Barry Goldwater, the Arizona Republican who'd served on the Rackets Committee. While they liked him personally, they believed any contest between the archconservative Westerner and the man now sitting in the Oval Office would wind up focused on their greatly diverging political philosophies. For just that reason, he was their favorite for a 1964 rival, a candidate they never doubted they could beat.

At this stage—March 1963—Bobby was struck by what he saw as inefficiency in his brother's administration. In his mind, it didn't serve the president well to compartmentalize his cabinet the way Jack did.

In a memo he sent Jack on the subject, Bobby said that he obviously hadn't learned an important lesson from the use of ExComm during the Missile Crisis.

"You talk to McNamara, but mostly on Defense matters," he noted. "You talk to Dillon but primarily on financial questions, Dave Bell on AID matters, etc. These men should be sitting down and thinking of some of the problems facing us in a broader context."

Bobby was well aware that these three Kennedy appointees, along with many of the others, were skilled and savvy Washington veterans. (McNamara was in charge at the Pentagon, Douglas Dillon at the Treasury. David Bell was now the administrator of the Agency for International Development but until recently had been director of the Office of Management and Budget.) He was urging Jack to stop and consider how to make use of these "best minds in government . . . in times other than deep crisis and emergencies."

This same memo also offered a teasing punch line. After the phrase "best minds," he'd added an asterisk. Below, its footnote read simply: "ME."

That April, Martin Luther King made the momentous decision to challenge the segregation laws of Birmingham, Alabama, a city where every restaurant, restroom, and good job was protected by unyielding rules of racial discrimination. King was now determined to expose—to his fellow Americans and the world beyond—the actual state of conditions in a country whose famed founding documents had committed it to the principle of human equality.

The demonstration he organized began with a march of defiance led by King himself on Good Friday, April 12. Denied the required license, they paraded anyway, and were arrested. Bobby Kennedy, who as we've seen didn't support such civil disobedience, became further angered when Dr. King refused to allow bail to be posted. Honoring the principles of civil disobedience, King and his fellow protesters were ready to accept legal consequences of their public actions. King now spent eight days behind bars during which time, denied paper, he wrote the essay "Letter from Birmingham Jail" on the margins of a newspaper his lawyer had brought him.

Now came one of those moments in history where a single event changed everything. In a new demonstration on May 2, hundreds, then thousands, of local schoolchildren, trained in the same civil disobedience, poured from the 16th Street Baptist Church, parading through the city again without a permit. They marched ahead steadily, straight into the ranks of the hostile local police led by Commissioner of Public Safety Eugene "Bull" Connor. The police met the oncoming crowd, some not yet teenagers, with high-pressure fire hoses. Though terrified, the young marchers kept singing as armed men with billy clubs bore down on them.

That night Americans, viewing these events in Birmingham from their living rooms, were shaken by what they were witnessing. In one scene caught by a news camera, a snarling police dog was sinking its teeth into the chest of a high school student.

Watching such scenes of mayhem, the United States attorney general, aware of his role as head of the Department of Justice, understood the dilemma he was facing. Dealing with it would require a careful balancing act between respecting local jurisdiction and the demands of conscience. Looking at the choices before him, he began, as he'd done on other occasions, to work through back channels.

Bobby's first goal was to strike at the same targets as King: the segregationist laws and culture of Birmingham. He dispatched Burke Marshall, head of the Justice Department's Civil Rights Division, to the city, where, quietly, he began to mediate between the city's business leaders and the civil rights activists.

The pressure for an agreement soon reached fever pitch. Twelve hundred children of various ages were now packed into jails meant to accommodate nine hundred. Cells meant for eight had seventy-five youths jammed into them. To add to the tension, King and top lieutenant Ralph Abernathy, both out on bail, were rearrested. Their condition this time for accepting bail was the release of the children.

Thanks to Burke Marshall's negotiating efforts, an agreement was reached to bring down the WHITE ONLY and BLACK ONLY signs from the city's restrooms and drinking fountains. Lunch counters were to be desegregated, and an ongoing program to upgrade African American employment opportunities was established. The historic end to these pillars of Jim Crow was to take effect within ninety days. King praised the invaluable job Burke had done "opening channels of communication between our leadership and the top people in the economic power structure" of Birmingham.

Still, fearing that this truce would falter without King's presence, Bobby now personally reached a local black leader in Birmingham who agreed to pay the civil rights leader's bail. And King accepted.

Next was the challenge of getting the two thousand children released. King and Bobby estimated it would cost $160,000 to meet bail for all of them, many of whom had been held for more than a week. Kennedy decided that a possible source for the necessary funds might be labor unions. He secretly asked Harry Belafonte, a friend of both his and King's, to serve as a secret intermediary with the protesters now being held in the Birmingham jails.

"I'm in an extremely vulnerable position," he told the singer, asking him to receive the hand-delivered checks.

Contacted and chipping in were Michael Quill of the Transport Workers, Walter Reuther of the United Auto Workers, George Meany of the AFL-CIO, and David McDonald of the United Steelworkers. Bobby remained in constant contact with Belafonte until the checks began arriving.

There were political considerations for Bobby to keep in mind, too. This extraordinary drama was not playing out in a vacuum: every citizen taking in what was happening was a potential voter. The challenge was to help King and the children while not getting too out front in the racial struggle. His brother, he knew only too well, was looking ahead to a tough reelection situation in the South the next year.

Bobby hoped that his efforts—that call to the Georgia judge to secure King's release in 1960; the desegregation of Ole Miss; and now bringing change to Birmingham—would send a clear signal to the civil rights movement that he was on their side. He'd come a long way from the days when he confessed to not staying awake nights worrying about civil rights.

The leaders of the burgeoning civil rights movement felt a different imperative. For them, this was no time to be patient and await government action. The images from Birmingham had burned their way into the national mind's eye. Now that all eyes were on Birmingham, there could be no turning back.

Bobby, understanding how high emotions on both sides of the issue were running, realized his position and that of the civil rights leaders were at odds when it came to both timing and public acts of defiance. He understood, too, that his calls for caution—fearing further havoc and harm—and public duty to uphold the law weren't enough to convince angry activists to cool their demands.

The step he now took, hoping for mutual benefit, was to ask celebrated black author and social critic James Baldwin, whom he'd met the year before, for help. Baldwin's first book, *Go Tell It on the Mountain*, had been published a decade earlier, and his newest one, *The Fire Next Time*, was a national bestseller. At Bobby's request, Baldwin now arranged—on very short notice—an informal get-together of his own friends and acquaintances to take place at the Kennedy family apartment in New York. This was two weeks after the successful conclusion of the Birmingham protest.

The guests included Belafonte, singer Lena Horne, playwright Lorraine Hansberry, who wrote *A Raisin in the Sun*, and psychologist Kenneth Clark, whose work on black youth had aided in the landmark 1954 Supreme Court *Brown v. Board of Education* decision, which outlawed segregation in U.S. public schools.

The attorney general opened the discussion by offering his own position and point of view. "We have a party in revolt," he explained, referring especially to Southern whites. "And we have to be somewhat considerate about how to keep them aboard if the Democratic Party is going to prevail in the next elections." He worried, he said, that black activism, now growing more extreme, could result in further backlash. Then he described the Justice Department's ongoing support for civil rights as demonstrated by the cases it was arguing.

He ended by appealing to a sense of who we are as Americans, both black and white, and the necessity, as a nation, to remain united. Don't we join together in defending this country? In that same spirit, shouldn't both races, he asked, be working together at home for civil rights?

It was all well intentioned, but naive as far as his listeners were concerned. Their lives and his couldn't be more different, and now they began to say so. Loudest and most belligerent in his objections to Bobby's remarks was twenty-four-year-old Jerome Smith, a CORE activist and early Freedom Rider who'd been beaten and jailed in Mississippi.

It made him sick, he burst out angrily, to have to beg for civil rights from the man whose job charged him with the duty to enforce laws guaranteeing them. "I've seen you guys stand around and do nothing more than take notes while we're being beaten," he said, referring to Justice Department attorneys.

Denouncing meaningless "cocktail party patter," Smith grew even more accusatory as he faced his host. Referring to the Vietnam War, he said, "What you're asking us young black people to do is pick up guns against people in Asia while you have continued to deny us our rights." The next time the police used fire hoses and dogs on him and his fellow protesters, he promised, he'd respond with a gun.

Now Baldwin asked Smith how he'd react if called upon to fight for his country. It was a provocative question. "Never! Never! Never!" Smith declared. Then, again alluding to Southeast Asia, said, "These are poor people who did nothing to us. They're more my brothers than you are."

Kennedy, unable to believe his ears, instantly challenged him.

"You won't fight for your country? How can you say that?" At this moment, Lorraine Hansberry—the first black woman to have had a play produced on Broadway—intervened.

"You've got a great many very, very accomplished people in this room, Mr. Attorney General," she said, "but the only man who should be listened to is that man over there." She pointed at Jerome Smith.

Though the evening ended in an unhappy standoff, its echoes would linger. Martin Luther King, hearing an account of it the next morning, hoped it would light a fire under the Kennedys. "Maybe it's what Bobby needed to hear. He's going to hear a lot more of it if the president keeps dawdling on that civil rights bill." But he also worried that insistence on keeping the struggle nonviolent was fast losing its appeal to angry and impatient young men like Jerome Smith.

Bob Kennedy's own reaction to the gathering—he'd, after all, requested it, seeing it as a reaching out—at first was exasperation. "They didn't want to talk about anything. They don't know the facts. They just wanted to shout."

Yet, with the days passing, he began to brood over what he'd heard that night in New York. "I guess if I were in his shoes," he told Ed Guthman, referring to Smith, "if I'd gone through what he's gone through, I might feel differently about this country."

"Segregation now, segregation tomorrow, segregation forever." That was the promise which rang out from George Wallace's inaugural address when—standing on the very spot where Jefferson Davis a century earlier took charge of the Confederacy—he'd been sworn in as Alabama governor that January.

Six months later, ignoring the country's shock at the police assault on those Birmingham children, he vowed to resist a federal court order to admit two students—Vivian Malone and James Hood—to the University of Alabama. He boasted he would "stand in the schoolhouse door" to prevent such an affront to his state.

Bobby, his department already moving to enforce the court order and gain the two students' admission, now saw an opportunity for broader action. In a meeting in the Oval Office, he called for the president to address the nation on the civil rights question. His brother, uncertain what was going to happen at the university, was against it.

Sitting around the table were the president, Bobby, Ted Sorensen, Ken O'Donnell, and political aide Larry O'Brien. Their conversation was being filmed for a documentary on the current impasse between the Justice Department and Governor Wallace. Bobby continued to make the case for a speech, arguing that the time was right, with the scenes from Birmingham seared into the mind of Americans. Wallace's resistance now revealed the urgency of the civil rights effort.

Malone and Hood were set to arrive the next day, June 11, on the Tuscaloosa campus. That morning, when they did, Governor Wallace, as he'd promised, had planted himself at the entrance to Foster Auditorium, where registration was taking place. He'd surrounded himself with state troopers. Deputy Attorney General Nicholas Katzenbach, representing the Justice Department and accompanied by federal marshals, now arrived to clear the way for the two new students, who were waiting in a car nearby.

Demanding from Wallace his "unequivocal assurance" that he'd do his "constitutional duty," Katzenbach made clear what both men knew: "From the outset, Governor, all of us have known that the final chapter of this history will be the admission of these students."

The stalemate lasted until nearly five hours later when National

Guard troops, summoned into service by President Kennedy, made sure the doors opened for Malone and Hood.

As Wallace could be seen on television leaving the doorway, President Kennedy turned to Sorensen, "I think we'd better give that speech tonight." Personally contacting all three networks, he requested a prime-time slot for a speech that night to air at eight. Until the moment he stepped before the cameras, he was editing what he would say.

It was the speech Bobby had pushed him to make, and for which he had assembled the arguments. "He urged it, he felt it, he understood it. And he prevailed," said Burke Marshall.

Opening with the announcement that the two black students had been admitted that afternoon, the president went on. "I hope," he declared, "that every American, regardless of where he lives, will stop and examine his conscience about this and other related incidents. This nation was founded by men of many nations and backgrounds. It was founded on the principle that all men are created equal, and that the rights of every man are diminished when the rights of one man are threatened."

He put the crisis in historic context: "One hundred years of delay have passed since President Lincoln freed the slaves, yet their heirs, their grandsons, are not fully free. They are not yet freed from the bonds of injustice. They are not yet freed from social and economic oppression. And this Nation, for all its hopes and all its boasts, will not be fully free until all its citizens are free."

He recognized, too, the issue thrown in his brother's face by Jerome Smith. "Today, we are committed to a worldwide struggle to promote and protect the rights of all who wish to be free. And when Americans are sent to Vietnam or West Berlin, we do not ask for whites only. It ought to be possible, therefore, for American students to attend any public institution they select without having to be backed up by troops."

The speech lasted fourteen minutes. Martin Luther King, in tears, while listening, called the address "the most sweeping and forthright ever presented by an American president." And to another activist watching with him, he expressed his admiration more colloquially: "Can you believe that white man not only stepped up to the plate, he hit it over the fence?"

The sense of accomplishment following the president's address was assaulted by news late that same night from Jackson, Mississippi. Shortly after midnight, Medgar Evers, an army veteran who'd served in the invasion of Normandy and was state field secretary of the NAACP, was shot in the back by a white supremacist. He'd been sitting in his car in his own driveway.

Taken immediately to the nearest hospital, Evers wasn't at first admitted, owing to the color of his skin. He died forty-five minutes after arriving. Five thousand people led by Martin Luther King marched in Jackson following his funeral.

The attorney general now could read the mood of the country in his mailbag, with harshly anti–civil rights letters daily arriving, postmarked from north as well as south. He'd hear other sorts of sentiments addressed to him in person. Guthman remembers their walking together in Manhattan one day. From above, a construction worker yelled down at him from the girder of a new building: "Hey, Bobby, don't forget about the Irish and the Italians!"

Just over a week later, President Kennedy submitted to Congress a strong civil rights bill. "How can we say to the Negro in Jackson," Bobby Kennedy asked in Senate testimony supporting it, "that when war comes you will be an American citizen, but in the meantime you're a citizen of Mississippi and we can't help you?" As in his brother's speech, the echoes from that evening in New York were still coming through to him. So was the tragedy of Medgar Evers.

Yet the Kennedy brothers held back from fully embracing Martin Luther King. Eleven days after his civil rights address, the president took advantage of a June White House meeting with civil rights leaders to take King aside. He told him that two of his most trusted aides, Stanley Levison and Jack O'Dell, were both known to have been active members of the Communist Party and could still be Soviet agents.

In the president's mind, and also Bobby's—as well as in that of J. Edgar Hoover, who was the source of such concerns—there existed the likelihood these men had infiltrated King's movement with an agenda different from his own. Whether it was a matter of stirring up unrest in the U.S., or simply embarrassing its government, either mission could have been dictated by Moscow. "Get rid of them," was the president's message to King.

But King hesitated. Reluctantly, he let O'Dell know that he would have to go. Yet soon relenting, he told him he could stay on until he found another job. Bobby, hearing of that delay, pushed King to enforce the firing. Despite his slowly increasing connection to the cause of civil rights, his anti-Communism far outweighed the other when it came to both his worldview and his conscience.

For King, finding himself strong-armed into banishing the invaluable Levison—a gifted speechwriter as well as a trusted adviser and confidant—was far from easy. In fact, the idea of it proved so wrenching that he attempted to strategize a way to work around the situation without the Kennedys knowing. Levison, it was decided, would stay away from King, and the two men would maintain their communication through intermediaries.

Levison had been under FBI surveillance. Now, as it became clear that there would be no real break between him and Dr. King, an angry Bobby Kennedy felt the need to act. Displeased at the sidestepping of the president's directive and convinced that Levison had to be under Kremlin control, he came to believe he had no choice but to have a wiretap put on King himself.

As the summer of 1963 was drawing to an end, President Kennedy was confronted by a Cold War struggle far more distant than Cuba, one that had been brewing through more administrations than his own. Eight years earlier, after the French army's defeat at the hands of the Vietminh—a Communist revolutionary force determined to overthrow the country's longtime French colonial masters—Vietnam was divided between a Vietminh-controlled North and a pro-Western South.

In 1955, Ngo Dinh Diem, a non-Communist nationalist, declared the Republic of South Vietnam with himself as president. Descended from a family of the earliest Vietnamese converts to Catholicism in the seventeenth century, he enjoyed strong backing from American Catholics, including then-Senator Jack Kennedy, who'd been an early member of the pro-Diem "American Friends of Vietnam." However, the corruption of his regime became increasingly an issue, as did his brutal persecution of the country's majority Buddhists, who in 1963 comprised 90 percent of the population.

With sixteen thousand American "military advisers" now stationed there, the United States was counting on the Diem government's ability to push back the Communist Vietcong guerrillas steadily encroaching from the North.

In Washington, the Kennedy government was divided over whom to support—the restive generals, who appeared to Washington the more aggressive anti-Communists, or President Diem. President Kennedy now named Henry Cabot Lodge, his onetime Senate opponent, as the new ambassador to South Vietnam.

On August 24, after Diem had ordered synchronized attacks on Buddhist pagodas across South Vietnam, Kennedy, who was spending the weekend in Hyannis Port, approved a cable to Lodge. It authorized him to side with an army coup against Diem—but only if Lodge's efforts to persuade the Vietnamese leader to separate himself from his unpopular brother, Nhu, who seemed to encourage his more oppressive impulses, were unsuccessful. "Diem must be given chance to rid himself of Nhu or Diem cannot be preserved," the cable read.

Yet Lodge took the cable as a license to immediately back the coup. "We are launched on a course from which there is no respectable turning back," he notified Washington five days later. "We should make all-out effort to get generals to move promptly."

Bobby, no fan of Lodge's, saw their man in Vietnam as out of order, failing to acknowledge the proper chain of command. "I told you he was going to be trouble," he reminded the president. "You know what's terrific about you?" Jack replied dryly. "You always remember when you're right."

By the end of October, Bobby was heard to say about Vietnam "that we're just going down the road to disaster." He was raising the radical possibility that the United States should cut its losses in South Vietnam and leave. The question he asked was whether a Communist takeover could be resisted successfully by *either* Diem or the generals.

On November 2, news arrived that the generals had overthrown Diem, and that he and Nhu were dead. Originally reported by the coup leaders as suicides, they had, in fact, been viciously executed.

Ted Sorensen recalled the "shock and dismay in JFK's face when he heard the news. "He'd had no indication or even hint that anything more than Diem's exile was contemplated."

In a memo he dictated to himself that Monday, President Kennedy took the blame for what had happened. He wrote of his government being "divided" as to whom to support in Vietnam, with the "attorney general" among those opposed to the coup.

That month, Jack Kennedy initiated the first major campaign meeting for 1964. Present were Bobby, Ted Sorensen, Ken O'Donnell, and Larry O'Brien. It was the same tight group that had met first in Palm Beach and later in Hyannis Port in 1959; they'd proven themselves before and were ready to do so again.

On Friday, November 22, two days after his thirty-eighth birthday, Bobby was interrupted by a phone call while having lunch at home. On the other end of the line was FBI director Hoover. "I have news for you," he said bluntly. His tone held no sympathy or softness. "The President's been shot."

Bobby immediately phoned Ken O'Donnell, who was traveling with the president in Texas. But he couldn't get through. "Jack's been shot," he told Ethel. "It may be fatal." Reaching the hospital, he wanted to make sure they'd found a priest. He wanted to save his brother's soul.

Then came a second call from Hoover. "The president's dead."

Ed Guthman arrived at Hickory Hill soon after that. "There's so much bitterness," Bobby said to him as they paced the lawn. "I thought they'd get one of us—but Jack, after all he'd been through, never worried about it. I thought it would be me."

He now wanted answers. Summoning CIA director John McCone, he asked him point-blank whether agency officials were involved. He took care—McCone being a fellow Roman Catholic—to phrase his questions "in a way that he couldn't lie to me." Thus, from McCone he learned, and was satisfied with his answers, that "they hadn't."

But his concern was with the succession. Even before seeing

McCone, he asked McGeorge Bundy to change the locks on his brother's files.

That night, after Air Force One, carrying its tragic cargo, had landed outside Washington, Robert Kennedy drove with his sister-in-law, Jacqueline, to Bethesda Naval Hospital where the autopsy was being performed. He listened carefully as she described to him her eye view of what had happened at Dealey Plaza when the motorcade passed through.

Afterward, he slept at the White House. Chuck Spalding accompanied him as he headed to the Lincoln Bedroom. When they'd arrived there and Bobby had walked in, Jack's old, dear friend closed the door. On the other side he could hear Bobby starting a conversation. What Spalding quickly realized was that he was talking to God. "Why?" he was asking. "Why? Why?"

As the president's body was readied to lie in state at the Capitol on Monday, Bobby decided to forgo the public viewing and close the coffin for the last time. He was, as always, looking out for his brother. What was left inside didn't look like Jack.

Bobby leads family at the Capitol, where Jack lies in state. Chief
Justice Earl Warren reads a tribute to the fallen president.

CHAPTER EIGHTEEN

RELIC

"I thought it would be me."
—ROBERT KENNEDY

On November 22, 1963, in my freshman year at Holy Cross, I was on my way to world history class. I was checking my mailbox after lunch when a classmate hit me with the incredible news that President Kennedy had just been shot. What? Could it be true? How bad was he hit? In my mind, "shot" didn't mean dead. Then, after learning we'd be allowed to skip classes I headed straight to the nearest TV and spent the afternoon watching Walter Cronkite anchoring the coverage on CBS. That evening I watched with others, flipping through the channels, to see the network features on Kennedy's life, his political career, and his presidency.

Heading home from Worcester that week on the bus, I needed to go through Port Authority in New York. There a woman stopped me, wanting to know where I went to school. Startled, I answered politely. Hearing my reply, she immediately commented how sad it must be up there now in Massachusetts, especially at a Catholic college.

This was the first person I'd spoken to beyond the insulated world of my campus. And our brief exchange there in the busy terminal gave me my first personal experience with the human impact of what had just occurred. I can truthfully say that I still see my life ever since as a before-and-after experience. If it felt like that for me, as well as for millions of others, what could it have been like for Bobby Kennedy, who'd spent his entire adult life devoted to his beloved brother?

Ed Guthman was with him. "His eyes were haunted, his complexion ashen and his mood desolate and stoic. The center of his life had been shot away; the brother he had idolized, to whom he had given so much and with whom he had worked so hard. For a dozen years he had been immersed in advancing his brother's career and the causes for which his brother stood, with no thought about what he would be doing at thirty-five or forty-five or fifty."

"He looked to me like a man who is just in intense pain," John Seigenthaler recalled. "Hurt, I mean, you know—just physically hurt."

Harris Wofford couched his description of what he witnessed in a different way, picturing Jack in the same situation. "I could not imagine John Kennedy sinking into such long, dark melancholy for any reason. Gaiety was the key to his nature. Robert Kennedy was a brooder who carried the agony of the world."

Even those who'd long been close to Jack and him were struck by the enormity of Bobby's near-paralyzing grief. Said Lem Billings, "Everything was pulled out from under him." His brother Ted's recollection was especially poignant: "It veered close to being a tragedy within a tragedy," he would write. "Ethel and my mother feared for his own survival; his psychic survival at least. He seemed to age physically."

At Jacqueline's suggestion, Bobby began to read poetry, which he'd never done, and found himself most drawn to the ancient Greeks. One line that seemed to reach him most deeply was from the playwright Aeschylus: "He who learns must suffer. Even in our sleep, pain that cannot forget falls drop by drop upon the heart, until, in our own despair, against our will, comes wisdom through the awful grace of God."

Early in the new year, Robert Kennedy traveled to Japan for the start of a diplomatic mission. He was being sent to Southeast Asia by the Lyndon Johnson administration in a spirit of goodwill, an attempt at positive distraction. It was less than two months since November 22 when he arrived in Tokyo for the first of two meetings with Indonesia's President Sukarno.

At Tokyo's Waseda University, he was greeted by thousands of cheering students, their enthusiasm providing a sharp contrast to the heckling he'd received on a visit there the year before. Next, in the Philippines, he experienced another rousing welcome. In the speech he delivered there, he emphasized the need for political involvement. "Dante once said that the hottest places in hell are reserved for those who in time of moral crisis maintain their neutrality. . . . And it's not sufficient just being against, just saying, 'Well, I don't think I like the way things are going.' We have a responsibility to offer an *alternative*."

It seems likely he was talking about himself and how he was beginning to see the way ahead. His brother Ted regarded that Far East journey as a turning point. "Bobby and Ethel witnessed a tumultuous outpouring of friendship from the people who wanted to show their respect and love for John Kennedy through Bobby's presence. I believe that reception restored his faith that life was worth living after all, and that President Kennedy had achieved something lasting and worthwhile."

One person who suspected the attorney general of more specific ambitions, including the idea of offering himself as that alternative to the status quo, was the man now in the White House. Their mutual hostility had never been very well kept in check. When LBJ now summoned Bobby to a one-on-one meeting after his return, it was to air a fresh grievance.

Johnson wanted him to know, in no uncertain terms, how unhappy he'd been to hear that Bobby's guy Paul Corbin had been recently spotted in New Hampshire stirring up interest in a Kennedy for Vice President write-in campaign. Corbin, a freewheeling political operative, was by now a true favorite of Bobby's. He'd made him part of his extended family. But Corbin held no such appeal for Johnson, who wanted him immediately fired from the Democratic National Committee where Bobby had arranged a spot for him.

"If he's such a good fellow, *you* pay him," an irate Johnson told Bobby. "He's around town knocking my head off and has been for three years—and I never met the bum in my life. Why should I have him on my payroll?"

For his part, John Seigenthaler thought that Bobby had been enjoying the Corbin gambit. "Knowing Paul, Bobby knew, probably, what was going on, didn't think it was too serious, and probably was amused by the fact that it created some discomfort for some of Lyndon Johnson's supporters."

Seigenthaler also felt Bobby didn't actually care whether or not Corbin's antics upset LBJ personally. As a result, the attorney general wasn't ready to give Johnson what he wanted. "He was loyal to

President Kennedy," Bobby now told Johnson, defending Corbin. "He'll be loyal to you."

"I know who he's loyal to," Johnson snapped back. "Get him out of there! Do it! President Kennedy isn't president anymore. I am."

"I know you're president," Bobby retorted. "And don't you ever talk to me like that again."

Johnson wasn't about to let it lie there. That night, he phoned Bobby to let him know Corbin was being fired, whether he liked it or not. If there was one thing the president, a political manipulator of the first order, didn't want, it was to have someone on the DNC who wasn't answering to him. After the conversation ended, Ed Guthman, in the room with Bobby, watched the AG cross the room and then stand silently at the window, staring into the night. When at last he spoke, it was to offer a single thought. "I'll tell you one thing. This relationship can't last much longer."

The New Hampshire write-in campaign continued even without Corbin keeping his hand in. It reached the point where it looked as if Bobby might outpoll Johnson, whose supporters were running their own write-in effort for head of the ticket. Finally, Bobby issued an official statement through the Justice Department: "The Attorney General has said that the choice of the Democratic nominee for Vice President will be made, and should be made, by the Democratic Convention in August, guided by the wishes of President Johnson and that President Johnson should be free to select his own running mate. The Attorney General, therefore, wishes to discourage any efforts on his behalf in New Hampshire, or elsewhere."

However, it had little effect on Granite State voters. On March 10, Lyndon Johnson received 29,630 votes for president in the New Hampshire primary, while Bob Kennedy received 25,861 for vice president. Such a strong showing naturally encouraged Democrats across the country to push the possibility of him as LBJ's running mate.

Early that June, Johnson's decision was dictated by the outcome of California's Republican primary. Senator Barry Goldwater, avatar of the new conservatism, beat New York governor Nelson Rockefeller and with the victory looked to be the inevitable GOP nominee to take on Johnson. Democrats, including the one in the White House, took the Arizonan's success as a sign the opposition party had chosen ideological purity over a truly competitive chance in November.

Edward Kennedy, who'd won the remainder of brother Jack's Senate term in 1962, was now running for reelection. In June, a plane carrying him from Washington to the Massachusetts state Democratic convention in Springfield crashed in an apple orchard due to a sudden thunderstorm. Although Kennedy survived, the pilot of the twin-engine craft and a Kennedy aide, Edward Moss, were killed. The two other passengers, Indiana senator Birch Bayh—who carried Teddy out of the wreckage—and his wife, also were spared. Still, Ted would be forced to spend five months in the hospital, recovering from multiple injuries.

Bobby, who'd raced across the state from Cape Cod, arrived at his brother's bedside at four in the morning. "Is it true you are ruthless?" the anesthetized and only barely conscious Ted whispered through the tubes sprouting around his face. His question targeted the inside-the-family irony that the one stuck with the tough-guy reputation was always the one most attentive to the others.

Bobby's concern now was not just for his gravely injured brother, but also for his mother and father. "How much more do they have to take?" he asked. "I just don't see how I can do anything now," he said to Guthman. "I think I should just get out of it all. Somebody up there doesn't like us." At this moment, any thought of his political career was put on hold.

In a matter of days, however, he had a long-standing commitment to honor. He was expected in West Berlin the following week where, as requested by Mayor Willy Brandt, he was to speak at the dedication of a memorial to President Kennedy. More than a quarter million West Berliners lined the streets for his arrival, honoring his brother's memory and the words of his rousing "*Ich bin ein Berliner*" speech, delivered in that divided city exactly a year earlier.

Speaking later the same day at the Free University of Berlin, he encouraged the students to keep faith with his brother's values. "There were many who felt that the torchbearer for a whole generation was gone, that an era was over before its time. But I have come to understand that the hope President Kennedy kindled isn't dead but alive. The torch still burns, and because it does, there remains, for all of us, a chance to light up the tomorrows and brighten the future. For me, this is a challenge that makes life worthwhile."

From there, Bobby, accompanied by Ethel and three of their children, traveled to Poland, where they attracted legions of thrilled admirers. When the family attended mass, thousands packed the Warsaw cathedral and the square outside. In Kraków, at the distinguished, ancient university there, the Jagiellonian, the excited students lifted him onto their shoulders in celebration.

Later, in a question-and-answer session at the City Council, he replied carefully when asked about his "version of the assassination." It was the first time he'd publicly discussed Lee Harvey Oswald, his brother's killer. The nearly nine-hundred-page report of the Warren Commission, tasked with investigating President Kennedy's assassination, was not yet completed. Yet, there in Kraków, Bobby called

Oswald a "misfit" and "antisocial," going on to say, as the commission would conclude, "There is no question that he did it on his own and by himself. He was not a member of a right-wing organization. He was a professed Communist, but even the Communists would not have anything to do with him."

Here, behind the Iron Curtain for the first time, Bobby and his family were allowed by the government the opportunity to pay their respects to Cardinal Stefan Wyszynski. He'd become primate of Poland when elevated to cardinal by Pope Pius XII in 1953. Given this rare chance by his state overseers to meet with Americans, Wyszynski explained to his guests what he saw as the positive side of his country's repressive rule, at least when it came to the Catholic Church. Depriving it of its historic wealth, he'd come to realize, "brought the priests and bishops much closer to the people."

Kathleen Kennedy was thirteen when she and two of her brothers accompanied her parents on this three-day trip. During the family's visit with Cardinal Wyszynski, she remembers that her mother, suddenly feeling hungry, asked one of those present if he might help find her something to tide her over. After the helpful cleric asked courteously what she thought she might like, Ethel soon received exactly the snack she'd asked for. (Twenty-one years later, when being introduced to Pope John Paul II, he reminded her: "I've met you once before. I made you a grilled cheese sandwich.")

Upon his return home, *The New York Times* praised Bobby's successes in Poland as "an act of unorthodox statesmanship," noting the way he'd shown the regime how much further it would have to go before it became a true "people's government."

It was hard for Bobby to be back in Washington, however, during the July 2 presidential signing of the historic Civil Rights Act. As Nick Katzenbach put it, it was difficult to stand there, with Johnson taking the credit "and not his brother." The moment proved equally difficult for LBJ: he had to be coaxed into handing his predecessor's brother one of the ceremonial pens.

At this point for Bobby, the idea of running for the Senate in New York had begun to hold strong appeal. The only problem, he noted, was the obvious one that he didn't live there. Such a candidacy, he said, presents "all the messiness of the arrogant outsider coming to take over." Looking to the immediate future, he had other thoughts. "I might just take a year off," he mused, "take the kids, go live in Europe."

The option of running for governor of Massachusetts, getting out of Washington altogether, no longer struck Bobby as the right move. He'd looked into exactly what holding the top executive office up there in the Boston State House entailed, and decided in the end he wasn't attracted. "That job doesn't have any real power," he concluded. "It's all divided up with the legislature and the governor's council." Besides which: "That's really Teddy's state now," he said. "I wouldn't want to interfere."

On July 15, the Republicans, meeting in San Francisco, nominated Goldwater. The nominee's acceptance speech contained a troubling call to arms. "Extremism in the defense of liberty is no vice and . . . moderation in the pursuit of justice is no virtue." As William Manchester would write of it, "the nominee deepened the division in the party by giving the moderates the rough side of his tongue in a memorable passage."

As the Democratic convention approached, against all logic and history—including his own with Johnson—Bobby continued to view the vice presidential nomination as a plausible goal. He may have been the only one to think so. It was an ambition, not different from Johnson's own in 1960, less about serving than succeeding. It made no sense otherwise. Neither man could stand the other. It would be like two dogs fighting over the same patch of sidewalk.

Two weeks after the Republicans chose their candidate, Johnson called the attorney general to the White House to end any suspense regarding his prospects for the ticket. It was obvious that Senator Goldwater's vote against the Civil Rights Act would be enough to promise strong support for the Republican in the South. Using that as his main argument, Johnson, now sure of his ground, pointed out that Bobby would hurt the ticket more than help it.

For his part, Bobby saw the bright side. "Being his vice president," he told Guthman, "could be a real dead end. He could put me in cold storage and I'd suffocate." Still, he'd longed, against all reason, for Johnson to take him anyway. It would set him on the path to a Kennedy restoration in 1972.

When, months earlier, he'd thought of running for the U.S. Senate from New York, Bobby had been honest about one very big reason *not* to do it. "It would be awful if I lost," he told Guthman. But now, putting that fear behind him, he was ready to declare his intention to enter the race. The contest would be against the Republican from upstate now seeking reelection, Senator Kenneth Keating from Rochester.

Two days later, the Democratic National Convention got under way in Atlantic City. For me, it was a local event, since my family had a summer home in Ocean City, the quiet resort just ten miles to the south. Getting word of an opening-night fundraiser where the big Democratic pols would meet and greet wealthy donors, I went to see for myself what was happening. At the famed Shelburne Hotel, I politely pestered those departing, and soon enough was handed a ticket that got me in the door.

Once inside, I found myself shaking hands with Hubert Humphrey, Scoop Jackson, Adlai Stevenson, and Eugene McCarthy, who seemed a bit surprised that I knew who he was. It was my first encounter with such figures, whom I'd avidly read about for years in the newspapers.

Having dismissed Bobby Kennedy as a vice presidential choice, Johnson was enjoying the opportunity to build suspense about his ultimate selection and was determined to keep his two finalists— both senators from Minnesota—dangling until the last possible minute. McCarthy, catching word of this power play, called it "sadistic" and publicly removed himself from contention. At the same time, he was no fan of any of the Kennedys, and was already criticizing Bobby's decision to try for the Senate.

"It was an antipathy on McCarthy's part that none of us ever understood," Ted Sorensen later said. Jack had contributed to McCarthy's Senate campaign—they'd served in the House together— yet began hearing in 1959 and 1960 that McCarthy was making adverse comments about him as he geared up to run for president.

The hostility was returned. Bobby even made it clear, when offered the chance by LBJ to make the vice presidential nominating speech, that he had no interest if that particular Minnesotan was the nominee. "If it's McCarthy, I can't do it. I just don't have any respect for that man at all," he told the president bluntly. And when the Texan finally, after building suspense until the eleventh hour, decreed the other senator from Minnesota, Hubert Humphrey, to be the one he'd run with, the Kennedy camp was relieved.

On the eve of the convention, Johnson had been unable to stop worrying that, somehow, the vice presidential nomination might be stampeded to Bobby. Fueling this fear was the effect a twenty-minute film about John Kennedy, introduced by his brother Robert, would have on the men and women from the fifty states soon to arrive in Atlantic City. None would need reminding that, under different circumstances, they'd have been there to nominate the man they now saw memorialized on the screen before them for a second term.

Thus, with such timing in mind, LBJ scheduled *A Thousand Days*—that being the number served by JFK before his assassination—for Thursday night, safely after the balloting. When Bobby arrived that evening, he found himself stuck by Johnson's minions in a dingy room well below the convention floor to await his cue. Yet, even if the anointed Democratic candidate was unwelcoming, the crowd, most emphatically, was not.

As he made his way to the stage, the entire Boardwalk Hall exploded into a standing ovation. Though he made efforts for them to stop, they had no effect. The exuberant clamor continued for twenty-two minutes, most of the time with Bobby attempting to end it. To no avail.

Scoop Jackson, his old colleague from the McCarthy committee, was standing there to introduce him. But whenever Bob raised his hand to try to stop the outpouring of emotion, Jackson discouraged him. "Why don't you let them get it out of their system, Bob?"

Though this address to the convention has come to be known as the "Stars" speech for the quotation from Shakespeare's *Romeo and Juliet* he applied to President Kennedy ("When he shall die take him and cut him out into stars . . ."), the first words Bobby uttered were these below. His rapt audience had no trouble taking them to heart.

> No matter what talent an individual possesses, what energy he might have, no matter how much integrity and honesty he might have, if he is by himself—and particularly a political figure—he can accomplish very little. But if he is sustained, as President Kennedy was, by the Democratic Party all over the United States, dedicated to the same things he was attempting to accomplish, he can accomplish a great deal.

And then, before concluding by quoting his brother's favorite poet, Robert Frost, he predicted that, "If we do our duty, if we meet our responsibilities and obligations, not just as Democrats, but as American citizens in our local cities and towns and farms and our states and in the country as a whole, then this generation of Americans is going to be the best generation in the history of mankind."

Afterward, alone on a fire escape, Robert Kennedy broke down in tears.

A carpetbagger is a candidate for public office who moves into a new area for that obvious purpose. Running for the Senate from New York, Bobby tried softening the charge with humor. "I could have retired. And my father has done very well and I could have lived off him," he told students at Columbia University in October. "And I don't need the money and I don't need the office space. Frank as it is—and maybe it's difficult to believe in the state of New York—I'd like to just be a good United States senator. I'd like to serve."

"I think it's going to be very difficult," he told an NBC interviewer. "I have the obvious problem of coming in from another state." He'd been clear on that point in his announcement. "I recognize that some voters have misgivings about considering a man for high office who has left that state and has only recently returned." He had, of course, lived in both Riverdale and Bronxville before heading off to England with his family.

Even those working on the campaign kept reminding him he was an outsider. "Inevitably, during the briefing sessions," Guthman remembered, "there were comments—some needling and some patronizing—about his lack of detailed knowledge of the state he hoped to represent."

Moreover, under the best of circumstances—and these were anything but—Bobby did not seem born for the part of candidate.

His mother admitted as much. "Although by this time Bobby knew all the ins and outs and behind-the-scene techniques of politics, he had never himself run for public office, never been a candidate in a way that would oblige him to come through to the general public as a personality," Rose Kennedy recalled. "And he was not overly endowed by nature and temperament for that different role. It hadn't been his style, and he had never had reason until then to develop it. He took on the challenge but not entirely happily and not easily."

Asked if he was going to "run against Keating's record," Kennedy dodged the issue. He tried turning the question to his own credentials, alluding to his experience in the Cuban Missile Crisis and the push for civil rights. However, the reporter, after listening to him, then simply repeated the question. "Are you going to run against Senator Keating's record?"

"I'm going to run in a positive way," Bobby finally replied.

Nor would he build his campaign on his brother's reputation. Peter Edelman was the campaign staffer assigned to studying the New York senator's record. "At the beginning, he was very reluctant to be negative about Senator Keating. Also, in terms of political tussle, he wasn't particularly interested in campaigning that way."

What he didn't want, Edelman went on, was "to trade on being his brother's brother. He didn't think that was right." At the same time, Edelman noted that Bobby hadn't yet managed to come up with an actual agenda of his own for the state of New York.

From the beginning, crowds could see Bobby acting out the mannerisms of his brother—for example, having one hand stuck in his suit coat, the other gesturing. Jack had done that. He also began smoking those little cigars the late president had liked.

But when Ed Guthman tried boosting his spirits with talk of the excited crowds he was drawing, he resisted. "Don't you know?"

he said. "They're for him." Watching the reception he received from his audiences, it seemed to him they were entirely about his brother's legacy. And about his own celebrity because of it.

Even now, he was still playing the role of strategist. He predicted a jump in the polls would follow his entry into the race. He could foresee, however, that once the torch-passing excitement had cooled off, the challenge would come in making the necessary recovery. There would be an inevitable period in which he would have to execute a comeback.

Early on, Bobby faced resistance from New York City's liberal community. Committed readers of the newspapers they trusted, they were intense in their politics, holding strong opinions and skeptical attitudes. This was true especially of how they felt toward Irish Catholic politicians. The reasons went back to the inbred politics of Tammany Hall, and its too often outright corruption. Their favorite politicians were those of memory—Franklin and Eleanor Roosevelt—and of defeat, Adlai Stevenson, and this made them resistant to the thrill of a Kennedy showing up asking to be made their United States senator. It didn't help that Bobby had shown he wasn't comfortable with them, either. Quite simply, he'd never called nor viewed himself as a part of the liberal faction.

He chose, in fact, to apply the term as one of values rather than affiliation. "I think labels are so difficult. What I think, what my idea is of a liberal, my concept of it is, somebody who has compassion for those who aren't well off. Now under that category, I'm a liberal and want to be a liberal."

His deeper challenge was more personal, the need to free himself of the emotional darkness haunting him from Dallas, still stalking his spirit out on the stump. Paul Corbin noticed one day that Bobby had chosen the same route through the state that his brother had once taken. "Get out of this mysticism! Get out of your daze! God damn, Bob, be yourself! Get hold of yourself! You're real. Your brother's dead." Only he could talk to him like that. ("God love Paul," Ethel said, hearing this recounted decades later.)

With a new poll showing Kennedy surging, the incumbent suddenly decided it was time to meet his challenger in a debate. However, when the two sides couldn't agree on a format, the Republican went ahead, appearing on camera seated across from an empty chair meant to represent his absent opponent. But Bobby called him on the move. Surrounded by television cameras and newspaper photographers, he showed up at the studio and demanded to be admitted. "Kindly inform Senator Keating I am here and ready to go on the air," he told those guarding the locked studio door.

All of this was being recorded by the media: Keating talking to that empty chair inside the studio, Bobby trying to enter from the outside. The half hour broadcast completed, the Republican was told reporters wanted to interview him about why he'd kept his opponent from entering the debate studio. At that, Keating panicked, running out of the building, turning over potted palms and furniture in his way.

The next day's newspapers showed Keating and the empty chair, Bobby standing at a door marked KEEP OUT—NO VISITORS—KEATING.

With this failed maneuver—and the resulting humiliation—Keating's campaign was basically doomed. On election night, Kennedy beat his rival by 700,000 votes. Though this was far less than Johnson's state margin of 2.7 million, it was Bobby's first election victory. "He was back on his feet, out of his brother's shadow," noted Guthman, "and he had the inner satisfaction of knowing that at the crucial moments in a difficult political struggle he had made the right decisions."

On election night, Bobby echoed what he'd said at the convention: "I believe this vote is a mandate to continue the efforts begun by my brother four years ago—the effort to get something started in this country."

But he also said: "If my brother were alive, I wouldn't be here. I'd rather have it that way."

Bobby is made an honorary Sioux and given a warrior's name: "Brave Heart."

CHAPTER NINETEEN

BRAVE HEART

"John Kennedy was a realist brilliantly disguised as a romantic;
Robert Kennedy, a romantic stubbornly disguised as a realist."

—ARTHUR SCHLESINGER

In September 1963, two months before Dallas, Bobby had traveled
to Bismarck, North Dakota, for a meeting of the National Congress
of American Indians. Earlier in the year, President Kennedy had
received these Native American leaders in the Rose Garden. He
said his administration was committed to getting them better edu-
cational and job opportunities. Now his brother was crossing the
country to affirm that.

The speech he gave at the Grand Pacific Hotel sounded the
theme that was more and more engaging him—the need to keep
moving America forward "toward the fulfillment of its destiny as
the land of the free, a nation in which neither Indians nor any other

racial or religious minority will live in underprivilege." Afterward, the Native Americans presented Bobby with a war bonnet, and gave him a warrior's name: *Brave Heart*.

In January 1965 Robert Kennedy's heart was still sore, its great wound in no way healed. He needed a warrior's courage to face the new world before him. He was being sworn in as the junior senator from New York. His brother Ted, meanwhile, was starting his first full term as the junior senator from Massachusetts. Not since 1803 had a pair of brothers served simultaneously in the United States Senate.

Both Kennedys arrived on Capitol Hill still in mourning for their cherished elder brother. It was unclear to Bobby whether the Senate was what he wanted or where he needed to be.

The problem for Bobby—taking his place in what's been called "the world's greatest deliberative body"—was that the challenge of these new responsibilities and duties wasn't enough to displace what James Stevenson, the *New Yorker* writer, observed to be his "resident, melancholy bleakness." The black necktie he hadn't yet stopped wearing could be seen as a symbol of the unlifting darkness he felt in a city filled with such sharply etched memories.

Adam Walinsky, his young legislative assistant, could sense the conviction Bobby seemed unable to dispel, that no matter what he did heading forward—"whether he got to be president or not . . . it had been the most fun before, when John Kennedy had been president, and that he would never be that young again, that he would never have that kind of joy again."

Yet the freshman senator knew the choice had been his and his alone. "I remember and regret the situation that gave rise to my being here," he said. "It will be a totally new life. But I would not be here unless I wanted to come."

Still, in those early weeks, as a friend noted, he seemed to be "impotent, frustrated, floundering." Today we might recognize his symptoms as similar to those displayed by a soldier back from war. We'd understand the inevitability of their grip on him. But in both Kennedy terms and those of the era—with Jack's death only fifteen years after the end of World War II—toughing it out was what was expected.

Restlessness, too, afflicted him, and in March he was offered a remarkable opportunity to indulge it—one that took him across North America to Canada's Yukon Territory. There, the Canadian government had just christened the continent's highest unclimbed peak Mount Kennedy in honor of the fallen president.

The National Geographic Society and the Boston Museum of Science now joined together to sponsor an expedition to map the unknown terrain. They invited both senators Kennedy to participate in the trek to the fourteen-thousand-foot summit. Ted, still not fully recovered from the previous year's plane accident, had to decline. Bobby, though having no experience as a mountain climber, and admittedly afraid of heights, accepted, seeing this as both a personal pilgrimage and a test of himself.

James Whittaker, the first American to have climbed Mount Everest, led the three-man party making the ascent. On the last ridge, fifty yards from their goal, Bobby was un-roped in order to head on alone. This way, he'd be the first at the top, and alone when paying homage to his brother. Arriving there, he bowed down on one knee and made the sign of the cross.

"I planted President Kennedy's family flag on the summit," Bobby wrote in a cover story that appeared in *Life* magazine the following week. "It was done with mixed emotion. [And] with a feeling of pain that the events of 16 months and two days before had made it necessary."

He also left behind a copy of his brother's inaugural address. The man who'd delivered that stirring call to his fellow citizens, and for whom the peak was named, would have been "greatly pleased" by the mountain and the views, Bobby wrote in the *Life* piece. Then, once having made the descent and eaten—steak, instant mashed potatoes, and ice cream—he traveled back to Whitehorse, the nearest city. There, he bought a round for everyone gathered in the bar at the local hotel. Its owner kept the check with which his guest had paid for the drinks and framed it. "I told him I wanted to keep it as a souvenir of the next president of the United States," he said.

Back in Washington, on Capitol Hill, he and Ted found themselves in new roles in the Senate. Seven years younger than Bobby but already in place for two years, Ted now took on the odd role of pathfinder, even mentor. It was clear—and surprising—that both enjoyed the change of pecking order. Of the two Senate buildings, Ted's office, owing to his seniority, was in the older, more historic one and his brother's in the newer.

A senator's position on any legislative issue is determined by voice vote in the Chamber, a proceeding carried out in alphabetical order. This put "Edward" ahead of "Robert," and gave Bobby the chance to hear whether his brother was voting "Aye" or "Nay." He'd then, often, choose to do the same.

Observers on the Senate floor could see the brothers communicating with each other, which they did by way of eye contact and facial expressions. As a reliable system, however, it was hardly foolproof.

Ted described one occasion when his brother came to the floor late:

He looked over at me from his seat to see how I was voting. I looked back at him, not understanding what he wanted. He kept looking at me, and finally shook his head as if to ask, "Is the vote no?"

I got it. I nodded back at him, meaning, "Yes, the vote is no." But Bobby thought I meant "The vote is yes."

So Bobby voted yes. I then voted no. Bobby then shook his head no—in agreement, he thought, with the no vote.

But I thought he meant, "No, I'm not voting no" so I vigorously nodded my head yes, as if to say, "Yes, you are supposed to vote no." Bobby shook his head, changed his vote to no.

It was like Abbott and Costello doing their "Who's on First?" routine.

The rules of seniority meant that the freshman senators had to wait their turn. Thus it happened that one day, Senator Kennedy (D-NY) sat from ten in the morning, when a committee hearing got under way, until two in the afternoon. His turn to question the witness had still not come.

"Is this the way I become a good senator?" he asked Ted, who was assigned to the same panel. "By sitting here and waiting my turn?" That's right, his brother told him. But then Bobby wanted to know just how many *more* hours he'd need to keep on sitting there "to be a good senator." Just "as long as necessary, Robbie," came the answer.

As Majority Leader Mike Mansfield, who'd served in the House and the Senate with Jack and had warm regard for the family, phrased it, Bobby was "in the Senate but not of it. He did not become a member of the club." Teddy, seeing this and knowing his brother's loner tendencies, worried simply that Bobby might never regain his relish for life, including the political life.

"He understood power well," the younger Kennedy would write of his brother's initiation into the hierarchical world of

Capitol Hill. "He knew that there was an inside Senate and an outside Senate, and that his fast-blossoming idealism made him an outsider." Ted noted that a number of historians had attributed the changes Bobby underwent in his Senate years—his growing concern for the downtrodden in American life—to Jack's death. He agreed.

Frank Mankiewicz, the Peace Corps regional director for Latin America, recalls getting a surprise phone call from Bobby. After first thinking a talented mimic was playing a trick on him, he realized it was Senator Robert Kennedy himself. He told Mankiewicz he was phoning because he hoped soon to make a fact-finding mission to South America. There his first stop would likely be Peru. Since Mankiewicz had been country director there from 1962 to 1964, Bobby was interested in hearing what he thought of the itinerary the State Department was suggesting for him.

Mankiewicz quickly saw that the prescribed trip was to be a classic in-and-out tour: a visit to the American school, lunch with the Peruvian-American chamber of commerce, dinner at the embassy. "Why are you going to Lima, Senator?" he asked, sensing a kindred spirit. "You could accomplish all that staying right here in Washington."

Intrigued by his forthrightness, Kennedy asked the Peace Corps official for an alternative schedule. Mankiewicz proposed the *barriadas*, shantytowns where millions of Peru's poor lived, along with a visit to the University of San Marco and one to a copper mine, a leading industry. He wanted Bobby to see the country from a Peace Corps volunteer's perspective, from that of the desperately poor. Those were the people Americans like Mankiewicz spent two years in Peru trying to help, not the well-off who'd spent generations taking care to help themselves.

Three days later, at a meeting at the State Department, Mankie-wicz was impressed by Bobby's handling of the officials organizing the trip. At one point, the senator interrupted the person instructing him on the U.S. boilerplate answers to give reporters: "I don't talk that way," he curtly informed the briefer.

In Chile, at the University of Concepción, the radical students there refused to let Kennedy speak, drowning out his attempts to address them. Even when he offered his hecklers equal time, they refused to let up. And when, at their invitation, he tried to join a group of student Communists, a protester spat in his face.

However, when he learned that much of the strength of this anti-government sentiment in Peru was related to the harsh and dangerous conditions in the copper mines, he insisted on being taken down in one. It was an extreme experience to go down 1,500 feet in an elevator, then five miles horizontally, out under the Pacific Ocean. Yet this was where the miners themselves year in and year out earned their pittance of a daily wage. The spectacle caused Bobby to ask a simple question.

Would you, he queried a high-level manager, be a Communist if you were working down in the mines? "I'm afraid I would," the man answered. "We breed them here."

Bobby, along with Ethel, had left Washington on the 1st of November. They were to visit five countries, finishing up in Venezuela. On November 22, the second anniversary of Jack's death, they attended mass in the state of Bahia in northeastern Brazil. He'd planned the trip so he could be out of his country when the day arrived.

Back in Washington, the senator phoned Mankiewicz to thank him again and also to report how impressed he'd been with the Peace Corps projects he'd seen on the trip. Then, a week or so later, he called him again, this time to ask if the man who'd given him such good advice was interested in becoming his press secretary.

Mankiewicz could see that Bobby wasn't looking merely for a spokesman—the duties of which he knew would take only a couple of hours a day—but for something more. Getting "advice on a million things" was how he described it.

Because of Bobby's stint working as minority counsel for the McCarthy committee, and later on the Rackets Committee, Mankiewicz saw that those who didn't really know him viewed him as an Irish cop. "He wasn't," Mankiewicz said, "but he permitted that image to get abroad and it was very tough to knock down." He also grew to appreciate Bobby's attitude toward the press, including his opinion of *The New York Times* as "an anti-Catholic newspaper." The senator once joked to columnist Jimmy Breslin that the newspaper's idea of a great story was "More Nuns Leave Convent than Ever Before."

One characteristic of Bobby's that Mankiewicz came to know well and increasingly admire was his willingness to change his mind. An example was his view on capital punishment. "I'm against it—in all cases," Robert Kennedy now declared. When reminded by Mankiewicz that he'd held the opposite view when serving as attorney general, Bobby paused a moment, then explained: "That was before I read Camus."

Eight years earlier, the French author and moral philosopher Albert Camus had been awarded the Nobel Prize for Literature, honored for his persistent efforts to "illuminate the problem of the human conscience in our time." In his essay "Reflections on the Guillotine," first translated into English in 1961, he'd made three main arguments against state execution: that it is no deterrent, and it therefore serves only as revenge, and that it harms the survivors of the executed in the same way as a victim's were.

It could well have been this last thought that resonated most strongly for Bobby, his own grief still so present. His interest in Camus's thought could have represented the evolution he was going through. His passion for bringing down predators was now giving way to an expanded empathy for life's victims.

His brother was an intimate witness to this transformation. "He decided," wrote Ted, "that he would take on issues that championed America's dispossessed, such as anti-poverty bills and further civil rights reform. He searched for injustices and moral causes. His involvement in them lent them a sense of urgency they might not otherwise have inspired. As he grew and learned, he became more and more interested in people as opposed to abstract ideas."

Yet while Bobby was changing in ways of his own, thoughts echoed also from the Kennedy presidency. Among a pile of final documents on Jack's desk was a sheet of paper with a word scribbled on it that held him in thrall. "Poverty," it read.

It may have been jotted following a conversation about Michael Harrington's recent book, *The Other America: Poverty in the United States*. A Holy Cross graduate, Harrington was a follower of Dorothy Day's Catholic Worker movement. He came to identify himself as a democratic socialist, which for him meant working for change within the Democratic Party. *The Other America*, his first book, was an immediate bestseller and was said to have triggered President Kennedy's and later Lyndon Johnson's interest in trying to reverse the deepening of America's economic divisions.

Bobby now became convinced that poverty was his brother's last unfinished agenda. The riots in the Watts neighborhood of Los Angeles worried him. For six days in August, this African American community had exploded in violence, looting, and arson. Thirty-four people were killed, and over one thousand were injured. Forty million dollars' worth of property was damaged or destroyed. It took the arrival of four thousand National Guards-men to bring order.

California governor Pat Brown appointed a commission to in-vestigate the causes of the lawlessness. Headed by John McCone, just retired from four years as director of the CIA, the commission met sixty-four times in a hundred days, interviewing 530 witnesses. Its conclusions blamed the riots on high unemployment, inferior schools, and poor living conditions.

Bobby, concerned about the same underlying causes, feared the protests would spread. There'd been earlier riots in Brooklyn's Bedford-Stuyvesant neighborhood as well. Finally, by year's end, he came to the decision to speak out on poverty and race. It turned into a series of addresses delivered in New York in January 1966, each on successive nights.

"I don't think that it's possible in our society and with our gov-ernment to tolerate lawlessness and disorder and violence. But at the same time I think that we've got to make more progress than we have in the past to be more effective with the programs that we've instituted. And to have some imagination to try to deal with the lack of hope that exists in many of these communities."

The plight of African Americans was getting worse, he believed. And this led him to question whether reliance on welfare—a stan-dard of liberal social policy—was working. Personally, he detested the term "Great Society," a proud coinage of the Johnson adminis-tration for its domestic programs of poverty and racial injustice. His own ideas focused on the residents of poor neighborhoods being able to participate in policy decisions. He also wanted to encour-age more private investment to act as economic engines in those communities.

In February, he toured a poor neighborhood in Brooklyn in

quest of ways to put his words into action. It would lead to the formation of the Bedford-Stuyvesant Restoration Corporation, whose purpose was to bring economic hope to one of New York's most desperate communities.

That same month, the Senate began two weeks of hearings on the Vietnam War, where Lyndon Johnson had greatly expanded American involvement. He'd begun the previous year with a major, ongoing air campaign against North Vietnam. To protect our airbases in South Vietnam, he had for the first time sent in U.S. combat troops: 3,500 marines to begin with, 125,000 by July, 184,000 by year's end. The strategy was to end North Vietnam's efforts to win control of the South through an expanding campaign of aerial bombardment.

One weakness in Washington's position lay in South Vietnam itself, meaning those now running it. In backing the military coup against President Diem, the country's last leader with the authority to ask America to leave, the U.S. had eliminated the only man with the same authority to ask the U.S. to stay.

As one military-led government in Saigon continued to replace another in successive coups, the U.S. bombing only hardened North Vietnam's commitment to reunite with the South at whatever cost. The Americans kept sending in troops only to have Hanoi match each buildup. However it had begun, it was fast becoming an American war against North Vietnam, with incessant bombing of the North and bloody combat in the South.

Also in early February, Robert Kennedy became absorbed by the hearings the Senate Foreign Relations Committee was holding on the war in Vietnam. The committee chairman, Senator J. William Fulbright (D-AR), had initiated them to challenge the Johnson administration's optimism that if the United States kept up its war of attrition "the communists would eventually give up." Fulbright played the role of prosecutor. For the first time the country was being offered a far different, far less rosy assessment of our chances. Often, Bobby would arrive, then stand in the back of the Senate Caucus Room, where the hearings were taking place, and listen.

On February 19, 1966, Bobby held a Senate press conference that marked his break with the Johnson administration on Vietnam. Proposing that the National Liberation Front, the political arm of the insurgent Vietcong forces, be invited to join in negotiations, he offered a simple rationale. "There are three things you can do with such groups," he argued. "Kill or repress them; turn the country over to them; or admit them to a share of power and responsibility." It was clear what option he was now advocating.

For expressing such thoughts, Robert Kennedy—who until this moment had been known throughout his career in Washington as a hard-line anti-Communist—was now accused of endorsing the unthinkable. He was saying the Communist insurgents should be included in a coalition government in South Vietnam. Vice President Hubert Humphrey was among those who rushed to attack. "It would be like putting a fox in the chicken coop," he jeered.

Such derision had the effect of making Bobby feel politically vulnerable. He'd allied himself with an antiwar movement that still represented only a minority of Americans. He expressed no further thoughts on Vietnam for the rest of 1966. His silence from that point on arose also from the belief that LBJ increased the U.S. commitment there after hearing criticism from him. "I'm afraid that by speaking out I make Lyndon Johnson do the opposite, out of spite."

President Johnson himself was convinced that pulling back from Vietnam would cast him as an appeaser. "Everything I knew about history," he would later write, "told me that if I got out of Vietnam and let Ho Chi Minh run through the streets of Saigon, then I'd be doing exactly what Chamberlain did in World War II. I'd be giving a big fat reward to aggression." Again, it was the shadow of Munich.

He was haunted, also, by a closer specter—the accusation that the Truman administration had been passive in allowing the Communist revolutionary leader Mao Zedong to take control of mainland China in 1949. He recalled the Republicans—and Jack Kennedy—taunting the Truman administration with "Who lost China?"

Johnson understood the role that Mao's crushing of the U.S.-backed Nationalists and his victorious establishment of the People's Republic of China had played in the rise of Joe McCarthy, whom he despised. He was convinced that both legacies, Munich and Mao, "taken together, were chickenshit compared to what might happen if we lost Vietnam."

In March, Bobby, serving on the Senate Subcommittee on Migratory Labor, flew to California to look into the causes of the strike being staged by migrant pickers in the grape-growing town of Delano. Its leader was a Mexican American named Cesar Chavez. His family had arrived in California's Central Valley during the Great Depression of the 1930s. Quitting school when he was fifteen, he worked in the fields until he joined the U.S. Navy in 1946, serving in the Western Pacific.

Chavez's career as a community organizer had begun in the early 1950s. In 1962 he founded what would become the United Farm Workers of America. At its inception, it had just ten members: Chavez, his wife, Helen, and their eight children. In 1960 he'd helped register voters for John F. Kennedy's presidential campaign.

Though he wanted higher wages, Chavez's primary goal was the right to organize and bargain collectively. In 1964 he won the backing of the United Auto Workers, a labor organization that had won Bobby's respect during his Rackets Committee days.

As often was the case, Bobby arrived on the scene in a mood of skepticism. "Why are we taking this trip?" he asked as they flew westward. That attitude quickly shifted to engagement. The fight was between the migrant laborers led by Chavez and the big farmers and the local governments they controlled. Senator Kennedy soon found himself outraged at the rationale he was given for the arrests of forty-four picketing workers. The local sheriff testified to the visiting subcommittee that they'd done so preemptively. They were "*ready*," he said, "to violate the law."

The former attorney general couldn't believe what he was hearing. "I suggest that during this lunch period that the sheriff and the district attorney read the Constitution of the United States."

Beyond that, Bobby had immediately taken sides, identifying instinctively with the farmworkers' struggle—especially that of their leader.

Chavez, whose heroic models were Gandhi and Martin Luther King, now saw Bobby as a champion for his cause. "He crossed a line that no other American politician ever crossed," he told Jack Newfield. What so impressed him, he said, was the intensity of Bobby's feeling for the poor, his authenticity as a human being, and his ability to grow and be changed by experience.

The feelings were mutual as witnessed by Kennedy aide Peter Edelman. "The chemistry was instant."

A "Day of Affirmation of Academic and Human Freedom" was proclaimed at the University of Cape Town for June 6, 1966. It had been organized to assert the students' commitment to human freedom and opposition to the oppression of black and mixed-race South Africans. Invited by the National Union of South African Students—whose president at the eleventh hour was banned from attending—to deliver a speech for the occasion, Robert Kennedy found eighteen thousand people waiting outside to welcome him when he arrived at the majestic Jameson Hall. It took him a half hour just to make his way through the enthusiastic welcomers.

His procession into the building had been led by a student holding an unlit torch to represent the extinguishing of academic freedom. According to those observing him, the American visitor had tears in his eyes as he climbed to the stage.

"I came here," he began, "because of my deep interest and affection for a land settled by the Dutch in the mid-seventeenth century, then taken over by the British, and at last independent; a land in which the native inhabitants were at first subdued, but relations with whom remain a problem to this day; a land which defined itself as a hostile frontier; a land which has tamed rich natural resources through the energetic application of modern technology; a land which once imported slaves, and now must struggle to wipe out the last traces of that former bondage."

Then he paused. "I refer, of course, to the United States of America."

With this perceptive matching of histories, that of his own country with that of his hosts, he offered a moral humility expected least of all by those defenders of the country's system of white supremacy who'd criticized his coming to South Africa in the first place. He was setting a marker down: the United States might be further along on its historic course regarding race, yet that did not put it on a higher national pedestal.

"For two centuries," he told them, "my own country has struggled to overcome the self-imposed handicap of prejudice and discrimination based on nationality, social class, or race—discrimination profoundly repugnant to the theory and command of our Constitution." He then reminded his audience of a reality he carried always with him, of how his grandfather, growing up in Boston, too often had been confronted by anti-Irish sentiment.

"Two generations later," he continued,

President Kennedy became the first Catholic to head the nation. But how many men of ability had, before 1961, been denied the opportunity to contribute to the nation's progress because they were Catholic, or of Irish extraction? How many sons of Italian or Jewish or Polish parents slumbered in slums—untaught, unlearned, their potential lost forever to the nation and human race? Even today, what price will we pay before we have assured full opportunity to millions of Negro Americans?

There is discrimination in New York, the racial inequality of apartheid in South Africa, and serfdom in the mountains of Peru. People starve in the streets of India, a former prime minister [Patrice Lumumba] is summarily executed in the Congo, intellectuals go to jail in Russia, and thousands are slaughtered in Indonesia; wealth is lavished on armaments everywhere in the world. They are differing evils; but they are the common works of man. They reflect the imperfections of human justice, the inadequacy of human compassion, the defectiveness of our sensibility toward the suffering of our fellows; they mark the limit of our ability to use knowledge for the well-being of our fellow human beings around the world. And therefore they call upon common qualities of conscience and indignation, a shared determination to wipe away the unnecessary sufferings of our fellow human beings at home and around the world.

He'd traveled to the tip of a distant continent and there had spoken, thrillingly. He called on the world's youth—which he said was "not a time of life but a state of mind"—to join the cause of greater human fairness. It was his greatest speech.

Bobby greets local residents in the Mississippi Delta.

CHAPTER TWENTY

AFFIRMATION

"It is from numberless diverse acts of courage and belief that human history is shaped. Each time a man stands up for an ideal or acts to improve the lot of others, or strikes out against injustice, he sends forth a tiny ripple of hope, and crossing each other from a million different centers of energy and daring, those ripples build a current that can sweep down the mightiest walls of oppression and resistance."

—ROBERT KENNEDY, SOUTH AFRICA, 1966

As 1967 dawned, nearly 400,000 U.S. troops were in South Vietnam. More than 6,000 Americans had been killed just in the previous year. At home, critics were calling the war an immoral pursuit unlikely to ever end. President Johnson dismissed them as "nervous Nellies" or "sunshine patriots." But a main target of his angry resentment was the junior senator from New York. This was despite the fact that, for months, Kennedy had been holding his fire ever since making that antiwar speech in February 1966.

At the end of January 1967, on a trip to Europe that included a stop in Paris, Bobby met there with Charles de Gaulle. It was the second time he'd been received at the Élysée Palace, having called on the French president once before, in 1962 when he was attorney general. On this visit, they discussed the situation in Vietnam, a conflict fraught with both human peril and political danger—as the French themselves knew only too well.

De Gaulle—a graduate of St. Cyr, the French West Point, and a heroic officer in both world wars—had headed the Free French against the German occupation. "I am an old man," he told Bobby, "and I have lived through many battles and wear many scars. So listen to me closely. . . . Do not become embroiled in the difficulty in Vietnam."

His advice was based on his belief, as both soldier and veteran statesman, that his American visitor should steer clear of divisive national debate in order to protect his chances for future leadership. Better to stand aside, de Gaulle urged, so that he could be available to later help his country "regain its proper course." It seemed unlikely advice from a man who'd become his country's greatest leader by his lonely act of opposition to the capitulation of 1940.

Bobby then spoke to reporters who clustered around as he left the meeting. "France and General de Gaulle," he replied to one questioner, "are going to play an important role in any successful effort we may have in finding a peaceful solution to the trouble in Vietnam. And if that's not recognized by the spokesman in Washington then we are in greater difficulty than I had thought."

But back in Washington in the Oval Office, the "spokesman" to whom he'd made the not-so-veiled reference was becoming steadily angrier. That was because Senator Kennedy had seen another French official in Paris, a representative of the Foreign Ministry. From this diplomat he'd learned that North Vietnam would now agree to participate in peace talks, though only if the United States agreed to halt its bombing campaign. When a State Department official who'd sat in on that meeting filed his report to his Washington superiors, the story was leaked.

The result was, first, a major piece in *Newsweek* describing how a "significant signal" from Hanoi had been conveyed to Senator Kennedy. A later one in *The New York Times* termed it a "peace feeler" from the North Vietnamese. For President Johnson, seeing these stories confirmed his suspicions. He imagined Bobby's own hand behind them, and an effort to portray himself as a leader searching for peace at the same time he, Johnson, was ramping up the war.

Meeting with Johnson upon his return, Bobby found himself, over the course of forty-five minutes, confronted by a furious president. His response to LBJ's charge that he'd tried to embarrass him was blunt. "The leak came from someone in your State Department," the senator informed him.

"It's not my State Department. Goddammit—it's *your* State Department!" Johnson shot back, his anti-Kennedy suspicions flaring up. It was his deeply held suspicion that New Frontier loyalists still lurked in his administration.

At one point, according to Ted Kennedy, Bobby now suggested that he himself act as a go-between, trying to work out a Vietnam peace agreement. He offered, said his brother, "to shuttle back and forth between Washington and Saigon and even travel to Hanoi and China if necessary—and Moscow—if Johnson would trust him to be the U.S. government's agent."

Bobby proposed that Johnson as a preliminary step stop the bombing of North Vietnam to see if its leaders would then agree to talks. "There isn't a chance in hell that I'll do that, not the slightest chance in the world," the president assured him.

Praising the increasing successes the U.S. military campaign was having, the president went on to insist that the war in Vietnam would soon be won, removing any need for the negotiations Bobby and others were calling for. Keep pushing for that, Johnson told him, and "I'll destroy you and every one of your dove friends. You'll be politically dead in six months!"

Bobby, who had learned over the years not to trust Johnson's rhetoric, now worried that he truly believed what he was saying. "These guys are out of their minds," he reported. "They think they're going to win a military victory in Vietnam by summer. They really believe it. The president was saying that, by July or August, the war will be over."

Still, despite the escalating hostility of that meeting, Bobby had told the president that he was ready, once again, to present his thoughts on Vietnam in another Senate speech. Going over it through the early morning hours of March 2, when he was to deliver it, he decided to start with a confession. The war, he said, when he stood to address his Senate colleagues, had been prosecuted by "three presidents," including his brother. "As one who was involved in those decisions, I can testify that if fault is to be found or responsibility assessed, there is enough to go around for all—including myself."

Continuing, he was unsparing when it came to the shared responsibility of all involved. "Let us reflect for a moment . . . on the horror. . . . It is our chemicals that scorch the children and our bombs that level the villages. We are all participants . . . we must also feel as men the anguish of what it is we are doing."

What followed was not an easy time for him when it came to public opinion. Bobby was now striving to keep his political and personal balance in the dual role he found himself playing—as both a reasoned but forceful critic of U.S. Vietnam policy and as an object of presidential wrath and resentment.

The war now threatened a new target, one at home. Up until the spring of 1967, sons of the American middle class had been largely protected from the draft. A young man could attend college for four years, gain admission to graduate or professional school, get married along the way, and never be called for induction.

In March President Lyndon Johnson simply up and announced an end to all graduate school deferments. No longer would the pursuit of a master's or doctoral degree safeguard those millions of college boys from a military hitch. For those of us in the class of 1967, that very June suddenly meant 1-A draft status.

I'll always remember the day of that announcement. Having worked hard to make the dean's list the last two years, I'd selected excellent universities to try for, any one of which I'd have been pleased to attend. My goal was a PhD in economics, followed by a college professorship. I have a strong memory of heading up to the field house to play basketball the afternoon of when I'd learned of Johnson's decree, convinced that my efforts were for nothing. Fortunately, however—and no doubt due to the furor he'd created—Johnson soon backed down, agreeing to a one-year moratorium. I'd have, at least, the chance to start grad school after all.

But as much as this temporary reprieve meant to me, along with my fellow Class of '67 seniors, it wasn't going to make much of a difference to the swelling anti–Vietnam War sentiment around the country. In demonstrations in New York and San Francisco, hundreds of thousands of Americans were making known their objections to Johnson's stubborn commitment to victory.

It was then that Dr. Martin Luther King chose to focus attention on a moral dimension of the war we were waging. Declaring that African Americans and "the poor, white and negro, . . . bear the heaviest burdens both at the front and at home," he pointed out the injustice of forcing young men with few other choices to do the fighting and the dying.

However, even as Bobby Kennedy opposed the official U.S. Vietnam policy, he refused to side with antiwar activists opposing the college draft. Speaking at the University of Oklahoma that March, he made clear the basis of his position against student deferments, declaring "the poor are carrying the burden of the struggle." And when a majority of the student audience indicated approval of the war with a show of hands, he shocked them by turning the tables, suggesting they be willing to match their support with a readiness to fight.

Late that spring, on both national television and radio, CBS presented an hour-long program titled *The Image of America and the Youth of the World*, billed as a "Town Meeting of the World." It was a debate between Senator Robert Kennedy and Ronald Reagan, the new Republican governor of California. Fifteen million Americans tuned in.

The war in Vietnam was the central subject. Although Bobby was willing to agree that the campus protests might signal encouragement to the North Vietnamese effort, he stopped there. He refused to go along with Reagan's belief that antiwar demonstrations were, in fact, actually prolonging the war and contributing to the rise in casualties.

More polished at projecting both himself and his message—he'd been, after all, a radio announcer, an actor, and also a TV host—Reagan proved the clear victor in the opinion of both sides watching. Frank Mankiewicz, who'd talked Bobby into participating, summed up the outcome this way: "One of Reagan's many strengths was that he did not indulge in nuances, and one of Robert Kennedy's many strengths was that he did indeed see, and ponder, nuance." The other difference was that Bobby sympathized with the student protesters. Reagan resented them and exploited his resentment.

In April, Kennedy traveled with three other senators to Mississippi on a fact-finding mission. They'd come south to study the effects of a local policy requiring indigent families applying for food stamps to make cash payments. Reports had reached Washington that too many hungry families could not afford to buy them.

Once those hearings were concluded, Kennedy and Senator Joseph Clark (D-PA) decided to go on to visit the Mississippi Delta, in order to see for themselves the stark conditions they'd heard described. At a stop in one household, a young boy shocked Bobby by telling him his diet consisted only of molasses. "I've been to Third World countries," the New York senator confided to an aide, "and I've never seen anything like this."

The next house at which they stopped belonged to a woman with seven children. Roaches were everywhere. A toddler, playing on the filthy floor, was covered in sores, his stomach distended. Bobby sat down and stroked the boy's cheek. "My God, I didn't know this kind of thing existed! How can a country like this allow it? Maybe they just don't know." When he talked to the child and couldn't get him to respond, the grown man began to cry.

Returning to Hickory Hill, standing at the doorway of his family dining room, Bobby now saw through a different prism the familiar sight of his wife and children seated around the table. Ethel described his response to me: "He was so passionate . . . and he was shaking. Saying, 'Do you know how lucky you are?' And he kept on repeating it."

Unable to dispel those lingering images, he continued to need to share with others what he'd seen and experienced. To the wife of one of his staffers, he lamented: "I've done nothing in my life . . . everything I've done was a waste . . . everything I've done was worthless!" For him, it was a searing reexamination of who he'd been and who he was. Now, as he saw it, the war being waged in a faraway Southeast Asian jungle was completely entangled with the failure of the country waging it.

It was Kennedy's idea to call child psychiatrist Robert Coles to testify before the subcommittee about the brutal and long-lasting effects of extreme poverty on young children. Later, as Bobby's guest for lunch at the Capitol, Coles found that his host's questions about child development—about fathers and sons, about kids who don't easily fit in, about trying always to prove oneself—seemed, really, to be about himself.

Coles was struck, too, by the interest his new acquaintance, a politician with a reputation for toughness, showed in the spiritual life of people like Dorothy Day and Cesar Chavez, both Catholics leading lives of Christian action. "He felt that he hadn't been tested the way that Day had been tested, that she had the true Catholic spirit," Coles told me. The total commitment of Chavez gripped him as well.

Bobby, Coles could see, was drawn to know more about "the

personal religious life of these people." Yet he was aware of the Kennedy family's history and understood that this third son "knew vulnerability alongside privilege and power." Tough but gentle, is how he described him. "He had a willingness to put himself in the shoes of others, as well as walk in his own."

Bobby and fellow antiwar candidate Eugene McCarthy.

CHAPTER TWENTY-ONE

THE MOVEMENT

"You know when I first thought I might have a chance? When I realized that you could go into any bar in the country and insult Lyndon Johnson and nobody would punch you in the nose."
—Eugene McCarthy

"The southern part of heaven" is Chapel Hill's town motto, and it sums up the way the University of North Carolina seemed to me when I arrived there in the fall of 1967. It had the further magic of being a world I'd come across by myself. Having followed my older brother to high school and college, I now felt myself an original settler.

One of the vintage buildings on the elegant campus, I was told, is where the occupying Union officers had stabled their horses during the Civil War. Nearly a half century before I came, novelist Thomas Wolfe had edited the student newspaper, *The Daily Tar Heel*. There was a genteel aura then to the campus town. Men thought nothing of showing up for varsity football games in three-piece suits. But even as it basked in its fine atmosphere, UNC was also the pride of the state's forward-looking education system.

Students from outside the state—including Yankees like myself—were welcomed in its strong academic departments, among which were political science, history, and English. Mainly graduate students lured by generous financial aid, they settled in, learning to speak more softly and slowly and becoming a subculture. I suppose I was part of it.

The Northerners' influence showed itself in political activism, which translated as *antiwar* activism. And it was all moving quickly. Within days of arriving, I was surprised to hear a fellow grad student use the term "fascists" in casual conversation. It was a word I associated with World War II—but this guy wasn't talking about Benito Mussolini and his Blackshirts. Instead, he was throwing the terms at prominent Americans in business and politics.

Another moment that took me aback happened at an anti–Vietnam War meeting when one of the participants yelled out "No pictures!" with the vehemence of someone expecting J. Edgar Hoover himself to pop in.

Much talk went on about "Vietnam Summer," which meant those efforts staged around the country against "The War" in recent months. Unlike participants in San Francisco's "Summer of Love," however, the Chapel Hill organizers wore no flowers in their hair. The people running the meetings I attended were deadly serious about the here-and-now. What mattered to them was stopping a war they found morally abominable, a conflict with the added immediacy of being a daily reality. It could pluck any of us from the comforts and intellectual stirrings of campuses like Chapel Hill and send us off to fight in the jungles of Southeast Asia.

There were frequent reminders of this. If you judged from the newspaper headlines, you might wonder if there could be any reasonable limit to the number of young American males needed to satisfy the Johnson administration's need to fight a war they said we were on the verge of winning. General William Westmoreland seemed to keep asking for more.

One of the antiwar speakers to appear on the UNC campus that fall was Allard Lowenstein, a member of the class of '48. As an undergraduate, he'd served as president of the National Student Association, an organization founded in 1947 to strengthen student government and student civil liberties. He'd gone on to Yale Law School and later worked for Eleanor Roosevelt, Adlai Stevenson, Hubert Humphrey, and North Carolina's Senator Frank Graham.

A charismatic leader of a one-to-one kind, he was a type rare in this country, an enduring youth activist. As Theodore White observed, "Even alone in a room, in private conversation, his talk quivered with the intensity of convention oratory."

Lowenstein was now masterminding a national "Dump Johnson" movement. With this as his starting point, he'd dedicated himself to finding a presidential candidate who could achieve what looked to many a daunting task. His hunt began with the most popular Democrat *not* in the White House. "I love Bobby Kennedy more than anyone else in public life," he said. But what he'd heard from New York's junior senator was a plainspoken rebuff: "I've tried to stop the war in every way I can, but Johnson can't be stopped."

Besides which, Bobby was reluctant to put himself forward, believing that his well-known antagonism toward Lyndon Johnson was a handicap. "People would say that I was splitting the party out of ambition and envy," he told Jack Newfield. "No one would believe that I was doing it because of how I feel about Vietnam and poor people."

Kennedy wasn't the only one to turn down Lowenstein. "I must have spoken to twenty senators or congressmen," he said in frustration. "Some thought I was a kook. Some of them listened. No one defended Lyndon Johnson or the war. I told them we had the strength.

I told them there was a base in the student movement. But no major figure would take the lead—I couldn't find a trigger or a fuse."

Deciding to call together a group of his most trusted advisers, Bobby scheduled a meeting for October 8. Up until that time, he'd said "nothing about running for president," Ted Kennedy later recalled. "Although he'd burned to challenge Johnson at least since the summer." He was aware that his brother was getting pushed to run by Lowenstein and by Jesse Unruh, an influential California Democrat who was speaker of the State Assembly.

Ted was one of those at the session at New York's Regency Hotel, which included aides who'd worked for Jack: Ken O'Donnell, Pierre Salinger, Richard Goodwin, Ted Sorensen, Fred Dutton, Chuck Daley, as well as brother-in-law Steve Smith, Jean's husband.

But, in fact, Bobby wasn't at the meeting. That was Ted's call. He thought it would keep the participants from speaking candidly about the pluses and minuses of Bobby running against a sitting Democratic president. His being there would also make it more difficult to keep the fact of the meeting from the press. Even though Bobby called at the last minute and said he wanted to come, Ted convinced him not to.

"The consensus of the meeting was not to challenge Johnson unless his political position became much weaker than it seemed to be at the time," wrote Bill vanden Heuvel, a Bobby ally who attended. "We had a good give-and-take and decided at the end of the day not to confront Johnson at that time, but not to *endorse* him either." The decision was profoundly political. The belief of those assembled, with one or two exceptions, was that if Bobby ran for president the following year, it would badly damage what seemed to them his otherwise sure shot in 1972.

Meanwhile, the antiwar movement was broadening itself. On October 21, the National Mobilization Committee to End the War in Vietnam organized the March on the Pentagon. A crowd of seventy thousand showed up on the Washington Mall in front of the Lincoln Memorial. Among the speakers were Dr. Benjamin Spock, Norman Mailer, and poet Robert Lowell. The folksinger Phil Ochs, famed for his antiwar ballads such as "What Are You Fighting For?," was a presence whose plaintive voice and passionate lyrics embodied the spirit of what was occurring. Once the Mall demonstration ended, fifty thousand women, men, and children walked across Memorial Bridge to the Department of Defense headquarters.

It was my first large-scale antiwar event. What I recall from that sparkling Saturday was the smell of trampled grass—the lawn kind—the innocence of the young parents pushing baby strollers and of the young nuns I saw, along with the prevailing good cheer of the vast crowd. Whatever politics—whether old-style or new—were being proselytized at the many tables and kiosks, one truth was clear: the one successful recruiter there was the chance to oppose the war.

Though I kept my emotional and physical distance—I chose to walk across the bridge along its sidewalks rather than in the ranks of the marchers—I found myself getting increasingly engaged. At the Pentagon parking lot, there was something about the crack U.S. infantry unit I saw there executing crowd-control maneuvers that struck me as disgustingly provocative. At that moment, I understood how you can find yourself caught up in mob psychology. I saw good people being treated as if they were bad people which they clearly weren't—and they knew it.

"It was like looking for your *father*." Al Lowenstein would say that his hunt for an anti–Vietnam War leader felt like looking for a father. I knew the feeling. Our own parents couldn't believe that their sons and daughters were daring to challenge a president's call to arms. "You were down there with those Communists!" Mom cried out when I came home to Philadelphia that Thanksgiving. Though I didn't know it at the time, I desperately wanted some grown-up to come along and say we were right, that it wasn't that we were just afraid to fight a war the way our fathers so unquestioningly had.

Senator Eugene McCarthy of Minnesota now rose to the challenge. A member of the Democratic-Farmer-Labor Party in that state, he'd been, variously, over the past three decades, a public school teacher, an army code breaker, a Benedictine novice, a college professor, and finally a U.S. congressman before entering the Senate in 1958. He was the one credible leader who said "yes" when Lowenstein came courting, the serious challenger who could bring the antiwar sentiment up to the surface and start Lyndon Baines Johnson tumbling down.

For a candidate to excite campuses, McCarthy was from central casting. He had the reserve of a popular lecturer along with the wit and apparent detachment of the professor you'd hope to have as a friend but liked him all the more for not needing someone like you. His diffidence, his lack of political bluster—seemingly even of personal ambition—made him the understated hero perfect for the taking down of the "my fellow Americans" orator sweating to us from the White House in prime time.

To use the descriptions popularized by media guru Marshall McLuhan, Gene McCarthy was cool. Johnson, on the other hand, was hot. We didn't need a lie detector to tell us which of the two we dearly wanted to believe.

As McCarthy began to ready himself to take the leap, Senator Robert Kennedy was moving to widen his difference with Johnson. Asked by a historian if his brother would have brought in 500,000 American troops to the Vietnam struggle, he was now sharp, direct, and impossible not to understand. "Never. The president would never have done it. He was determined not to send troops. If the

South Vietnamese could not do it, the United States could not win it for them." He said his brother had been hoping to neutralize Vietnam, in the same way he'd done with neighboring Laos in 1962.

Then, in an appearance on CBS's *Face the Nation*, Kennedy re-asserted his conviction that Lyndon Johnson had deviated from his brother's Vietnam policy. The war, he said, had become "immoral."

Still, he wasn't running, not even now. "His general feeling is that it would be a great mistake for him to challenge Johnson at this point," Arthur Schlesinger jotted in his journal after a Saturday-night dinner at Hickory Hill in early November. The historian felt that his host thought it "would be considered evidence of his ruth-lessness, his ambition and a personal vendetta. On the other hand, he fully recognizes that the situation has changed a great deal and may change a lot more."

Schlesinger also observed: "He thinks that McCarthy's entry into the primaries will help open things up, though he is perplexed as to how he should handle this himself. He acknowledges the danger that McCarthy might be successful enough to prevent the emergence of another anti-LBJ candidate, but feels he has no alternative but to wait. His hope is that, as McCarthy beats LBJ in primaries, state political leaders, faced with the prospect of local disaster if LBJ heads the ticket, will come to him and ask him to run in the interests of the party. In the meantime, he is refurbishing his national contacts."

Unlike Bobby, Gene McCarthy had kept to himself his actual feelings about the man sitting in the White House. Outwardly, he'd positioned himself as a loyalist, supporting him on matters before the Senate that were of specific Texas interest. The rousing speech he'd given nominating Adlai Stevenson at the 1960 Democratic convention was another example of his careful Johnson allegiance. It was, in effect, an LBJ blocking maneuver, a ploy to prevent Jack Kennedy from a first-ballot win.

But there was, perhaps, payback in Eugene McCarthy's candidacy. Four years earlier in Atlantic City, Johnson had shown his disrespect for the senator by dangling the vice presidency in his face, just to gin up some needed convention drama. Now, going to see Bobby, Senator McCarthy let him know he planned to run in New Hampshire—the earliest Democratic primary—even if he didn't expect to get more than five thousand votes to Johnson's projected forty thousand.

On November 30, McCarthy made it official. His hat was in the ring. "They say I'm committing suicide," McCarthy said, following his announcement. "Well, I'd rather do that and face up to the wrongness of the war than die of political old age." For him, he emphasized, it was more about principles than personal political gain. He also explained that he wanted no future regrets, no thinking "I should have made myself available in 1968."

Bill Clinton, a Georgetown University student at the time, was one of those college students impressed by what they saw: "As the party's heir apparent to Adlai Stevenson's intellectual liberalism, McCarthy could be maddening, even disingenuous, in his efforts to appear almost saintly in his lack of ambition. But he had the *guts* to take on Johnson."

Meanwhile, the men around Bobby Kennedy were considering the new situation. A meeting at Bill vanden Heuvel's New York apartment—to discuss what now—was scheduled. This time, with the potential candidate there in the room, the advisers were divided. Arthur Schlesinger and Richard Goodwin backed Bobby's entering the race. Salinger and O'Donnell, too, leaned heavily in that direction. The two Teds, Kennedy and Sorensen, were firmly against.

"We both believed that Johnson would win reelection and that my brother should wait until 1972 when he would be the logical successor," the younger Kennedy recalled. To this, Bobby wondered aloud if the world could endure another Johnson term.

Schlesinger would sum up the meeting as "troubled and inconclusive" and Bobby as "torn, rueful," though clearly "sorely tempted." Persisting in the need for caution, the noncandidate's own summation was, "We haven't decided anything—so I guess I'm not running."

In the year-end issue of *The Village Voice*, Jack Newfield wrote an astute appraisal:

> If Kennedy does not run in 1968, the best side of his character will die. He will kill it every time he butchers his conscience and makes a speech for Johnson next autumn. It will die every time a kid asks him, if he is so much against the Vietnam War, how come he is putting party above principle? It will die every time a stranger quotes his own words back to him on the value of courage as a human quality.
>
> Kennedy's best quality is his ability to be himself, to be authentic in the existential sense. This is the quality the best young identify with so instinctively in Kennedy. And it is this quality Kennedy will lose if he doesn't make his stand now against Johnson. He will become a robot mouthing dishonest rhetoric like all the other politicians.

The subject's reaction to the article was direct and candid. "I just have to decide now whether my running can accomplish anything. I don't want to run only as a gesture. I don't want it to drive Johnson into doing something really crazy.

"I don't want it to hurt the doves in the Senate who are up for re-election," he continued. "I don't want it to be interpreted in the press as just part of a personal vendetta or feud with Johnson.

"It's all so complicated. I just don't know what to do."

Bobby touring a tenement in New York's Lower East Side.

CHAPTER TWENTY-TWO

VIGIL

"My problem is that I don't have anyone to be
for me what I was for my brother."

—ROBERT KENNEDY

Ted Kennedy was the one person close to Bobby who'd remained firmly opposed to a run for president in 1968. The reason he gave whether at meetings or alone with his brother had to do with the pure politics of the matter. He believed an attempt in 1968 would fall short, with Johnson handily securing the nomination. And if that were to happen, then the solid chance his brother might otherwise have for the 1972 nomination and the presidency would be in ashes. His was the seasoned pol's conviction that *timing is everything*.

Deep within Bobby was the dream of restoring the banner of the New Frontier to the American presidency. Beneath Teddy's earned political savvy, however, was the concern he'd brought into all those sessions debating a second Kennedy run for the White House. What he had was a real worry he'd never shared with Bobby, whom he'd feared for so long wouldn't survive the loss of Jack. It was a specter he'd admit to only years later: "We weren't that far away from '63, and that still was very much of a factor."

Ted knew their father would have advised against running, just as he'd counseled against Jack's trying for the vice presidential nomination back in 1956. Then, too, the timing had been off. The early 1968 dynamic, though, was complicated. Ted figured that Jack, were he now in Bobby's circle of advisers, might have looked at the current moment and cautioned him against jumping in. Yet Ted also was willing to bet that if it were now Jack himself faced with the dilemma, he'd not have hesitated.

What finally pushed Ted to relent and soften his opposition was his grasp of the way Bobby's conscience and compassion were now driving him. "It was not just the war," he would explain. "It was . . . how the war was propelling the direction of America, especially the young people, the underprivileged, the underserved, those struggling for their civil rights. It was the inflaming of the cities and the failure to deal with the root causes of the flames."

Ted believed his brother—growing more and more aware of the equality and fairness missing from so many American lives—at the same time was feeling greater pressure to find remedies. "When people came to Bobby—as they did, saying, '*You* can change this. *You* can do it'—he felt an obligation to do something."

Even so, Bobby continued to hesitate. At a New York dinner in early January, he told his companions he couldn't help but fear the traps Johnson might be setting for him if he declared. Sitting with Schlesinger, actor Sidney Poitier, astronaut John Glenn, and others, he told them he believed there were politicians urging him on whose agendas were their own, not his. He worried, too, that the wily occupant of the Oval Office might immediately shift his Vietnam policies the moment he declared his candidacy.

"Suppose, in the middle of the California primary, when I'm attacking him on the war, he should suddenly stop the bombing and go off to Geneva to hold talks with the North Vietnamese? What do I do then? Either I call his action phony, in which case I am lining up with Ho Chi Minh, or else, I have to say that all Americans should support the president in this search for peace. In either case, I'm likely to lose."

At a dinner later that month, he remained fixed on the idea of Johnson's possible vindictiveness. How could he stand against a president "prepared to escalate or de-escalate, to bomb or stop bombing"—anything to turn the tables and make Bobby the villain?

At a meeting with reporters on January 30, Bobby put his decision on the record. "I have told friends and supporters who are urging me to run that I would not oppose Lyndon Johnson under any conceivable circumstances."

But almost immediately after he'd spoken, Mankiewicz stopped the departing reporters to ask them to change one word his boss had just used—from "conceivable" to "foreseeable." The reason for the sudden edit, approved by Kennedy, could be found in the information on a slip of wire service copy he'd just passed to the senator. It contained early reports from Vietnam of a devastating Communist incursion into the South.

Later that day, *The Washington Evening Star*, the capital's afternoon daily, featured Bobby's decision not to run on the front page. But the far more prominent story was captured in the headline, "Reds Launch Mightiest Offense." The Tet Offensive, as the driving onslaught came to be known, consisted of vicious attacks made across the country by eighty thousand North Vietnamese and Vietcong troops. In one city, Hue, alone, thousands of civilians were executed. It was the largest military operation by either side up until then, and its lethal scope stunned an American public that until that moment had been convinced such areas, including Saigon, were safe from attack.

Whatever actually had been occurring on the ground in Vietnam, it bore little resemblance to the carefully tailored propaganda fed by U.S. officials there to the U.S. press corps based in Saigon. Though they had little choice but to transmit the official version of the grim reality, the increasingly skeptical newsmen dubbed those daily briefings among themselves "the Five O'Clock Follies." Tet had proven those skeptics right.

With more than 535,000 troops in his command, General Westmoreland followed Tet by requesting 206,000 more. Meanwhile, back in Chapel Hill, common sense told me, a grad student in economics, that if we weren't able to win with more than a half million soldiers, it was unlikely additional troops would make the difference. The same common sense said we weren't winning—and that we weren't *going* to win.

As the people around him realized, each day it was becoming harder for Bobby to sit on the sidelines. Yet however powerful his instinctive need to respond, he held himself back. During an appearance on *The Tonight Show*, he expressed to guest host Harry Belafonte his view that a successful challenge to President Johnson would be "very difficult" politically.

"The views that I represent," he told him, "I don't think they're supported by anything other than a minority in the United States." Looking around, however, one could see that this reality was daily changing.

The power of the war opponents was about to get a boost. CBS news anchor Walter Cronkite, just returned from a reporting assignment in South Vietnam, said this on the evening broadcast of February 27:

We have been too often disappointed by the optimism of the American leaders, both in Vietnam and Washington, to have faith any longer in the silver linings they find in the darkest clouds. Any negotiations must be that—negotiations, not the dictation of peace terms. For it seems now more certain than ever that the bloody experience of Vietnam is to end in a stalemate.

Not long after this, the trusted Cronkite startled Mankiewicz by requesting to meet privately with Bobby. When the press secretary had arranged this, the newsman—ignoring the ground rules of journalistic neutrality that in ordinary times he'd have observed—spoke frankly and forcefully to the senator. "You must run for president against LBJ. It's the only way to stop this awful war."

And still Bobby felt unsure of the road forward. And while he waited and watched, unable to commit, excitement over the McCarthy campaign continued to mount. Across New Hampshire, its citizens found eager students—polite and persuasive—at their front doors. If they were young men, they had shaved off their beards, and cut their long hair, to get "Clean for Gene." It was accepted that resembling the raucous protesters seen on the nightly news would never be the way to convince Granite State voters to back their man.

Heading to the UNC Student Union each evening to watch the news with the other regulars, I savored hearing Cronkite and his colleague Eric Sevareid recount the latest progress of the McCarthy volunteers up there tromping determinedly through "the snows of New Hampshire." Ever since Dallas, the spirit of American politics had seemed to me to be dead and buried. Now, it felt like it was being reborn.

As the March 12 primary drew closer, the strategic advantage enjoyed by the McCarthy camp was arithmetical. It was about the odds. With state polls showing him hardly in double digits, he was nonetheless in a win-win situation. All he had to do, he said, was "beat the spread." He even liked to joke that his name could turn out to have an added-bonus effect: conservative Republicans might write him in thinking he was that other McCarthy.

On primary night, as it turned out, he exceeded expectations, winning over 42 percent to Johnson's 49.5 percent. Throwing in the Republican write-ins for each of them, he'd lost to the president by a bare 230 votes.

In New York that night, Robert Kennedy admitted he was feeling boxed in. McCarthy certainly wouldn't quit the race now. Bobby understood. "I don't blame him at all," he said. "Of course he feels that he gave me my chance to make the try, that I didn't and that he has earned the right to go ahead. I can't blame him."

He could see, also, the implicit advantage for him in McCarthy's strong showing. "He has done a great job in opening the situation up." The political landscape now looked different. He, Bobby, could no longer be tagged as the outlier dividing the Democratic Party. It was divided already.

Near midnight he reached Richard Goodwin, who'd been writing speeches for McCarthy and who now felt certain President Johnson was down for the count. "What do I do now?" Bobby asked him.

As they talked, Bobby went on to try, though without success, to reenlist Goodwin to his own team. "He failed to realize," Goodwin wrote later, "that the triumph in New Hampshire had transformed McCarthy into a national figure—fresh, attractive, with a powerful hold on the imagination of the electorate—a shining knight from Minnesota assaulting the battlements of established power."

But Bobby was moving away from indecision and toward commitment. "I'm reassessing the possibility of whether I will run against President Johnson," he told reporters when he returned to Washington the next morning.

Ted Sorensen now brought forth a proposal to Bobby that made sense, one that addressed the Vietnam War directly. His idea was to ask Lyndon Johnson to assemble a high-level commission to review all aspects of America's Vietnam policy. It would amount, the thinking went, to an implicit admission that current U.S. strategy wasn't working. This would permit Johnson, and presumably his successor, to move toward a negotiated settlement.

President Johnson, approached privately by Sorensen, had indicated interest. "If it could be done without looking to the Communists as though we're throwing in our hand," the man Jack Kennedy had once likened to a riverboat gambler said, "it might be useful."

On Thursday morning, two days after New Hampshire, Sorensen and Bobby went together to the Pentagon to present the idea of the commission, meeting secretly with the new secretary of defense, Clark Clifford. His predecessor, Robert McNamara, had resigned, owing to his own increasing dissatisfaction with President Johnson's policies.

A cornerstone of the presentation made to Clifford that morning was Bobby's insistence that the commission be set up as a sincere and valid effort and not merely a "public relations gimmick." His clear conviction was, from the start, that the appointed members would need to demonstrate their "clear-cut willingness" to seek a peaceful settlement on Vietnam. However, it didn't take long for Clifford to return to Bobby with his new boss's thumbs-down. Acknowledging anything even resembling failure held no interest for Lyndon Johnson.

That initiative and its dead-end result ended the months of hanging back. At eleven o'clock Friday morning, Robert Kennedy instructed Frank Mankiewicz, "Better reserve the Senate Caucus Room for tomorrow."

"Martin Luther King was shot and killed tonight."
Bobby Kennedy, Indianapolis, April 4, 1968.

CHAPTER TWENTY-THREE

DEFIANCE

"To take arms against a sea of troubles."
—WILLIAM SHAKESPEARE, *HAMLET*

Once he'd decided to declare—on Saturday, March 16—Bobby hoped to avoid a fight that would divide the antiwar forces. Seeking to solve the problem before it became one, he dispatched brother Ted to Wisconsin the day before to try to persuade McCarthy to split the upcoming primary races between them.

It would be a form of sharing their mutual effort to unseat LBJ, and it meant each agreeing to step aside in states where the other had the best chance. In that way, the antiwar vote's strength might be maximized and, together, they might bring down Johnson.

By the time he reached Green Bay, however, Senator McCarthy had already gone to bed. Awakened, he and his wife, Abigail, listened to Ted, rejecting his proposal out of hand. Gene McCarthy was determined to keep the electoral edge he'd gained in New Hampshire.

He told his late-night visitor to let his brother know that if he was joining the fight, he'd have to take his chances—and not just with Lyndon Johnson. McCarthy, the man who'd gone first, was adamant. He wasn't going to move over simply because a Kennedy wanted in.

Returning east by chartered plane, Ted made it to Bobby's house before dawn Saturday with the disappointing news. "What do you think I should do?" Bobby asked Arthur Schlesinger, who had joined them for the announcement.

"Why not come out for McCarthy?" he answered, saying that all of the Minnesotan's delegates were potential Kennedy ones. "He can't possibly win, so you'll be the certain inheritor of his support."

"I can't do that," Bobby shot back. "It would be too humiliating. Kennedys don't act that way."

The group surrounding him that Saturday morning at Hickory Hill—the two Teds, Bill vanden Heuvel, as well as Schlesinger—was wary. They sensed the resentment his entry would trigger, especially among the antiwar liberals. If Bobby entered now, as far as they were concerned he'd be jumping McCarthy's claim. Worse still, he'd be blamed for splitting the anti-Johnson forces, thus allowing the president to win the nomination after all.

"Look, fellows," Bobby told them. "I can't do it. I can't come out for McCarthy. Let's not talk about it anymore. I'm going ahead, and there's no point in talking about anything else." Still, he, too, was able to see what was happening, grasping the real possibility that his goal—stopping the Vietnam War—might be defeated by the very act of becoming a candidate.

But it didn't deter him. In his mind, the die was cast. Eager to get on with it, he now started work on the speech he soon would deliver. He wrote of his desire to heal the country's wounds, and of the need to close the gaps between black and white, rich and poor, even between generations. Yet, aware of the tremors ahead, he couldn't help but joke grimly that he'd be creating a gap of his own "by splitting the Democratic party in three pieces."

Certainly, after playing Hamlet for so many months, Bobby now was facing his own "sea of troubles." He had to beat Lyndon Johnson with one hand, brush back McCarthy with the other. He needed to win the primaries—preferably, as his brother had done, taking all of them. Simultaneously, he needed to woo that bulk of the country where party leaders, not primaries, selected their states' delegates.

This meant splitting his time between battling primaries, one at a time, and getting his poll numbers up nationwide. He'd not be able to let up, not before the critically important California primary in early June. Still, it wouldn't really slow down after that. Up until the end of August, when delegates began arriving in Chicago for the convention, he had to be trawling for them whenever and wherever he was able. To most political onlookers, the task facing him—to lock up the Democratic nomination for president—verged close to impossible.

There was, as well, a challenge he saw as particularly his own. He was looking to maximize his popularity among minorities, exciting them enough to turn out at the polls in large numbers. Yet it would be a balancing act. He'd need to accomplish that feat while at the same time not scaring off the white working-class voters who'd formed the base of Kennedy support since his brother first ran for office in 1946.

Plus, there was the hard truth that he was starting out so very late. His brother Jack had believed that starting early—seriously early, long before any opponents—was the only way to launch a political campaign. By deciding to enter the presidential contest on March 16, with the primary season already in progress, Bobby had lost the opportunity to obey the rule.

Coming in now as he was, he was asking those who'd already endorsed Johnson or who supported Gene McCarthy to switch sides. Such timing, too, made it difficult for governors, senators, and party chairmen to join him. Yet these were the very party stalwarts he'd need to win over, even if he won the major primaries lying ahead. Democratic leaders across the country were about to be put on notice: they had to decide for or against him.

Most Democrats were already committed to Lyndon Johnson. He, after all, was the incumbent. Kennedy's one hope, given Johnson's wily strength and McCarthy's idealistic challenging of it, was to make use of a special power he and he alone possessed. He could excite people with the undeniably romantic notion of another Kennedy era, a New-er Frontier.

To help with the process of rounding up delegates, Dave Hackett signed on to put together an operation like he'd carried through for Jack in 1960. His loyalty hadn't faltered. Knowing Bobby so well for so long and now watching him mature, he believed his old friend had evolved from the misfit he'd known at Milton to a potential unifier on the national stage.

After announcing, Bobby headed west to start his roving campaign—the plan was sixteen states in two weeks—at Kansas State University. Frank Mankiewicz, who walked into the giant field house with Kennedy, was stunned by the reaction he received. "Roars rolled out one after another as he entered. I'd never seen anything like it." The tumult felt like being on the "inside of Niagara Falls"—as another seasoned political observer, Jack Newfield, described it.

Standing there before a fifteen-thousand-strong crowd, Kennedy admitted to having once been a cheerleader for the country's commitment in Vietnam. "But past error is no excuse for its own perpetuation. All men make mistakes, but a good man yields when he knows his course is wrong and repairs the evil."

He went on to offer a stunning philosophical question: "If it becomes necessary to destroy all of South Vietnam to save it, will we do that, too? And if we care so little about South Vietnam that we are willing to see its land destroyed, and its people dead, then why are we there in the first place?"

Later that day, at the University of Kansas, he introduced what was to be his campaign's overarching theme, the idea he placed at "the root of all of it." Driving him, he declared, was the quest to find again "the national soul of the United States."

What he saw in the country gravely worried him. "Our young people—the best educated and the best comforted in our history, turn from the Peace Corps and the public commitment of a few years ago to lives of disengagement and despair—many of them turned on with drugs and turned off on America." Personal excellence and community values, he observed, were being sacrificed to "the accumulation of material things."

He spoke, too, of those whom he, in sorrow, called the country's "unknowns"—the children of the Mississippi Delta with their distended stomachs and "destroyed minds"; the Indians living on reservations where the most common cause of death is suicide; of the impoverished whites in Appalachia and the families in the black ghettos of the big cities. In each case, he pronounced the conditions there "unacceptable."

But it was when he vehemently opposed the Vietnam War that the crowd's response was the strongest. It was as if he could "feel the fabric ripping," he told one of the reporters covering him as they flew back to New York. "If we don't get out of this war, I don't know what these young people are going to do. There's going to be no way to talk to them. It's very dangerous."

Yet there were journalists who now saw Bobby himself as the danger. The *Washington Post's* Richard Harwood, a former marine, referred to him as a "demagogue" for blaming Lyndon Johnson for all the country's ills—ranging from youthful drug addiction to draft resistance to urban rioting. In his view, Robert Kennedy was trying to win the nomination by "revolution."

Later that week, Kennedy addressed 8,500 students at the University of Alabama in Tuscaloosa, scene of the tense confrontation with Governor Wallace five years earlier. "When a man leaves his home to risk death 12,000 miles away, while we live and study in comfort, I want him to find the door of opportunity open when he returns." This attempt to identify civil rights with basic patriotism was greeted with considered applause.

When he was asked if he'd ever consider accepting second place on a Lyndon Johnson ticket, his reply was swift, and sharp. "You don't understand. I said I was for a coalition government in *Saigon*, not here."

Returning to New York, an airport bystander gave him the startling news. On prime-time television earlier that evening, Lyndon Johnson had announced he wouldn't seek renomination. He said he was unwilling to allow "partisan personal causes" to distract him from his presidential duties. It's likely, however, that a quite different and very specific motive lay behind that bombshell: he'd had twenty-four hours to think over the news that late-breaking polls showed that Eugene McCarthy, the man he'd failed to manipulate back in Atlantic City, was about to beat him—two-to-one—in the April 2 Wisconsin primary.

What Johnson did not announce that dramatic night was his decision to throw his support to Hubert Humphrey. That would come later as, backed by LBJ's influence, his vice president picked up loyal state delegations across the country. Fearful of entering primaries, where antiwar sentiment would run strong, Humphrey intended to win the nomination entirely in the back rooms.

It wasn't McCarthy LBJ cared about. "The thing I feared from the first day of my presidency," he'd recall years later, "was actually coming true. Robert Kennedy had openly announced his intention to reclaim the throne in the memory of his brother. And the American people, swayed by the magic of his name, were dancing in the streets."

Speaking at Notre Dame University in South Bend, Indiana, on April 4—that state's primary was still a month away—Robert Kennedy held fast to his course of being antiwar while at the same time supporting the cause of a fair draft policy. There he told an audience of five thousand that student deferments discriminated against those who were eligible but couldn't afford college. The next stop that day was Ball State University in Muncie, where a crowd of nine thousand awaited him. "For all the advantages that we have, don't we have a major responsibility to those that don't have those advantages?" he questioned.

"You're placing a great deal of faith in white America," a black student now questioned him. "Is this faith justified?" Bobby, accepting the challenge, noted first that there were "black extremists who do not like white people and . . . are teaching violence and lawlessness and disorder." At the same time, he acknowledged that there are also "white people who say . . . black people are inferior and therefore don't want to treat them equally."

Finally, he offered hope. "I think the vast majority of the American people want to do the decent and the right thing."

As they were about to leave Muncie, there came sudden word that Martin Luther King had been shot in Memphis, Tennessee. The reply he'd just given to the Ball State student—which had offered no assurances but had talked about "the decent and the right thing"—now haunted Bobby. "It grieves me," he said to a reporter. "I just told that kid this—and then walk out to find that some white man has just shot their spiritual leader."

In Indianapolis that night, a Kennedy rally was scheduled to take place in the Broadway neighborhood, an inner-city African American community. Civil rights leader John Lewis, who'd joined the Kennedy campaign, had helped organize the event. "There were some people saying that . . . maybe he shouldn't come, because, maybe there would be violence. But some of us said he *must* come." The candidate himself agreed. "Our local campaign leadership, and the city leaders," Mankiewicz recalled, "urged that the meeting be canceled, because security could not be guaranteed. But Kennedy insisted that was one of the reasons he had to keep the date."

A situation fraught with risk was now made riskier: the local police who'd been assigned to escort the motorcade to the rally site refused to proceed into the black neighborhood. Instead, the cars bringing in the candidate and his staff had to go it alone. "What am I going to say?" Bobby asked as they drove past thronged sidewalks where no one yet knew the terrible news.

Having climbed atop a flatbed truck, he went to the microphone. "Do they know about Martin Luther King?" you can hear him ask his hosts on the tape. It's clear that they don't.

"Ladies and gentlemen," he began, speaking without notes. "I am only going to talk to you just for a minute or so this evening because I have some very sad news for all of you . . . and I think sad news for all of our fellow citizens and people who love peace all over the world. And that is that Martin Luther King was shot and was killed tonight in Memphis, Tennessee."

There was a collective gasp. At first, his listeners didn't believe what they were hearing. There was even scattered applause from those excited at his presence and so ready to cheer that they didn't make out his words. Bobby then continued:

Martin Luther King dedicated his life to love and to justice between fellow human beings. He died in the cause of that effort. In this difficult day, in this difficult time for the United States, it is perhaps well to ask what kind of a nation we are and what direction we want to move in.

For those of you who are black—considering the evidence evidently is that there were white people who were responsible— you can be filled with bitterness, and with hatred, and a desire for revenge. We can move in that direction as a country, in great polarization—black people amongst black, and white amongst whites, filled with hatred toward one another.

Or we can make an effort, as Martin Luther King did, to understand and to comprehend and replace that violence, that stain of bloodshed that has spread across our land, with an effort to understand compassion and love.

For those of you who are black and are tempted to be filled with hatred and mistrust of the injustice of such an act, against all white people, I would only say that I can also feel in my own heart the same kind of feeling. I had a member of my family killed—but he was killed by a white man. But we have to make an effort in the United States. We have to make an effort to understand, to get beyond or go beyond these rather difficult times.

A favorite poem, my favorite poet—was Aeschylus. He once wrote: "Even in our sleep, pain which cannot forget falls drop by drop upon the heart until, in our own despair, against our will, comes wisdom through the awful grace of God."

What we need in the United States is not division. What we need in the United States is not hatred. What we need in the United States is not violence and lawlessness, but is love and wisdom, and compassion toward one another, a feeling of justice toward those who still suffer within our country—whether they be white or they be black.

We can do well in this country. We will have difficult times. We've had difficult times in the past. We will have difficult times in the future. It is not the end of violence. It is not the end of lawlessness; it is not the end of disorder. . . .

Let us dedicate ourselves to what the Greeks wrote so many years ago: to tame the savageness of man and to make gentle the life of this world. Let us dedicate ourselves to that, and say a prayer for our country and for our people. Thank you very much.

It took this tragic moment in America's racial history to forge the bond that Robert Kennedy had been seeking. The recognition of shared victimhood played a part. His reference to a "member of my family" was the sole public mention he was ever to make regarding his own relationship to what he would call "the events of November 1963."

As the evening went on, riots broke out in a hundred American cities, Indianapolis not among them. Dozens were killed, thousands injured. Stunned as many white Americans were by the killing of Martin Luther King, the more powerful electoral effect resulted from the widespread urban violence. Fueled by a powerful mix of anger, grief, resentment, and a need for revenge that became known as "white backlash," the term itself became a license for more of the same.

Bobby knew what he believed. That certainty kept him from being swept along in the collective emotion. Though a man of growing compassion, he believed in law and order and didn't hesitate to employ the phrase. He fought discrimination, despaired over the tragedy in Memphis, but also was unable to tolerate seeing the nation's capital burning in response.

His daughter Kerry, then eight, remembers watching with him scenes of the rioting on TV. He said he understood their frustration, but described the people they saw as "bad." A former attorney general, after all, he believed justice impossible without enforcement of the law.

At the City Club in Cleveland, Ohio, on the day after King's assassination, he addressed the topic of violence in America. "Whenever any American's life is taken by another American unnecessarily—whether it's done in the name of the law or in the defense of law, by one man or a gang, in cold blood or in passion, in an attack of violence or in response to violence—whenever we tear at the fabric of life which another man has painfully and clumsily woven for himself and his children, the whole nation is degraded."

For Bobby, Eugene McCarthy remained the obvious roadblock. In Schlesinger's opinion, the basic problem was that McCarthy had seized the loyalty of the young and idealistic. The pioneer tends to be the hero. "McCarthy," he said, "by the single act of prior entry, captured Bobby's constituency and, with it, a lot of the dynamism of the campaign."

With the Indiana primary drawing nearer, Bobby's hope was to carry a substantial white vote that would match his dominant strength among African Americans. He saw it as a positive sign when he experienced appreciative welcomes from both groups in Gary, Indiana, four days before voters would go to the polls.

There, he rode in a convertible seated between Mayor Richard Hatcher, the city's first African American leader, and Gary's most famous citizen, the prizefighter Tony Zale. Known as the "Man of Steel" for the mills where he'd once worked and always had lived near, Zale was a two-time middleweight champion. Bobby would end the day with his own hands bloody, cuff links and even shoes missing, so frenzied were his reaching fans. "That being touched all the time," he told a reporter. "I don't like it. But people can hear everything about a candidate; and it's the touching him they never forget."

"The people here were fair to me," he said late on election eve. "They gave me a chance. They listened to me. If they don't like you they let you know; if they do like you they let you know that, too."

In the end, Bobby Kennedy won the Indiana Democratic primary, receiving 42 percent of the vote. The popular governor, Roger Branigin, running as a favorite son, won 31 percent, Senator McCarthy 28.

Richard Goodwin, who'd left the McCarthy campaign and returned to the Kennedy fold, believed Bobby had found his message. "His inner urge toward defiance—of unjust privilege, indifferent power, concentrated wealth, which provide so much hatred among some—was also the source of his greatest strength, arousing the hopes and expectations of millions who felt themselves victimized."

As Bobby himself saw it: "I've proved I can really be a leader of a broad spectrum. I can be a bridge between blacks and whites without stepping back from my positions."

Bobby and Ethel celebrate victory in the California primary, June 5, 1968.

CHAPTER TWENTY-FOUR

SACRIFICE

"Blest are those whose blood and judgment are so well commingled."
—Hamlet

The week after Indiana, Bobby trounced the competition in a second primary, this time in Nebraska. It was a convincing margin: 52 percent to Gene McCarthy's 31. This victory gave hope that he could well be on a streak with McCarthy gradually fading with each contest.

Missing from the headlines, though, was the attention that could have been paid to the Minnesotan's shrewd retreat. McCarthy had touched down in Nebraska for a single day, merely to show his flag, then headed off to Oregon where the political landscape looked more welcoming.

Bobby's optimism after Indiana and Nebraska, if not exactly wishful thinking, ignored a basic truth. "At every stage of the campaign," Bill vanden Heuvel recalled, "Kennedy was to underestimate McCarthy's strength. He did not perceive . . . how the mystique of the New Hampshire triumph had transformed McCarthy from the political gadfly of January to a fresh, attractive figure with a powerful hold on the imagination of the electorate."

He also hadn't yet grasped how McCarthy appeared to those meeting him at home on their TV screens. Dry and a tad disappointing in person, he came across on television—despite his liberal voting record and still-unpopular call for a negotiated end to the Vietnam War—as, essentially, a Midwestern moderate of the we-should-listen-to-him sort. No matter how close to radical was his position, his professorial mien suggested peaceful compromise, not disagreeable rabble-rousing.

To many, Robert Kennedy gave the opposite impression, a man whose intention was to shake things up. On the last weekend before the May 28 balloting in Oregon, for example, he visited Roseburg, a county seat in the southern part of the state. There, despite the local sheriff's warning about hostile demonstrators, Bobby took up the issue of gun control. Standing before a crowd that included a good many hunters in this lumber industry town, he made his case with angry indignation. A fellow "on death row" in Kansas, he told his listeners, a murderer who'd killed a half dozen people, sent away to Chicago for a mail-order rifle and had it arrive.

"Does that make any sense?" he demanded to know. "That you should put rifles and guns in the hands of people who have long criminal records, of people who are insane, of people who are mentally incompetent or people who are so young they don't know how to handle rifles and guns?" Yet even this drew boos from his listeners. "They'll get them anyway!" one fellow shouted.

Yet even riding for forty minutes in an open convertible in the rain didn't dampen his spirits: "Name something you've done that was more fun than this!" he challenged Jim Whittaker, his mountain-climbing pal who'd come along to help.

As Whittaker described his experiences accompanying Bobby: "He threw himself into the crowds and tried to reach as many people as possible. They responded with frightening enthusiasm." Nonetheless, Gene McCarthy took Oregon with 45 percent of the vote, Kennedy getting only 38. It was the first time he'd lost an election, either as Jack's campaign manager or now as a candidate himself. "He was devastated by that loss," Goodwin recalled.

Bobby refused to pass the blame. "If I'd won it, it would have been my victory, and I've lost it and it's my defeat. I sometimes wonder if I've correctly sensed the mood of America. I think I have. But maybe I'm all wrong. Maybe the people don't want things changed."

Pat Buchanan, then a Nixon campaign researcher and speech-writer, found himself impressed by the way that Kennedy absorbed the shock of losing. "His graciousness in conceding defeat and con-gratulating Gene McCarthy was impressive. This is the first time I'd seen Bobby in person. He could not have shown himself better in victory than he did in defeat that night."

In the hours following the Oregon results, Bobby now showed himself willing to rethink his tactics. This included taking a more respectful attitude to his rival. The people had spoken, and Eugene McCarthy had earned the right to be taken seriously. Having re-sisted his rival's call for a debate, he relented. "I'm not in much of a position now to say he's not a serious candidate. Hell, if he's not a serious candidate after tonight, then I'm not a candidate at all."

So now it was on to California, where the primary was sched-uled for the next Tuesday, June 4. On the morning after he lost Ore-gon, Bobby arrived in Los Angeles. Once again he stood in an open convertible as it drove slowly through streets of black and Mexi-can American neighborhoods en route from the airport to Beverly Hills. Once more, his cuff links were grabbed away, his shirt torn, and his clothing soaked with sweat. "I will work with all of you," he promised. "Give me your help."

John Lewis watched, amazed. "People treated him like he was some rock star. It was young people. It was blacks, white, Hispanic, just pulling for him." As historian Ronald Steel viewed it, Kennedy was using "hysteria as an electoral device, plunging into the crowds his advance men organized . . . presenting his body to the crowds as virtually a sacrificial offering."

But the increasingly wild excitement of those crowds greeting Bobby came at a price. For one thing, it didn't play well in living rooms when glimpsed on the evening newscasts. Seen in thirty-second bites, it scared white voters. For political chronicler Theodore White, the impression conveyed by the sight of Robert Kennedy welcomed by an excited crowd was "almost demoniac, frightening."

Though Bobby's desire was to bring together citizens from all communities, the fear born of the urban riots following the death of Martin Luther King was pulling Americans in a very different direction. Across the country, from Watts to Washington, it seemed as if a different, closer-to-home war was erupting in America's backyards.

Bobby had worries on another front—the campus. McCarthy's candidacy had done what Bobby's hadn't. By starting early, he had worked a magnetic effect on college students, pulling them to his cause. I remember seeing on television CBS's Roger Mudd confronting Kennedy with that fact as the two sat together in an airport waiting area. How much did this hurt? Mudd wanted to know. The expression on Bobby's face, after hearing the question, showed the answer.

How could he ever forget his visit to the University of San Francisco, where a student had spat in his face or when he'd heard another yelling "Fascist pig!" only to realize the epithet was directed at him? Somehow, in the perversity of competitive politics, this rebellious spirit, this born *misfit*, had allowed himself to be positioned as a defender of the status quo.

In mid-May, Jim Whittaker reported receiving a phone call from Ethel. "He's getting more and more death threats," she told him, "and I'm worried."

But Bobby, who'd refused to worry about his personal safety, now revealed a fatalism about his electoral chances. "I can accept the fact I may not be nominated now," he told Jack Newfield. "If that happens, I'll just go back to the Senate and say what I believe, and not try again in '72. Somebody has to speak up for the Negroes, the Indians and the Mexicans, and poor whites. Maybe that's what I do best. Maybe my personality just isn't built for this. The issues are more important than me now."

On Saturday, June 1, came the debate with McCarthy, broadcast nationwide on ABC's *Issues and Answers*. This "first official confrontation" took place in the network's San Francisco studios and lasted an hour. It was a question-and-answer format, with the two politicians seated at a round table with three newsmen. When Bobby was asked the question he'd most been dreading—if, as attorney general, he'd authorized a wiretap on Martin Luther King—he sidestepped. The civil rights leader was a "great and loyal American," he said, and left it at that. McCarthy did not follow up. By the end, it was clear the two men were more in agreement than not.

Though the press, by and large, pronounced it a draw, what mattered in the end was the public's reaction, captured afterward. McCarthy's supporters, who'd imagined their man's smoothly polished verbal skills would prevail, were hoping for a decisive win. Instead, they were presented with the opposite result: 60 percent scored it for Kennedy.

Reporters assigned to the Democratic primary race were starting to look more closely at this Kennedy who'd spent years growing beyond being Joseph Kennedy's son and John Kennedy's brother. What many wound up with was a deepening respect for the authenticity they now saw in him. Richard Harwood, who'd asked his *Washington Post* editor to be assigned to a different candidate, told him: "I'm falling in love with this guy." Explaining his request later, he said, "I think we were getting partisan. We hadn't quite become cheerleaders, but we were in danger of it."

An exhausted Bobby spent primary day, June 4, with his wife and family at a friend's beach house in Santa Monica. When his son David was caught in the surf, his father swam out and brought him back.

By evening, with projections showing Robert Kennedy the winner—the New York primary looming two weeks later—Bobby told Richard Goodwin, already at work on a victory speech, that he wanted to mend fences with McCarthy. His rival's Oregon win, along with the strong challenge he'd presented in California, demanded open respect. Dave Hackett had just showed him his tally of the up-to-date delegate count; it indicated that Bobby wouldn't be able to catch Hubert Humphrey's backroom campaign as long as he was in open combat with McCarthy.

Praising the McCarthy movement to Goodwin, he added, "I'd like to say something nice about him personally." He was ready to offer a deal. "I think we should tell him if he withdraws now and supports me, I'll make him secretary of state." His brother had proposed this, though without success, back in 1960 to encourage Adlai Stevenson to leave the fight.

Reaching Ken O'Donnell back east at Washington headquarters, he summed up how the moment seemed to him. "You know, I feel now for the first time that I've shaken off the shadow of my brother. I feel I made it on my own."

With an hour to go before addressing the crowd late that night at the Ambassador Hotel, Bobby dropped into a conversation with reporters a telling phrase. It was one he'd picked up from John Buchan, the author of *Pilgrim's Way*, Jack's favorite book. Buchan, Bobby said, had called politics an "honorable adventure." What struck him about the phrase, I think, was how it summed up what he'd come to believe: it was all worth it if the journey had a purpose.

"I have an association with those who are less well off, where perhaps we can accomplish something," he told an interviewer that night, "bringing the country back together—and that we can start to put into effect, all of us working together—some programs that will have some meaning. If the division continues, we're going to have nothing but chaos and havoc here in the United States."

Later, addressing the excited crowd there in the hotel with Ethel standing beside him, he said, "I think we can end the divisions within the United States, whether it's between blacks and whites, between the poor and the more affluent or between age groups or on the war in Vietnam. We can start to work together. We are a great country, an unselfish country. I intend to make that my basis for running."

He had found a good in politics, its purpose, *his* purpose. He had found his mission in life. He wanted to go on, wanted *dearly* to go on.

Robert Kennedy campaigns before a poster of Jack.

CHAPTER TWENTY-FIVE

SALUTE

"Is everybody else all right?"
—Bobby Kennedy
June 4, 1968

In early June of 1968, a fellow grad student of mine was headed up to Montreal to check out a job. He was thinking about moving there to avoid the Vietnam draft and invited me to join him for the weekend. The city was beautiful, sparkling and sunny, alive with excitement about Canada's youthful and progressive new prime minister, Pierre Elliott Trudeau. The new political atmosphere put all of the city's French charm and commercial bustle on radiant display.

For me, an important personal moment that long weekend came as I sat on a park bench several blocks up from Saint Catherine Street studying a list of notes to myself. These were my options on what to do now that my student deferment was turning into a pumpkin. The one that jumped out at me—promising adventure, patriotism, and good values—was the Peace Corps. My preference: Africa.

I was still in Montreal when Bobby was shot. Turning on the radio in the dark that Wednesday morning what I heard sounded like a reprise of Dallas. It took a couple of minutes for me to realize a new horror had come to pass. Later, as I traveled to the airport, the cab driver kept repeating aloud the same idiotic sentence: "The giant has stubbed its toe." Rather than honor the calamity, he was striking some weirdly small blow for Canadian nationalism. "The giant has stubbed its toe," he continued to say, with growing pride at his cleverness.

It was still a question of whether Bobby would make it. I'd prayed for his victory in the California primary. For me, he seemed to offer the only real hope of stopping the war. Hubert Humphrey wasn't going to do it—he was too much in Johnson's shadow. Now my prayers were different. They were simply for Bobby.

I was back in Chapel Hill when the awful news came. To this day I can still hear the anguish in Frank Mankiewicz's words in the official announcement that were repeated throughout the day. "Senator Robert Francis Kennedy died at 1:44 this morning . . . June 6, 1968. . . . He was forty-two years old."

Saturday, a week after his debate with McCarthy, dawned grim and gray. There was none of the pageantry of five years before, none of the brilliant theater that had fit so intuitively to the country's need for a proud mourning, no sign of Yeats's "terrible beauty," no "day of drums," no riderless horse. As Robert Francis Kennedy was carried in the dark to the gravesite on the sloping hill in Arlington, near his brother, it was just about loss.

It's what I felt as I watched the news footage of the Penn Central train, carrying him south from his funeral at New York's St. Patrick's Cathedral down through New Jersey, Delaware, and Maryland to Washington's Union Station. His presidential campaign had lasted eighty-two days. "The Impossible Dream" was Bobby's song. He knew the odds against him. Conscience, not glory, was what had called this Kennedy into service. Now his death left a void as large as his promise.

What made Robert Kennedy so unique, Jack Newfield wrote, "was that he felt the same empathy for white workingmen and women that he felt for blacks, Latinos and Native Americans. He thought of cops, waitresses, construction workers and firefighters as his people." And they were all there, perhaps two million of them massed along the tracks on that hot late-spring day, holding American flags and saluting, waiting to see him pass. GOD BLESS YOU, RFK and WE LOVE YOU, BOBBY, their signs read. As the train entered Philadelphia, nearly twenty thousand people, mostly African American, began to sing "The Battle Hymn of the Republic."

The Democratic National Convention in Chicago that August was far from politics as usual. It was America at war with itself. It was the clash Bobby had wanted to prevent, between the police and the college kid, between the working guy and the better-off, between father and son.

For me, that autumn was bittersweet. I was leaving my parents, my brothers, and my friends to head off to southern Africa, to the newly independent Kingdom of Swaziland as a Peace Corps volunteer. I would be there as a trade development adviser, working with rural businessmen.

I was leaving behind a country that had been robbed, again, of a leader.

On the morning after the shooting, Ethel Kennedy had asked her friends John Glenn and his wife, Annie, to take six of her children back across the country to Virginia. With Ethel at the hospital that Wednesday morning, it fell to Glenn to tell them what had happened:

"We flew back across the country in an Air Force jet dispatched by the president," Glenn would write. "We took the kids out to Hickory Hill and stayed the night with them. I was in Bobby's study when I saw on his desk a collection of Ralph Waldo Emerson's poems and essays. Leafing through it, I saw he'd marked in the margin a pair of passages he liked.

" 'If there is any period one would desire to be born in, is it not the age of Revolution; when the old and the new stand side by side and admit of being compared; when the energies of all men are searched by fear and by hope; when the historic glories of the old can be compensated by the rich possibilities of the new era? This time, like all times, is a very good one *if we but know what to do with it.*'

"Then there was the other:
" 'Always do what you are afraid to do.'"

ACKNOWLEDGMENTS

I want to thank Jonathan Karp of Simon & Schuster for this great assignment. After my two books on John F. Kennedy, I relished the chance to write about a central figure in the Kennedy story.

I began thinking seriously about Bobby Kennedy from the time he emerged into national leadership on his own. That was in the later months of 1967 and early months of 1968 when Eugene McCarthy and he converged in their struggle for the banner of the anti–Vietnam War movement.

In the years since, there were those who introduced Bobby Kennedy to me in unique ways. Wayne Owens was RFK's Rocky Mountain coordinator in 1968. Three years later, he was the top aide to Senator Frank Moss of Utah. It was Wayne who hired me on my return from service with the Peace Corps in Africa. His heartfelt devotion to Bobby Kennedy brought me in personal touch with the influence Kennedy had on young people like him.

Paul Corbin was another, very different figure who was very close to the man he called "Bob." I will never forget how this roguish character became emotional after reading a speech I'd written praising his hero. Nor will I ever forget his colorful stories of real-life politics he unloaded on me one winter night in a Chinese restaurant a floor above Brooklyn's Court Street.

There are others who allowed me to better complete my portrait of Bobby Kennedy. Ethel Kennedy contributed a Palm Beach afternoon answering every question about her husband. Their daughter Kathleen, who joined us, was insistent in keeping the conversation both lively, penetrating, and genuine.

Another family witness I've relied upon is Bobby's younger sister, Jean, who was helpful in my producing *Jack Kennedy: Elusive Hero*. Her book *The Nine of Us* offers the rare inside perspective on growing up a Kennedy.

I must once again acknowledge Helen O'Donnell for transcribing the oral history of her father, Kenneth O'Donnell. His account of the 1952 Senate race, especially of his successful recruitment of Bobby to manage the campaign, was indispensable. Kenny knew it all, including the backroom tactics Bobby used to swing big-shot support to his brother in 1960. He was my inside witness throughout.

I want to thank the many other people who helped me tell the Bobby Kennedy story. They include those who helped me with my books on Jack Kennedy. Charles Bartlett, Paul "Red" Fay, John Glenn, Eugene McCarthy, Thomas P. "Tip" O'Neill, Jr., George Smathers, Ted Sorensen, Charles Spalding, and Bill Wilson. Also: Mortimer Caplin, Peter Edelman, Dr. William Kennedy Smith, George Stevens, James Symington, William vanden Heuvel.

I have relied, too, on the memoirs of those who were close to Bobby at various stages of his life.

Lem Billings and Chuck Spalding were friends he inherited from Jack. Joseph P. Kennedy, Sr., accepted both men as proven family loyalists. Ed Guthman, who brought Bobby into the Rackets investigation and later served as his press secretary at the Justice Department, has been a seasoned guide for me to those years. I came across Ed later when he was editor of *The Philadelphia Inquirer*. He was a great journalist and trustworthy memoirist. I want to thank Frank Mankiewicz for his memoir of serving Bobby during his Senate tenure and Jack Newfield for inspiring me years ago with his dramatic witness to Kennedy's run for president. Both men richly understood the man.

Certain people deserve my special appreciation. Michele Slung helped get this book into shape while correctly noting that my daily writing for broadcast had weakened my will to write in full paragraphs. Tina Urbanski, *Hardball* senior producer, made it possible for me to perform my job at MSNBC and meet all the deadlines for this book. Another contributor was Lauren Mick, who did a great job reading two stacks of books and gathering together all my underlinings, adding some of her own. I also need to thank Meghan Cunningham for her excellent work. For his fine contribution to the photographic artwork, I again thank the estimable Vincent Virga.

I want to thank the people who allow me to produce *Hardball* editions five evenings a week. They include MSNBC president Phil Griffin; my two executive producers, Court Harson and Ann Klenk; senior producers Tina Urbanski, Robert Zeliger, and Jennifer Mulreany; director Ray Herbert; and producers Adam Garnett, Makayla Humphrey, Geet Jeswani, Christine Kim, Valerie McCabe, Tiffany Mullon, Nkechi Nneji, Will Rabbe, and Rachel Witkin.

At Simon & Schuster, I want to thank Richard Rhorer, Stephen Bedford, Cary Goldstein, Larry Hughes, Marie Florio, Eloy Bleifuss, Kristen Lemire, Amanda Mulholland, Paul Dippolito, Jonathan Evans, Jackie Seow, and Misha Hunt.

Above all, I owe Kathleen, my loving spouse and my ambassador to the rest of mankind, for elevating my life.

NOTES

Two biographies of Robert F. Kennedy have stood the test of time. The first, Arthur M. Schlesinger, Jr.'s, *Robert Kennedy and His Times*, 1978, bears the keen intelligence of a great historian who knew his subject as a personal friend. Evan Thomas's *Robert Kennedy: His Life*, 2000, is an essential second look at RFK by one of a later generation's most respected biographers. His trustworthy narrative was my essential scaffolding in writing this personal account of Bobby Kennedy's life and legacy.

My sources include interviews I conducted for *Kennedy & Nixon: The Rivalry That Shaped Postwar America*, 1996, and *Jack Kennedy: Elusive Hero*, 2011. They include Charles Bartlett, Ben Bradlee, Mark Dalton, Fred and Nancy Dutton, Paul Fay, Lester Hyman, Thomas P. "Tip" O'Neill, Jr., Terri Robinson, George Smathers, Ambassador Jean Kennedy Smith, Ted Sorensen, Chuck Spalding, and Billy Sutton. I've been able to add new interviews with Mortimer Caplin, Peter Edelman, John Glenn, Ethel Kennedy, Dr. William Kennedy Smith, George Stevens, James Symington, Kathleen Kennedy Townsend, and William vanden Heuvel.

As with *Jack Kennedy: Elusive Hero*, my indispensable resource for this book is Sander Vanocur's interviews of Kenneth O'Donnell, which were made available to me by his daughter Helen. O'Donnell was a central figure in the Kennedy story from his days as Bobby's Harvard teammate. I refer to his oral history as KOD interview.

There have been a good number of books written on Robert Kennedy by those who worked with him and by reporters who covered him. Together with the two masterworks by Schlesinger and Thomas, they are the foundation of my storytelling in each period of our subject's brief—fifteen-year—public life. I will credit each of these authors in the notes below.

PROLOGUE

2 *"I am announcing today":* Robert F. Kennedy, Washington, D.C., March 16, 1968.

3 *"the throne in the":* Jeff Shesol, *Mutual Contempt: Lyndon Johnson, Robert Kennedy and the Feud That Defined a Decade* (New York: W. W. Norton, 1997), p. 439.

5 *"the most generous little boy":* Evan Thomas, *Robert Kennedy: His Life* (New York: Simon & Schuster, 2000), p. 30.

5 *"It's pretty easy to":* Charles Spalding, John F. Kennedy Presidential Library, Oral History Collection.

6 *"puny," even "girlish":* Thomas, p. 30.

6 *"All this business about Jack":* Arthur M. Schlesinger, Jr., *Robert Kennedy and His Times* (New York: Ballantine, 1978), p. 96. Note: Unless otherwise indicated all Schlesinger cites are to *Robert Kennedy and His Times.*

6 *Bobby was smaller:* Lem Billings quote: Jean Stein, *American Journey: The Times of Robert Kennedy* (New York: Harcourt Brace, 1970), p. 37.

7 *"you were at a fair or something":* Author interview with Chuck Spalding.

7 *"make difficult decisions":* Jean Kennedy Smith, *The Nine of Us: Growing Up Kennedy* (New York: HarperCollins, 2016), p. 111.

7 *"Black Robert" he called him:* Thomas, p. 47.

8 *it's estimated that a million admirers:* "RFK, RIP, Revisited," *New York Times,* June 1, 2008.

10 *famous toast at an alumni dinner:* John Collins Brossidy, Holy Cross Alumni Dinner, 1910.

1. ALTAR BOY

Jean Kennedy Smith is Bobby's younger sister. He was the seventh in the family, she the eighth, both sharing the "little kids' table" in their early years. Her brief, remarkable *The Nine of Us: Growing Up Kennedy*, 2016, refers to Bobby as the family "gem." The same can be said of her memoir. I could find no better guide to his early years.

15 *"The Child is father":* William Wordsworth, *The Poetical Works of William Wordsworth*, Volume 3 (London: Edward Moxon, 1836), p. 3.

16 *Robert Kennedy would remark:* Robert F. Kennedy speech, Friendly Sons of St. Patrick of Lackawanna County, Scranton, Pennsylvania, March 17, 1964.

16 *NO IRISH NEED APPLY:* Thomas, p. 33.

16 *"Our forefathers": Pittsburgh Press,* March 18, 1964.

17 *tradition had dictated:* "Primogeniture and Ultimogeniture in Rural Ireland," *The Journal of Interdisciplinary History* 10, no. 3 (Winter 1980): 491–97.

18 *What separated Joe Kennedy:* Schlesinger, p. 14.

18 *"The castle or the outhouse":* Jack Newfield, *RFK: A Memoir* (New York: E. P. Dutton, 1969), p. 42.

18 *left Boston to settle:* Arthur Krock, *Memoirs: Sixty Years on the Firing Line* (New York: Funk & Wagnalls, 1968), p. 339.

19 *"in his own railway":* Schlesinger, p. 6.

19 *"Yes, but it was symbolic":* Ibid.

19 *It was young Bobby who took:* Ibid.

19 *It made him more Irish:* Thomas, p. 33.

21 *Once he raced so hard:* Rose Fitzgerald Kennedy, *Times to Remember* (New York: Doubleday, 1995), p. 88.

21 *"I was very awkward":* Ronald Steel, *In Love with Night: The American Romance with Robert Kennedy* (New York: Thorndike Press, 2000), p. 38.

21 *"It showed either":* Schlesinger, p. 23.

21 *soon became her favorite:* Thomas, p. 31.

21 *overlooked by his father:* Robert Dallek, *Camelot's Court: Inside the Kennedy White House* (New York: HarperCollins, 2013), p. 39.

21 *calling him her "pet":* Schlesinger, p. 42.

21 *"thoughtful and considerate":* Rose Fitzgerald Kennedy, *Times to Remember,* p. 89.

21 *"And probably the most religious":* Ibid., 89.

22 *The most Irish of:* Thomas, p. 33.

22 *At night from his room:* Steel, p. 35.

22 *invited to join their:* Thomas, p. 30.

22 *"He longed to explore":* Jean Kennedy Smith, *The Nine of Us,* p. 113.

22 *"Bobby strained his":* Ibid., p. 31.

22 *Jean remembered how:* Ibid., p. 118.

23 *"never really loved him":* Jacqueline Kennedy interview with Theodore White, Camelot Papers, John F. Kennedy Presidential Library.

23 *"History made him what he was"*: Ibid.

24 *became an altar boy:* Thomas, p. 2.

2. AMBASSADOR'S SON

David Nasaw's *The Patriarch: The Remarkable Life and Turbulent Times of Joseph P. Kennedy*, 2012, scrutinizes this grandly influential man as no one has before. It is hard to imagine another historian attempting to climb again to this peak. I owe his work for the background of this and the succeeding chapter.

27 *"For the second time"*: Neville Chamberlain speech, September 30, 1938.

28 *"I was really worried"*: David Nasaw, *The Patriarch: The Remarkable Life and Turbulent Times of Joseph P. Kennedy* (New York: Penguin, 2012), p. 171.

29 *he began enthusiastically:* Ibid.

29 *He went to his pal William Randolph Hearst:* Ibid., pp. 173–74.

29 *Joe Kennedy expected in return a swift:* Ibid., p. 186.

29 *It wasn't until the spring of 1934:* Ibid., p. 207.

30 *He proposed making Joseph Kennedy its first chairman:* Ibid., p. 208.

30 *asking him to chair:* Ibid., p. 255.

31 *"laughed so hard"*: Ibid., p. 272.

31 *the golden trio:* Thomas, p. 30.

32 *"acutely embarrassed"*: Nasaw, p. 297.

33 *"keep America out of any conflict"*: Ibid., p. 310.

33 *"it was not so much"*: Ibid.

33 *"Such pronounced attitudes"*: Ibid.

33 *the United States ambassador:* Ibid., p. 311.

33 *"While telling them what they wanted"*: Ibid.

34 *avoiding another European war:* Ibid., p. 338.

34 *In the last week:* Ibid., p. 346.

34 *"We have sustained a defeat"*: Winston Churchill, Speech to the House of Commons, October 1938.

35 *"It is unproductive"*: Doris Kearns Goodwin, *The Fitzgeralds and the Kennedys* (New York: Simon & Schuster, 1986), p. 566.

35 *began sending his family:* Nasaw, p. 410.

3. HONOR THY FATHER

37 *"The most important obligation":* Caoimhín Ó Danachair, "The Family in Irish Tradition," *Christus Rex* 16, no. 3.

37 *St. Paul's in Concord, New Hampshire:* Thomas, p. 29.

38 *despised red cap:* Nasaw, p. 297.

38 *never troubled by being alone:* Thomas, p. 31.

38 *Within a month:* Ibid., p. 29.

38 *put the blame on the Protestantism:* Ibid.

38 *relied solely upon the King James Bible:* Schlesinger, p. 30.

38 *education of her "pet":* Thomas, p. 30.

38 *her strong-willed husband's attention:* Ibid.

39 *More even than an appeaser:* Krock, p. 335.

39 *flown famed aviator:* Nasaw, p. 339.

39 *idea . . . of reaching "good relations":* Ibid., p. 354.

40 *"I'll bet you five to one":* Ibid., p. 474.

40 *Roosevelt pushed him further:* Ibid., p. 442.

41 *he transformed the paper:* Thomas, p. 32.

41 *belief that the British would lose the war:* Krock, p. 337.

41 *persisted in fighting Roosevelt's plan:* Nasaw, p. 458.

42 *backed Roosevelt's opponent:* Ibid., p. 457.

42 *signaling his wish to come home:* Ibid., p. 335.

42 *Lyndon Johnson, then a junior Texas:* Robert A. Caro, *The Years of Lyndon Johnson: The Passage of Power* (New York: Vintage, 2012), p. 62.

42 *What gratified him most:* Ibid.

43 *Bobby Kennedy took it:* Ibid.

43 *Joe had been interviewed at:* Nasaw, p. 498.

43 *assuming the session was off the record:* Krock, p. 337.

43 *"Democracy is all done":* Louis M. Lyons, "Kennedy Says Democracy All Done in Britain, Maybe Here," *Daily Boston Globe*, November 10, 1940.

43 *offered his resignation:* Krock, p. 336.

44 *Recounting to me his first visit:* Author interview with Chuck Spalding.

44 *"the first of the tragedies":* Nasaw, p. 537.

45 *Greatly more handicapped:* Thomas, p. 34.

45 *Rosemary's surgery had been performed:* Nasaw, p. 535.

45 *Joe Kennedy, Jr., and his brother Jack:* Thomas, p. 40.

45 *Joe was down in Jacksonville:* Nasaw, p. 540.

45 *Its presence provided him and other students:* Ibid., p. 41.

45 *Bobby stayed intent on what was happening:* Thomas, p. 35.

45 *"If he got a 77 he would argue":* Ibid., p. 36.

46 *"Mrs. Kennedy's little boy Bobby":* Ibid., p. 31.

46 *he was caught and:* Ibid., pp. 36–37.

46 *"Don't, I beg you":* Ibid.

46 *His next stop would be:* Ibid., p. 37.

47 *"Bobby ran every practice":* Schlesinger, p. 43.

47 *liked playing, "The Mick":* Thomas, p. 47.

47 *Hackett was both a legendary:* Ibid., p. 38.

47 *"I think we became friends right away":* David L. Hackett, John F. Kennedy Presidential Library, Oral History Collection.

47 *"There was no altar boy":* Ibid.

48 *"From the moment I met him":* Schlesinger, p. 45.

48 *"He would move into those situations":* Ibid.

48 *He had once asked him if something could be done:* Thomas, p. 39.

48 *"I think what he did have was":* Ibid.

48 *"I think if you talked to most people":* Ibid.

49 *"Once a person was his friend":* Chris Matthews, *Jack Kennedy: Elusive Hero* (New York: Simon & Schuster, 2012), p. 45.

4. RITES OF PASSAGE

51 *"After every charge":* James Joyce, *A Portrait of the Artist as a Young Man* (UK: Penguin Classics, 1916).

51 *"I want to go over there":* Author interview with Paul Ferber.

52 *She did this by conspicuously:* Thomas, p. 41.

52 *"Dad just phoned from N.Y.":* Nasaw, p. 549.

52 *A Japanese pilot:* JFK letter to Lem Billings, in David Pitts, *Jack and Lem: John F. Kennedy and Lem Billings: The Untold Story of an Extraordinary Friendship* (New York: Da Capo, 2007), p. 96.

52 *In the dark early-morning:* Description of JFK's command vessel, thirteen men including JFK, on *PT-109*, in Robert Donovan, *PT-109: John F. Kennedy in World War II* (New York: McGraw-Hill, 1961), p. 128.

53 *I don't think he should:* Schlesinger, p. 52.

53 *Bobby went on his own:* Ibid.

53 *Bobby began the V–12 officers training program:* Rose Fitzgerald Kennedy, *Times to Remember*, p. 255.

54 *"We haven't really had too much action":* Ibid., p. 53.

54 *"Say hello to all the Irish Catholics":* Thomas, p. 44.

54 *recovering from back surgery:* Herbert S. Parmet, *Jack: The Struggles of John F. Kennedy* (New York: Doubleday, 1982), p. 121.

54 *mistaking him for Jack:* Thomas, p. 42.

54 *"the father of our hero, our own hero":* Matthews, *Jack Kennedy*, p. 62.

54 *"We don't have any losers around here":* Schlesinger, p. 14.

55 *"By God, I'll show them":* Nigel Hamilton, *JFK: Reckless Youth* (New York: Random House, 1993), p. 640.

55 *Joseph Kennedy associate:* Krock, p. 348.

55 *The lieutenant's assigned target was:* Hamilton, pp. 659–60.

55 *"I can quite understand how you feel":* Nasaw, p. 569.

56 *"Children, your brother Joe has been lost":* Adam Clymer, *Edward M. Kennedy: A Biography* (New York: William Morrow, 1999), p. 15.

56 *went for a walk alone on the beach:* Thomas, p. 43.

56 *"Success was so assured":* Schlesinger, p. 56.

56 *In November of 1944:* Thomas, p. 44.

56 *"usual moody self":* RFK letter to Dave Hackett, January 1945, John F. Kennedy Presidential Library.

56 *"more and more like a draft dodger":* Ibid.

57 *"Your brother is a jerk":* Thomas, p. 44.

57 *"It looks like I will fly like a bird":* RFK letter to Dave Hackett, March 13, 1945, John F. Kennedy Presidential Library.

57 *By month's end:* Parmet, p. 131.

58 *"Am not going to fly":* RFK letter to Dave Hackett, May 4, 1945, John F. Kennedy Presidential Library.

58 *"My heart is with it":* Joan Blair and Clay Blair, *The Search for JFK* (New York: Putnam, 1976), p. 473.

58 *Without telling his father, Bobby headed:* Schlesinger, p. 60.

58 *It was then, in early 1946:* Blair and Blair, p. 518.

59 *"a lot of something a lot of those guys":* Schlesinger, p. 60.

59 *"The war makes less sense to me now":* JFK letter to war buddies, in Arthur M. Schlesinger, Jr., *A Thousand Days: John F. Kennedy in the White House* (Boston: Houghton Mifflin, 1965), p. 88.

60 *"I had never lived very much in the district"*: Presidential recordings, John F. Kennedy Presidential Library.

61 *"I didn't realize how Bobby worshipped him"*: KOD interview.

61 *"Black Robert"*: Thomas, p. 41.

61 *"It's damned nice of Bobby"*: Paul B. Fay, Jr., *The Pleasure of His Company* (New York: Harper & Row, 1966), p. 145.

61 *"One picture of the two"*: Schlesinger, p. 63.

62 *"From his expression"*: Fay, pp. 145–46.

62 *He'd chosen three wards:* Parmet, p. 157.

62 *On a group skiing trip:* Schlesinger, p. 66.

62 *"He asked me to work on the campaign"*: KOD interview.

63 *"I couldn't believe this skinny"*: Thomas P. O'Neill, *Man of the House: The Life and Political Memories of Speaker Tip O'Neill* (New York: Random House, 1987), p. 73.

63 *Locating another Joe Russo:* Joe Russo newspaper ad, *Boston Magazine*, June 1993.

63 *But when it came to getting his:* Fay, p. 147.

63 *"Then, very quietly, the candidate"*: Ibid.

64 *In* The New Yorker *for June:* O'Neill, p. 77.

64 *"He was as thin as a straw"*: Kevin Cullen, "A Loyalty Much Richer than Any Bank Account," *Boston Globe*, November 7, 2010.

65 *"His real field of"*: Schlesinger, p. 67.

65 *"I read in the* Boston Post*"*: Stein, p. 38.

65 *They shared, incidentally, an antipathy:* Thomas, p. 50.

65 *But upon seeing Spee reject another:* Ibid.

65 *"Bobby began to meet other kinds"*: Ibid.

67 *"None of us liked him"*: Ibid.

68 *"I remember being kind of"*: Ibid.

69 *"He had a broken leg"*: *Ethel* HBO documentary, Moxie Firecracker Films, 2012.

5. COMMITMENT

71 *"For anyone to achieve something"*: "Kennedy Children Groomed for Careers in Politics," United Press International, August 7, 1969.

71 *"responsive to the will of the people"*: "Joint Statement with Winston

Churchill and Joseph Stalin on the Yalta Conference," Miller Center, University of Virginia, February 11, 1945.

72 *The spring of 1947:* This account first appeared in Christopher Matthews, *Kennedy & Nixon: The Rivalry That Shaped Postwar America* (New York: Simon & Schuster, 1996).

72 *Two tragedies:* Ibid.

73 *A grieving Bobby made his way to London:* Thomas, p. 56.

74 *"the new type of Catholic":* Dominic Sandbrook, *Eugene McCarthy: The Rise and Fall of Postwar American Liberalism* (New York: Alfred A. Knopf, 2007), p. 22.

74 *Bobby became especially vehement:* Schlesinger, p. 81.

75 *"We can look back over the last four or five years":* Robert Kennedy article in the *Boston Advertiser.*

75 *The one who held his heart:* Thomas, p. 57.

76 *"The responsibility for the failure":* *Congressional Record,* January 29, 1949.

76 *second trial for perjury:* William R. Conklin, "Hiss Guilty on Both Perjury Counts; Betrayal of U.S. Secrets Is Affirmed; Sentence Wednesday; Limit 10 Years," *New York Times,* January 22, 1950.

76 *"The conspiracy would have":* Richard Nixon speech, U.S. House of Representatives, Matthews, *Kennedy and Nixon,* p. 68.

77 *"most traitorous":* Joseph McCarthy speech, Wheeling, West Virginia, February 9, 1950.

77 *In fact, the official assessment:* National Security Council Report No. 68, April 12, 1950.

78 *"Bobby turned and saw the person in trouble":* Author interview with Ethel Kennedy.

80 *That November, Congressman Jack Kennedy:* John P. Mallan, "Massachusetts: Liberal and Corrupt," *New Republic,* October 13, 1952.

80 *"the Dinosaur Is Dead":* Thomas, p. 55.

81 *Bobby's response was an eloquent five-page letter:* "Robert F. Kennedy and the Desegregation of the 1951 Ralph J. Bunche Lecture," Andrew Mc-Canse Wright, *Savannah Law Review* 2, no. 1, 2015.

82 *It was the "safest place":* Author interview with Ethel Kennedy.

83 *"the final step from which":* Schlesinger, p. 82.

6. BROTHER

This and the succeeding chapter's account of the 1952 Senate race are drawn heavily from Kenneth O'Donnell's interviews with Sander Vanocur (KOD interview).

85 *"Every politician in Massachusetts":* Schlesinger, p. 214.

86 *As Jack had recently pointed out: Meet the Press,* NBC, December 3, 1951.

88 *"a pain in the ass":* Robert Hilty, *Robert Kennedy: Brother Protector* (Philadelphia: Temple University Press, 1997), p. 64.

88 *"We flew to the military hospital":* John F. Kennedy, *Profiles in Courage* (New York: Harper & Brothers, 1956), Foreword.

89 *"He was a war veteran":* KOD interview.

89 *But O'Donnell's assessment:* Ibid.

89 *Speaker Tip O'Neill, Jr.:* Author conversation with Tip O'Neill, which first appeared in Matthews, *Jack Kennedy.*

90 *"He started getting our attention":* KOD interview.

90 *"I'm seriously considering running":* Ibid.

91 *He was afraid to take even:* Ibid.

93 *"I knew Bobby was the one with":* Ibid.

93 *"Well, that's fine":* Ibid.

7. THE KENNEDY PARTY

The bulk of this chapter is based on the oral history of Kenneth O'Donnell (KOD interview).

96 *"anything to distract you":* Author interview with Ethel Kennedy.

96 *"I told him you've got to":* KOD interview.

96 *For O'Donnell, this was a window:* Ibid.

96 *Bobby was annoyed at Ken:* Ibid.

96 *"He just made it very clear":* Ibid.

97 *Now came the task of convincing:* Ibid.

97 *Jack didn't like hearing:* Ibid.

97 *"Why don't you come up":* Ibid.

97 *"His brother asked him":* Author interview with Ethel Kennedy.

97 *"It was a very tough thing":* Ibid.

98 *Handling their father was at the top:* Stein, p. 43.

99 *Ethel would defend her husband's:* Author interview with Ethel Kennedy.

99 *build a total political network:* KOD interview.

102 *Joe's ties to Senator Joe McCarthy:* Nasaw, p. 667.

103 *"How dare you compare":* Parmet, p. 245.

103 *"trying to ruin my":* Nasaw, p. 667.

104 *McCarthy never entered the state:* David M. Oshinsky, *A Conspiracy So Immense: The World of Joe McCarthy* (New York: Oxford University Press, 2005), p. 242.

104 *On the night before the election:* KOD interview.

104 *When he got Bobby on the phone:* Ibid.

104 *"He went town by town":* Ibid.

105 *Outside the window:* Ibid.

105 *ability to* make decisions: Author interview with Ethel Kennedy.

105 *"What a bunch of bums":* KOD interview.

8. CLAN

107 *"What are you going to do now?":* Stein, p. 45.

109 *"I'm tired of it":* Helen O'Donnell, *The Irish Brotherhood: John F. Kennedy, His Inner Circle, and the Improbable Rise to the Presidency* (Berkeley: Counterpoint, 2015), p. 89.

110 *Joe Kennedy was working to convince:* Nasaw, p. 671.

112 *One morning in the Senate cafeteria:* Caro, *The Passage of Power*, pp. 61–62.

112 *"It's about Roosevelt and his father":* Ibid.

112 *"Did you ever see two dogs":* Caro, *The Passage of Power*, p. 63.

113 *a subcommittee assignment:* Nasaw, p. 672.

114 *Liberal columnist Doris Fleeson:* Shesol, p. 18.

114 *According to* The Boston Post*:* Schlesinger, p. 102.

116 *Bobby gave notice:* Nasaw, p. 672.

117 *"I was particularly impressed":* Schlesinger, p. 107.

117 *Joe McCarthy's wedding gift:* Author conversation. The cigarette box is in the possession of Robert Shrum, a professor at the University of Southern California.

117 *McCarthy's honeymoon in the:* Richard Reeves, *President Kennedy: Profile of Power* (New York: Simon & Schuster, 2011), p. 513.

118 *"coddling Communists":* Donald Crosby, *God, Church, and Flag: Senator Joseph R. McCarthy and the Catholic Church, 1950–1957* (Chapel Hill: University of North Carolina Press, 2011), p. 147.

118 *Sixty-two percent of Republicans:* Reeves, p. 534.

118 *When it came to Catholics:* Crosby, p. 148.

119 *"He had a lot of frustration":* LeMoyne Billings quote in Stein, p. 48.

119 *"many people formed their ideas about him":* Ibid.

119 *Democratic members boycotted:* Schlesinger, p. 109.

119 *McCarthy agreed to give the:* Ibid.

119 *"Put your mind at rest":* Stein, p. 50.

120 *"You can't believe it":* Author interview with Ethel Kennedy.

121 *Ken O'Donnell saw his friend's conflict:* Stein, p. 49.

123 *1,200 men at a St. Patrick's Day dinner:* Crosby, p. 152.

125 *"Tell Jackson we're going to get":* Oshinsky, p. 478.

125 *"We've got letters he wrote":* Shesol, p. 19.

126 *"half my voters in Massachusetts":* Crosby, p. 206.

127 *"To understand the situation":* Ibid.

128 *given the last rites of the Catholic Church:* KOD interview.

128 *"Why do you reporters":* Arthur Herman, *Joseph McCarthy: Reexamining the Life and Legacy of America's Most Hated Senator* (New York: Simon & Schuster, 2000), p. 10.

9. HAIL MARY

131 *"Well, I guess you could call it a Hail Mary":* Jarrett Bell, interview with Roger Staubach, "Origins of 'Hail Mary': Cowboys Legend Roger Staubach Remembers How It Stuck," *USA Today,* January 13, 2017.

131 *Bobby Kennedy his chief counsel:* James Neff, *Vendetta: Bobby Kennedy Versus Jimmy Hoffa* (New York: Little, Brown, 2015), p. 38.

131 *Bobby's thoughts began shifting:* Thomas, p. 72.

132 *The strategy was to make:* Parmet, p. 366.

132 *gathered the data and wrote:* Harris Wofford, *Of Kennedys and Kings: Making Sense of the Sixties* (Pittsburgh: University of Pittsburgh Press, 1980), p. 31.

133 *"To me, he was a self-important":* David Pietrusza, *1960: LBJ vs. JFK vs. Nixon: The Epic Campaign That Forged Three Presidencies* (New York: Sterling Publishing, 2008), p. 63.

134 *Stevenson's public justification:* Parmet, p. 375.

135 *"Call Dad and tell him":* O'Donnell, p. 147.

135 *He was calling him:* Parmet, p. 376.

135 *"Whew!" Bobby said:* Ibid.

135 *despite frantic attempts:* KOD interview.

135 *"What can you do":* Ibid.

136 *he thought his brother would:* Ibid.

136 *now had to be candid:* Ibid.

136 *"find out who has the power":* Ibid.

137 *"Why are you against my brother?":* Thomas Oliphant and Curtis Wilke, "When JFK Won by Losing," *Politico,* May 14, 2017.

137 *The first ballot had:* Larry J. Sabato, *The Kennedy Half-Century: The Presidency, Assassination, and Lasting Legacy of John F. Kennedy* (New York: Bloomsbury, 2013), p. 38.

137 *Southerners were out in force:* Nasaw, p. 711.

137 *"The second ballot":* Reeves, p. 466.

137 *"Texas proudly casts its vote":* Wofford, p. 31.

138 *"Forget it!":* Thomas Oliphant and Curtis Wilkie, *The Road to Camelot: Inside JFK's Five-Year Campaign* (New York: Simon & Schuster, 2017), p. 49.

138 *he instead recognized Edmondson:* Stein, p. 65.

138 *"He was very depressed":* Author interview with Jean Kennedy Smith.

139 *"It's the best thing":* Ibid.

139 *The outlook now was:* Nasaw, p. 708.

139 *it left him seething:* Barbara Leaming, *Jacqueline Bouvier Kennedy Onassis: The Untold Story* (New York: Thomas Dunne Books, 2014), p. 83.

140 *they had to create from scratch:* Shesol, p. 25.

140 *Jack Kennedy headed to:* Nasaw, p. 708.

140 *It was Bobby who:* Robert Caro, *The Years of Lyndon Johnson: Means of Ascent* (New York: Vintage, 1991), p. 234.

141 *finally heard her husband's:* Leaming, *Jacqueline Bouvier Kennedy Onassis,* p. 84.

141 *Bobby set off to join:* Parmet, p. 385.

142 *"I came out of our":* Ibid.

142 *"You wouldn't believe it":* O'Donnell, p. 161.

142 *Kennedy thought Stevenson quite simply spent too:* Stein, p. 66.

142 *Bobby had watched his brother:* RFK wedding reception interview.

143 *"After the traditional Thanksgiving":* Edward Kennedy, *True Compass,* p. 116.

143 *acting as a bridge between:* Thomas, p. 73.

143 *"It was understood":* Rose Fitzgerald Kennedy, *Times to Remember,* p. 307.

10. IRISH COP

Edwin Guthman met Robert Kennedy as he began his investigation of crooked labor leaders on the Senate Rackets Committee. A dedicated investigative reporter, he joined Kennedy as a top aide at the Justice Department. His memoir, *We Band of Brothers*, 1971, has served as a personal, inspiring, credible guide to these years. While I had only a single encounter with Guthman, I have gained the highest respect for him.

145 *"I thought Teamster meant mob":* Author interview with Kathleen Kennedy Townsend, March 4, 2016.

145 *returning to the Senate's:* Nasaw, p. 710.

145 *"He did his investigations":* Neff, p. 31.

146 *Bobby could do* exactly: Edwin Guthman, *We Band of Brothers* (New York: Harper & Row: 1964), p. 4.

146 *This meant taking on:* Thomas, p. 74.

146 *Mollenhoff told Kennedy:* Neff, p. 33.

146 *"A young lawyer from":* Guthman, p. 96.

146 *"Can you trust him":* Thomas, p. 74.

147 *Mollenhoff was the perfect man:* Guthman, p. 4.

147 *digging into the activities:* Neff, p. 31.

147 *Bobby informed his father:* Nasaw, p. 710.

147 *"the worst ever":* Thomas, p. 76.

147 *Two days after Christmas:* Ibid.

147 *To accommodate that:* Ibid.

147 *McClellan as chairman:* Neff, p. 38.

147 *Among the Republicans were:* Ibid.

147 *"Bobby wanted me on that committee":* Thomas, p. 76.

148 *"If the investigation flops":* Kenneth P. O'Donnell and David E. Powers, *Johnny, We Hardly Knew Ye: Memories of John Fitzgerald Kennedy* (New York: Open Road Media, 2013), p. 132.

148 *Kennedy declared two rules:* Thomas, p. 85.

148 *"If we allowed witnesses":* Guthman, p. 32.

148 *"The most important advantage":* Ibid.

149 *"more concerned with what the":* Shesol, p. 20.

149 *Bobby received a call:* Thomas, p. 78.

149 *Hoover instructed him:* Neff, p. 46.

149   *met face-to-face with Hoffa:* Thomas, p. 77.

149   *"Here's a fella thinks he's doing me a favor":* Neff, p. 47.

149   *"spoiled jerk":* Ibid., p. 55.

149   *"Bob, who had an underlying":* Steel, p. 52.

150   *FBI sting operation:* Thomas, p. 79.

150   *"It was Ethel Kennedy who roused":* Guthman, p. 57.

150   *"He stared at me for three minutes":* Neff, p. 61.

150   *"I'll jump off the Capitol":* Thomas, p. 79.

150   *Rackets Committee turned its attention:* Neff, p. 69.

151   *raised $76,000 in contributions:* Guthman, p. 64.

151   *"Bob kept his word":* Ibid., p. 56.

151   *the most cooperative Republican:* Ibid., p. 24.

151   *"Drunk the last three times":* Schlesinger, p. 172.

151   *"It was typical of Bobby":* Ibid., p. 173.

151   *That May, Bobby's former boss:* Ibid.

152   *"I was in the car with Daddy":* Author interview with Kathleen Kennedy Townsend.

152   *"It was all very difficult for me":* Steel, p. 49.

152   *The burial took place the next day:* Neff, pp. 41–42.

152   *Representing him was a rising:* Thomas, p. 80.

153   *two thirds of whom were African American:* Ibid.

153   *arrange for former heavyweight champion:* Ibid.

153   *Louis offered a warm greeting:* Schlesinger, p. 155.

153   *A record company hired Louis:* Robert F. Kennedy, *The Enemy Within: The McClellan Committee's Crusade Against Jimmy Hoffa and Corrupt Labor Unions* (New York: Harper, 1960), p. 61.

153   *The dramatic evidence:* Thomas, p. 80.

154   *"I'm going to send Bobby Kennedy":* "Labor: Out of the Trap," *Time,* July 29, 1957.

154   *"He divided everyone up":* Neff, p. 150.

154   *"driven by a conviction":* Ibid., p. 91.

154   *Kennedy called Hoffa before:* Guthman, pp. 66–67.

154   *"Don't you know I could have you":* Robert F. Kennedy, *The Enemy Within,* p. 160.

154   *"Since you've been with the Teamsters":* Neff, p. 93.

155   *claiming the Fifth Amendment right:* Ibid., p. 96.

155 *"was glaring at me across the counsel":* Ibid., p. 97.

155 *"It would drive the bastard":* Thomas, p. 80.

155 *Again and again, the Teamster:* Neff, p. 103.

155 *Finally, the chairman had it:* Ibid., p. 104.

155 *could see what was driving:* Guthman, pp. 29–30.

156 *"With McClellan and Bob":* Ibid., p. 30.

156 *he was elected to replace:* Robert F. Kennedy, *The Enemy Within*, p. 118.

156 *"You have carried a candle":* Neff, p. 127.

156 *"This year seems to":* Shesol, p. 22.

157 *"Look at him":* Ibid.

157 *"He wasn't frustrated":* Thomas, p. 83.

157 *"My first love":* Schlesinger, p. 169.

158 *"Now he was dead":* Robert F. Kennedy, *The Enemy Within*, p. 35.

158 *Bobby accused Jimmy Hoffa:* Ibid., p. 62.

158 *You also meet here:* Ibid., p. 75.

158 *Frank Kierdorf, the arsonist:* Ibid., p. 84.

158 *"Sam" Giancana:* Thomas, p. 83.

158 *"Every man has his price":* Robert F. Kennedy, *The Enemy Within*, p. 58.

158 *"I have every politician in town":* Ibid., p. 67.

158 *the Kennedy brothers would be lionized for the quest:* KOD interview.

159 *"toughness and idealism that guided":* Robert F. Kennedy, *The Enemy Within*, p. 325.

11. ENFORCER

161 *"How do you expect to run":* Fay, p. 6.

161 *"How would you like":* Ibid., p. 7.

161 *"It doesn't matter if they like":* Steel, p. 56.

162 *Bobby, on Jack's orders:* Shesol, p. 10.

163 *Observing those early days:* David L. Hackett, John F. Kennedy Presidential Library, Oral History Collection.

164 *"What we basically did":* Ibid.

164 *"loyalty index":* Ibid.

164 *"To get a ten":* Ibid.

12. THE ENEMY WITHIN

This chapter relies heavily on Jeff Shesol's *Mutual Contempt*. His is the best account of Kennedy's decision to select Lyndon Johnson as his vice presidential running mate.

176 *He called him a "riverboat gambler":* Benjamin C. Bradlee, *Conversations with Kennedy* (New York: W. W. Norton, 1984), p. 18.

176 *They revealed that:* Shesol, p. 35.

178 *"He's my choice":* Ibid., p. 43.

179 *"I wasn't any Chamberlain":* Caro, *The Passage of Power*, p. 105.

179 *"You've got your nerve!":* Robert Dallek, *An Unfinished Life: John F. Kennedy* (New York: Little, Brown and Company, 2003), p. 57.

179 *Johnson had one further trick:* Shesol, p. 39.

179 *"Do not reject this man":* Sandbrook, p. 105.

180 *had broken his third promise:* Ibid., p. 39.

180 *Bobby was now in total command:* Caro, *The Passage of Power*, p. 245.

180 *They'd arrived with 600:* Sabato, p. 53.

180 *Jack sent a message to:* Guthman, p. 77.

181 *asked Johnson if he'd like to be his:* W. H. Lawrence, "Johnson Is Nominated for Vice President; Kennedy Picks Him to Placate South," *New York Times,* July 15, 1960.

181 *events become murkier:* Shesol, pp. 52–54.

181 *"so savagely attacked":* Ibid., p. 57.

182 *fell to Bobby:* Shesol, p. 52.

182 *They'd guessed wrong:* Ibid., p. 54.

182 *"Bobby's been out of touch":* Ibid.

182 *"Don't worry, Jack":* Thomas, p. 98.

183 *"Yesterday was the best day":* Ibid.

13. VICTORY

186 *"I think it so unfair of people":* Leaming, *Jacqueline Bouvier Kennedy Onassis*, p. 94.

186 *"Jack, who'd needled Hubert Humphrey":* Edward M. Kennedy, *True Compass: A Memoir* (New York: Warner, 2009), p. 155.

187 *"I was in the green room":* Author interview with Bill Wilson.

187 *The Kennedy plan now:* Matthews, *Jack Kennedy*, p. 295.

188 *"What the hell is this?":* Author interview with Bill Wilson.

189 *"There was a guy standing":* Ibid.

189 *"the glaring failure of American":* Senator John F. Kennedy speech, Cincinnati, Ohio, Democratic Dinner, October 6, 1960.

190 *"We must attempt to":* Statement on Cuba by Senator John F. Kennedy, October 20, 1960.

191 *"There was hardly a place":* The account of Martin Luther King's arrest and the Kennedys' effort to free him is drawn from Harris Wofford's *Of Kennedys and Kings*, p. 16.

194 *"I am deeply indebted":* Martin Luther King, *The Papers of Martin Luther King, Jr.*, Volume V, edited by Clayborne Carson, Tenisha Armstrong, Susan Carson, Adrienne Clay, and Kieran Taylor (Berkeley: University of California Press, 2005).

195 *"Hi, Johnny. How are you?":* Schlesinger, p. 219.

195 *"Last week, Dick Nixon":* Fay, p. 60.

196 *Bobby's house in Hyannis Port:* Rose Fitzgerald Kennedy, *Times to Remember*, p. 321.

196 *"Each state has certain bellwether":* KOD interview.

196 *"Bobby found me and pulled":* Ibid.

196 *"We called the Senator":* Ibid.

196 *"I don't mind him":* Ibid.

196 *"I think, around eleven":* David L. Hackett, John F. Kennedy Presidential Library, Oral History Collection.

197 *Jack went off to bed:* Thomas, p. 107.

197 *presented Bobby with a special:* Hilty, p. 193.

14. FREEDOM FIGHTER

199 *"At last, Bobby's moral center seemed to stir":* Harry Belafonte, *My Song: A Memoir of Art, Race, and Defiance* (New York: Vintage, 2011), p. 234.

199 *"We're going to do what":* Hilty, p. 184.

199 *"Not necessarily young men":* Ibid.

200 *One of the earliest to land:* KOD interview.

200 *Over O'Donnell's opposition:* Ibid.

200 *"understandably reluctant to call":* Fay, p. 75.

201 *"suggested to me the possibility":* Arthur M. Schlesinger, Jr., *Journals: 1952–2000* (New York: Penguin, 2007), p. 101.

201 *"For the last four years":* Dallek, *An Unfinished Life*, p. 308.

201 *Soon after the election:* Neff, p. 205.

201 *"I said I didn't want":* Shesol, p. 65.

202 *"I didn't want to spend":* Nasaw, p. 759.

202 *Jack dispatched Clark Clifford:* Ibid.

202 *"I made up my mind today":* Dallek, *An Unfinished Life*, p. 64.

202 *"I need to know that":* Thomas, p. 110.

203 *"It's the first thing he's":* Shesol, p. 67.

203 *"If I learned anything":* Ibid., p. 66.

203 *Three months later, on April 12:* Thomas, p. 120.

203 *"The great mass of Cuban":* Ibid.

204 *Monday, just hours after:* Ibid.

204 *"I don't think it's going":* Reeves, p. 92.

204 *"I think we've made":* Guthman, pp. 110–11.

204 *"You can start praying":* Ibid.

205 *"There's an old saying":* President John F. Kennedy press conference, April 21, 1961.

205 *"Those sons-of-bitches":* Reeves, p. 103.

206 *"There can be no long-term":* Ibid., p. 264.

206 *On May 4, thirteen "Freedom Riders":* Thomas, p. 128.

206 *"During those days":* RFK, *American Experience*, PBS, July 1, 2004.

207 *But the worst violence:* Thomas, pp. 128–29.

207 *"Stop them!":* Ibid., p. 129.

207 *Just a month later:* Barbara Leaming, *Jack Kennedy: Education of a Statesman* (New York: W. W. Norton & Co., 2007), p. 299.

207 *The new attorney general:* Sabato, p. 79.

207 *"To them, the Freedom Riders":* Belafonte, p. 233.

207 *Bobby also felt a genuine concern:* Thomas, p. 129.

208 *"that's the last thing":* RFK, *American Experience*, PBS, July 1, 2004.

208 *"I just leaped out":* Ibid.

209 *"Troops are on the way":* NBC News Archives.

209 *"Robert Kennedy became educated":* RFK, *American Experience*, PBS, July 1, 2004.

209 *"At last, Bobby's moral center":* Belafonte, p. 230.
209 *On a Voice of America broadcast:* Guthman, p. 181.

15. GENERAL

211 *"He would have taken a bolt":* Peter Collier, *The Kennedys: An American Drama* (San Francisco: Encounter Books, 2002), p. 450.
211 *pursuing organized crime:* Thomas, p. 115.
212 *One of his first acts:* Neff, p. 217.
212 *crime-busting potential:* Ibid., pp. 215–17.
212 *His first step was contacting:* Ibid.
212 *"One of the things I'm going":* Ibid.
212 *"From the moment he was":* Ibid., p. 233.
212 *"unstable as an animal":* Thomas, p. 162.
212 *Bobby also found himself engaged:* Guthman, p. 226.
213 *President's Committee on:* Godfrey Hodgson, *JFK and LBJ: The Last Two Great Presidents* (New Haven: Yale University Press, 2016), p. 140.
213 *"It goes back to the very":* David L. Hackett, John F. Kennedy Presidential Library, Oral History Collection.
213 *"Perhaps a juvenile delinquent":* Schlesinger, *Robert Kennedy and His Times,* p. 409.
213 *"I started in the Department":* Guthman, p. 88.
213 *it was important that they trust:* Schlesinger, *Robert Kennedy and His Times,* p. 241.
214 *"Maybe at one o'clock":* John Seigenthaler, John F. Kennedy Presidential Library, Oral History Collection.
214 *"I'm Bob Kennedy":* Ibid.
214 *The lawyers working for him:* Thomas, p. 112.
214 *"In the next three and a half":* Guthman, p. 92.
214 *"Did you see any Negroes?":* John Seigenthaler, John F. Kennedy Presidential Library, Oral History Collection.
215 *"We're not seeking":* Ibid.
215 *an event took place that changed:* Reeves, p. 272.
215 *issue of* Life *magazine featured:* "The No. 2 Man in Washington," *Life,* January 26, 1962.
216 *"wondrously qualified for":* Ibid.
216 *Once coming across a:* Ibid.

216 *"He seems to be genuinely":* Ibid.

216 *Forgoing a wage increase:* Reeves, p. 295.

217 *Four days after signing:* Ibid., p. 296.

217 *"You've made a terrible":* Ibid.

217 *five other steel companies:* Ibid.

217 *"Some time ago":* Ibid., p. 298.

217 *"There shouldn't be any":* "Today's Titans Can Learn from Fall of U.S. Steel," Floyd Noris, *New York Times,* July 3, 2014.

217 *The orders to the FBI agents:* Guthman, p. 233.

218 *already raised a ruckus:* Ibid., p. 231.

218 *"I get some credit":* Ibid., p. 234.

218 *"Why is it that all the telephone calls":* Ben Bradlee, *A Good Life* (New York: Simon & Schuster, 2011), p. 240.

218 *He went on:* Ibid.

218 *"And, of course":* Ibid.

218 *who'd been tracking him:* Steel, p. 66.

219 *was involved in an ongoing:* Neff, p. 239.

219 *Hoover had logs of:* Ibid.

219 *It took the director's visit:* Reeves, p. 290.

219 *"Johnny, you just can't associate":* Ibid., p. 292.

219 *And so was their friendship:* Steel, p. 68.

220 *"I trust that if you ever":* Schlesinger, *Robert Kennedy and His Times,* p. 493.

222 *"like the Alamo":* Thomas, p. 18.

222 *"Shoot anybody that puts":* Reeves, p. 362.

222 *"the mightiest internal struggle":* Schlesinger, *Robert Kennedy and His Times,* p. 325.

223 *"It seemed to me very clear":* Hilty, p. 347.

16. TWO GREAT MEN

225 *"Every time they have a conference":* Shesol, p. 107.

225 *Bobby Kennedy was haunted:* Thomas, p. 146.

225 *"Cuba means a great deal to the old Bolsheviks":* Reeves, p. 105.

226 *"It was almost as simple as":* Thomas, p. 146.

226 *Code-named Operation Mongoose:* Ibid., p. 149.

226 *below-the-radar mission:* Ibid., p. 133.

226 *At their first meeting:* Ibid.

227 *On October 15, a U-2 spy plane:* Reeves, p. 379.

227 *The president was in his bedroom:* Caro, *The Passage of Power*, p. 208.

228 *emergency meeting in the West Wing:* Reeves, p. 368.

228 *Bobby's response: "Shit":* Ibid., p. 369.

228 *"Ken Keating will probably":* Ibid., p. 370.

229 *"We kidded ourselves":* Guthman, p. 118.

229 *he made a strong case:* Reeves, p. 378.

229 *both Kennedys found themselves:* Caro, *The Passage of Power*, p. 210.

229 *"This thing is falling apart":* Thomas, p. 217.

230 *"I remember going into":* Author interview with Ethel Kennedy.

231 *Bob Kennedy and Ted Sorensen:* Reeves, p. 418.

231 *The president asked his brother:* Dallek, *An Unfinished Life*, p. 561.

232 *"I should say that during":* Thomas, p. 228.

232 *"In order to save the world":* Ibid., p. 230.

232 *"Looking back on it":* Wofford, p. 408.

232 *he brought in James B. Donovan:* Guthman, p. 131.

17. CIVIL RIGHTS

235 *"What I didn't fully appreciate":* Guthman, p. 90.

235 *In early 1963: Newsweek,* March 18, 1963.

236 *"No Kennedy likes":* Caro, *The Passage of Power*, p. 250.

237 *"You talk to McNamara":* Wofford, p. 409.

241 *"We have a party in revolt":* Belafonte, p. 267.

242 *Loudest and most belligerent:* Ibid.

242 *"What you're asking us":* Ibid.

242 *"Never! Never! Never!":* Thomas, p. 244.

243 *"Maybe it's what Bobby":* Belafonte, p. 270.

243 *"They didn't want to talk":* Guthman, p. 221.

243 *"I guess if I were in his shoes":* Ibid.

243 *"Segregation now, segregation tomorrow":* Inaugural Address of Alabama governor George Wallace, January 14, 1963.

244 *Bobby continued to make the case:* Ted Sorensen, John F. Kennedy Presidential Library, Oral History Collection.

245 *President Kennedy turned to:* Belafonte, p. 267.

246 *Martin Luther King, in tears:* Ibid., p. 271.

246 *The sense of accomplishment:* Ibid.

246 *"How can we say to the Negro in Jackson":* Guthman, p. 223.

247 *"Get rid of them":* Reeves, p. 530.

247 *Reluctantly, he let:* Belafonte, p. 275.

249 *"We are launched on a":* Cablegram from Ambassador Lodge to Secretary Rusk, *New York Times,* July 1, 1971.

249 *"I told you he was going":* Reeves, p. 642.

249 *"that we're just going":* Thomas, pp. 270–71.

249 *On November 2:* Reeves, p. 649.

250 *On Friday, November 22:* Schlesinger, *Robert Kennedy and His Times,* p. 608.

250 *"Jack's been shot":* Neff, p. 4.

250 *"There's so much bitterness":* Steel, p. 86.

250 *He now wanted answers:* Thomas, p. 277.

250 *Even before seeing McCone:* Ibid.

251 *"Why?" he was asking:* Charles Spaulding interview, *RFK, American Experience,* PBS, July 2004.

18. RELIC

253 *"I thought it would be me":* Schlesinger, p. 609.

254 *"His eyes were haunted":* Guthman, pp. 244–45.

254 *"He looked to me like a man":* John Seigenthaler interview, *RFK, American Experience,* PBS, July 2004.

254 *"I could not imagine":* Wofford, p. 388.

254 *"Everything was pulled out":* Schlesinger, p. 612.

254 *"It veered close to being":* Edward Kennedy, *True Compass,* p. 210.

255 *"He who learns must suffer":* Steel, p. 96.

255 *He was being sent to Southeast Asia:* Richard Goodwin, *Remembering America,* p. 247.

255 *"Bobby and Ethel witnessed":* Edward Kennedy, *True Compass,* p. 211.

256 *One person who suspected:* Guthman, 254.

256 *Paul Corbin had been recently spotted:* Caro, *The Passage of Power,* p. 583.

256 *was by now a true favorite of:* John Seigenthaler interview, *RFK, American Experience,* PBS, July 2004.

256 *"If he's such a good fellow":* Thomas, p. 651.

256 *"Knowing Paul, Bobby knew":* John Seigenthaler interview, *RFK, American Experience,* PBS, July 2004.

256 *Bobby didn't actually care:* Shesol, p. 182.

257 *"I know who he's loyal to":* Schlesinger, *Robert Kennedy and His Times,* p. 248.

257 *Johnson wasn't about to let:* Guthman, p. 254.

257 *The New Hampshire write-in:* Ibid.

257 *"The Attorney General has said":* Ibid., pp. 255–56.

258 *arrived at his brother's bedside:* Rose Fitzgerald Kennedy, *Times to Remember,* p. 392.

258 *"How much more do they":* Guthman, p. 285.

259 *"There were many who felt":* Ibid., p. 274.

259 *"version of the assassination":* Ibid.

260 *"There is no question that":* Ibid., p. 277.

260 *allowed by the government:* Ibid.

260 *The moment proved equally:* Shesol, p. 165.

261 *Senate in New York:* Clymer, p. 58.

261 *"all the messiness of the arrogant":* Richard Goodwin, *Remembering America,* p. 297.

261 *"That job doesn't have":* Schlesinger, *Journals,* p. 230.

261 *"That's really Teddy's state":* Richard Goodwin, *Remembering America,* p. 297.

261 *Bobby continued to view:* Bradlee, *A Good Life,* p. 296.

262 *Johnson called the attorney general:* Richard Goodwin, *Remembering America,* p. 298.

262 *"could be a real dead end":* Guthman, p. 283.

262 *"It would be awful if I lost":* Ibid., p. 284.

263 *"If it's McCarthy":* Sandbrook, p. 11.

263 *Johnson had been unable:* Sabato, p. 272.

264 *"Why don't you let them":* John Seigenthaler interview, *RFK, American Experience,* PBS, July 2004.

265 *Robert Kennedy broke down:* Thomas, p. 296.

265 *"Inevitably, during the briefing":* Guthman, p. 289.

266 *"Although by this time":* Rose Fitzgerald Kennedy, *Times to Remember,* p. 393.

266 *"At the beginning":* Author interview with Peter Edelman.

267 *Bobby faced resistance:* William Jacobus vanden Heuvel and Milton Gwirtz-

man, *On His Own: Robert F. Kennedy, 1964–1968* (New York: Doubleday, 1970), p. 44.

267 *"I think labels are so difficult":* NBC News Archives.

267 *Paul Corbin noticed one day:* Schlesinger, p. 670.

268 *decided it was time to meet:* Ibid., p. 675.

268 *"Kindly inform Senator Keating":* vanden Heuvel and Gwirtzman, p. 53.

268 *Keating panicked, running:* Ibid.

268 *"He was back on his feet":* Guthman, p. 311.

19. BRAVE HEART

Frank Mankiewicz was Bobby's loyal press secretary. His posthumous *So As I Was Saying* . . . is a colorful, inside guide to Bobby through his Senate years to the end.

271 *"John Kennedy was a realist":* Schlesinger, p. 602.

271 *Bobby had traveled to Bismarck: New York Times*, September 16, 1963.

272 *presented Bobby:* Ibid.

272 *"resident, melancholy bleakness":* Jim Stevenson, *The New Yorker*; Schlesinger, *Robert Kennedy and His Times*, p. 817.

272 *black necktie he hadn't yet:* Shesol, p. 233.

272 *"whether he got to be":* Ibid., p. 234.

273 *"impotent, frustrated, floundering":* RFK, *American Experience*, PBS, July 1, 2004.

273 *Canadian government had just:* Schlesinger, p. 811.

273 *The National Geographic:* Ibid.

273 *"I planted President Kennedy's":* "Robert F. Kennedy," *Life.*

273 *He also left behind:* RFK, *American Experience*, PBS, July 1, 2004.

274 *"He looked over at me":* Edward Kennedy, *True Compass*, p. 230.

275 *"Is this the way":* vanden Heuvel and Gwirtzman, p. 64.

276 *After first thinking:* Frank Mankiewicz, *So As I Was Saying . . . My Somewhat Eventful Life* (New York: Thomas Dunne Books, 2016), p. 141.

277 *"I don't talk that way":* Ibid., p. 142.

277 *the radical students:* vanden Heuvel and Gwirtzman, p. 168.

277 *when he learned:* Ibid., p. 169.

277 *"I'm afraid I would":* Ibid.

277 *On November 22:* vanden Heuvel and Gwirtzman, p. 171.

278 *"I'm against it—in all cases":* Mankiewicz, p. 190.

20. AFFIRMATION

289 *"It is from numberless diverse":* Robert Kennedy "Day of Affirmation" speech, University of Cape Town, South Africa, June 6, 1966.

289 *"nervous Nellies":* Lyndon B. Johnson remarks at a Democratic Party dinner in Chicago, May 17, 1966.

290 *"I am an old man":* vanden Heuvel and Gwirtzman, p. 209.

290 *"regain its proper course":* Ibid.

290 *"France and General de Gaulle":* "Must Accept French Peace Help, Bobby," *Chicago Tribune*, February 1, 1967.

291 *A later one in:* "Kennedy 'Signal' in Capital: Report of Peace Feeler from Hanoi Strains Senator's Relations with Johnson," *The New York Times*, February 6, 1967.

291 *over the course of:* Schlesinger, p. 768.

291 *"It's not my State Department":* Ibid.

292 *"to shuttle back and forth":* Edward Kennedy, *True Compass*, p. 249.

292 *Bobby proposed:* Mankiewicz, p. 164.

292 *"There isn't a chance in hell":* Schlesinger, p. 768.

292 *"I'll destroy you and every one":* Ibid.

292 *"These guys are out of their minds":* Ibid.

292 *"As one who was involved":* Newfield, p. 137.

293 *"Let us reflect for a moment":* Schlesinger, p. 733.

294 *"the poor, white and negro":* Address by Martin Luther King, Jr., The Nation Institute, Los Angeles, California, February 25, 1967.

294 *he refused to side with antiwar:* Schlesinger, p. 774.

294 *presented an hour-long:* "The Image of America and the Youth of the World," RFK with Governor Ronald Reagan, CBS Television and Radio, May 15, 1967.

295 *"One of Reagan's many":* Mankiewicz, p. 166.

295 *"My God, I didn't know":* Schlesinger, p. 795.

296 *"He was so passionate":* Author interview with Ethel Kennedy.

21. THE MOVEMENT

301 *One of the antiwar speakers:* Theodore H. White, *The Making of the President 1972* (New York: HarperCollins: 2010), p. 81.

301 *"I love Bobby Kennedy more":* Ibid., p. 84.

301 *"People would say that":* Steel, p. 140.

301 *"I must have spoken":* White, p. 82.

302 *Deciding to call together:* Schlesinger, *Journals*, p. 273.

302 *He was aware that his brother:* Schlesinger, *Journals*, p. 273.

302 *Ted was one of those:* vanden Heuvel and Gwirtzman, p. 278.

302 *Bobby wasn't at the meeting:* Newfield, p. 192.

302 *"The consensus of the meeting":* vanden Heuvel and Gwirtzman, p. 279.

302 *On October 12, the National Mobilization:* Jeff Leen, "The Vietnam Protests: When Worlds Collided," *Washington Post*, September 27, 1999.

303 *"It was like looking for your* father": White, p. 82.

305 *"His general feeling is that":* Schlesinger, *Journals*, p. 264.

305 *"He thinks that McCarthy's":* Ibid.

306 *"They say I'm committing":* Sandbrook, p. 172.

306 *"As the party's heir apparent":* Bill Clinton, *My Life: The Early Years* (New York: Vintage, 2005), p. 118.

306 *A meeting at Bill vanden Heuvel's apartment:* Edward Kennedy, *True Compass*, p. 252.

306 *The two Teds:* Newfield, p. 193.

307 *"We haven't decided anything":* Schlesinger, *Journals*, p. 270.

307 *In the year-end issue:* Newfield, pp. 195–96.

307 *"I just have to decide now":* Ibid., p. 196.

307 *"I don't want it to hurt":* Ibid.

22. VIGIL

309 *"My problem is that":* Newfield, p. 199.

309 *Ted Kennedy was the one person:* Clymer, p. 105.

310 *"We weren't that far away":* Ibid.

310 *Ted knew their father:* Edward Kennedy, *True Compass*, p. 262.

310 *Yet Ted also was willing:* Ibid.

310 *"It was not just the war":* Ibid., p. 264.

310 *Ted believed his brother:* Ibid.

310 *At a New York dinner in early January:* Schlesinger, *Journals*, p. 273.

310 *urging him on whose agendas were their own:* Ibid.

311 *"Suppose, in the middle":* Ibid., p. 274.

311 *"prepared to escalate or de-escalate":* Ibid., p. 277.

311 *"I have told friends and supporters":* Steel, p. 144.

311 *Mankiewicz stopped the departing reporters:* Clymer, p. 104.

311 *But the far more:* Ibid., p. 104.

311 *In one city, Hue, alone:* "The Massacre at Hue," *Time*, October 31, 1969.

312 *"The views that I represent":* Joan Walsh, "44 Years Ago, Harry Belafonte Hosted the Tonight Show—And It Was Amazing: He Interviewed RFK and MLK Months Before Their Death. Fifteen of Twenty-five Guests Were African American," *The Nation*, February 16, 2017.

312 *"We have been too often disappointed":* CBS News, Walter Cronkite editorial on the Vietnam War, February 27, 1968.

313 *"You must run for president":* Mankiewicz, p. 198.

313 *"Clean for Gene":* Ken Rudin, "Remembering Eugene McCarthy," NPR, December 12, 2005.

313 *"beat the spread":* Sandbrook, p. 177.

314 *winning over 42 percent to Johnson's:* White, p. 102.

314 *"I don't blame him at all":* Schlesinger, *Journals*, p. 280.

314 *"What do I do now?":* Richard Goodwin, *Remembering America: A Voice from the Sixties*, 1st ed., p. 516.

314 *"He failed to realize":* Ibid., p. 520.

314 *"I'm reassessing the possibility":* Clymer, p. 107.

315 *"If it could be done":* Ted Sorensen, John F. Kennedy Presidential Library, Oral History Collection.

315 *On Thursday morning, two days after:* Newfield, p. 221.

315 *A cornerstone of the presentation:* Ibid.

315 *with his new boss's thumbs-down:* vanden Heuvel and Gwirtzman, p. 312.

315 *"Better reserve the Senate Caucus Room for tomorrow":* Mankiewicz, p. 173.

23. DEFIANCE

I credit Jack Newfield for my appreciation of Robert Kennedy, both as public figure and close-up human being. No one else has written as well about the tragic last months of this heroic figure.

317 *"To take arms against a sea of troubles":* William Shakespeare, *Hamlet*.

317 *he dispatched Ted to Wisconsin:* Clymer, p. 109.

317 *Abigail, listened to Ted:* Ibid.

318 *"What do you think I should do?":* Schlesinger, *Journals*, p. 283.

318 *"Why not come out for":* Ibid.

318 *"I can't do it":* Ibid.

319 *"by splitting the Democratic party":* Ibid., p. 284.

320 *Dave Hackett signed on to put together:* David L. Hackett, John F. Kennedy Presidential Library, Oral History Collection.

320 *the plan was sixteen states:* Steel, p. 170.

320 *"Roars rolled out one after another":* Mankiewicz, p. 175.

321 *Standing there before a fifteen-thousand:* Thomas, p. 362.

321 *"But past error is no excuse":* Guthman, p. 239.

321 *Driving him, he declared:* Robert F. Kennedy remarks at the University of Kansas, March 18, 1968, John F. Kennedy Presidential Library.

322 *"feel the fabric ripping":* Clark, p. 50.

322 *referred to him as a "demagogue":* Shesol, p. 426.

322 *8,500 students at the University of Alabama:* Newfield, p. 236.

322 *"You don't understand":* Ibid.

322 *Lyndon Johnson had announced:* Ibid., p. 243.

323 *"The thing I feared from the first day":* Doris Kearns Goodwin, *Lyndon Johnson and the American Dream* (New York: Open Roads Media, 2015), p. 343.

323 *"For all the advantages that we have":* Transcript of Robert F. Kennedy remarks at Notre Dame University, Irving Gymnasium, April 4, 1968.

323 *"You're placing a great deal":* Ibid.

324 *As they were about to leave Muncie:* Mankiewicz, p. 179.

324 *"It grieves me":* Robert F. Kennedy to John J. Lindsay of *Newsweek*, in Schlesinger, p. 874.

324 *"There were some people saying":* Christopher Matthews, "Of Kennedy and King," *Image Magazine, San Francisco Examiner*, June 6, 1993.

324 *"Our local campaign leadership":* Mankiewicz, p. 179.

324 *the local police who'd been assigned:* Ibid.

324 *"What am I going to say?":* Matthews, "Of Kennedy and King."

325 *his listeners didn't believe:* Ibid.

325 *"Martin Luther King dedicated his life":* Robert F. Kennedy statement on assassination of Martin Luther King, Jr., Indianapolis, Indiana, April 4, 1968, John F. Kennedy Presidential Library.

326 *"member of my family":* Matthews, "Of Kennedy and King."

327 *he believed in law and order:* Richard Goodwin, *Remembering America*, p. 530.

327 *scenes of the rioting on TV:* Ibid.

327 *At the City Club:* Robert F. Kennedy speech transcript, Cleveland City Club, April 5, 1968, John F. Kennedy Presidential Library.

328 *"That being touched all the time":* Clark, p. 212.

328 *"The people here were fair to me":* Newfield, p. 261.

328 *receiving 42 percent of the vote:* "How Bobby Kennedy Won the '68 Indiana Primary," *Newsweek,* May 19, 1968.

328 *"His inner urge toward defiance":* Richard Goodwin, *Remembering America,* p. 529.

329 *"I've proved I can really be":* Clark, p. 219.

24. SACRIFICE

331 *McCarthy had touched down in Nebraska for a single day:* vanden Heuvel and Gwirtzman, p. 351.

331 *"At every stage of the campaign":* Ibid., p. 322.

332 *"Name something you've done":* Guthman, p. 241.

333 *It was the first time he'd lost:* Thomas, p. 382.

333 *"He was devastated by that loss":* RFK, *American Experience,* PBS, July 2004.

333 *"His graciousness in conceding defeat":* Patrick J. Buchanan, *The Greatest Comeback: How Richard Nixon Rose from Defeat to Create the New Majority* (New York: Crown, 2014), p. 264.

333 *"I'm not in much of a position":* Richard Goodwin, *Remembering America,* p. 533.

334 *"I will work with all of you":* RFK, *American Experience,* PBS, July 2004.

334 *a student had spat in his face:* Richard Goodwin, *Remembering America,* p. 533.

335 *"He's getting more and more death threats":* Jim Whittaker, *A Life on the Edge: Memoirs of Everest and Beyond* (Seattle: Mountaineers Books, 2013).

335 *"I can accept the fact I":* Newfield, p. 271.

336 *asked his* Washington Post *editor:* Ibid., p. 262.

336 *"I'd like to say something nice":* Richard Goodwin, *Remembering America,* p. 537.

336 *"You know, I feel now":* KOD interview.

337 *Pilgrim's Way, Jack's favorite book:* Thomas, p. 40.

337 *"I have an association with those":* KOD interview with Sander Vanocur, NBC News.

25. SALUTE

339 *"Is everybody else all right?":* Thomas, *Robert Kennedy*, p. 391.

340 *"Senator Robert Francis Kennedy died":* Mankiewicz, p. 150.

341 *"was that he felt the same empathy":* Newfield, p. 8.

341 *On the morning after the shooting:* John Glenn, *A Memoir* (New York: Bantam, 1999), p. 425.

342 *"If there is any period one'":* "The American Scholar," an address delivered by Ralph Waldo Emerson, Cambridge, MA, August 1837.

BIBLIOGRAPHY

Belafonte, Harry. *My Song: A Memoir of Art, Race, and Defiance.* New York: Vintage, 2011.

Blair, Joan, and Clay Blair. *The Search for JFK.* New York: Putnam, 1976.

Bradlee, Benjamin C. *Conversations with Kennedy.* New York: W. W. Norton, 1984.

———. *A Good Life.* New York: Simon & Schuster, 2011.

Buchanan, Patrick J. *The Greatest Comeback: How Richard Nixon Rose from Defeat to Create the New Majority.* New York: Crown, 2014.

Caro, Robert. *The Years of Lyndon Johnson: Means of Ascent.* New York: Vintage, 1991.

———. *The Years of Lyndon Johnson: The Passage of Power.* New York: Vintage, 2012.

Clinton, Bill. *My Life: The Early Years.* New York: Vintage, 2005.

Clymer, Adam. *Edward M. Kennedy: A Biography.* New York: William Morrow, 1999.

Collier, Peter. *The Kennedys: An American Drama.* San Francisco: Encounter Books, 2002.

Crosby, Donald. *God, Church, and Flag: Senator Joseph R. McCarthy and the Catholic Church, 1950–1957.* Chapel Hill: University of North Carolina Press, 2011.

Dallek, Robert. *Camelot's Court: Inside the Kennedy White House.* New York: HarperCollins, 2013.

———. *An Unfinished Life: John F. Kennedy.* New York: Little, Brown and Company, 2003.

Donovan, Robert. *PT-109: John F. Kennedy in World War II.* New York: McGraw-Hill, 1961.

Fay, Paul B., Jr. *The Pleasure of His Company.* New York: Harper & Row, 1966.

Glenn, John. *A Memoir.* New York: Bantam, 1999.

Goodwin, Doris Kearns. *The Fitzgeralds and the Kennedys.* New York: Simon & Schuster, 1986.

———. *Lyndon Johnson and the American Dream.* New York: Open Roads Media, 2015.

Goodwin, Richard. *Remembering America: A Voice from the Sixties.* Boston: Little, Brown and Company, 1988.

Guthman, Edwin. *We Band of Brothers.* New York: Harper & Row, 1964.

Herman, Arthur. *Joseph McCarthy: Reexamining the Life and Legacy of America's Most Hated Senator.* New York: Simon & Schuster, 2000.

Hilty, Robert. *Robert Kennedy: Brother Protector.* Philadelphia: Temple University Press, 1997.

Kennedy, Edward M. *True Compass: A Memoir.* New York: Warner, 2009.

Kennedy, John F. *Profiles in Courage.* New York: Harper & Brothers, 1956.

Kennedy, Robert F. *The Enemy Within: The McClellan Committee's Crusade Against Jimmy Hoffa and Corrupt Labor Unions.* New York: Harper, 1960.

Kennedy, Rose Fitzgerald. *Times to Remember.* New York: Doubleday, 1995.

King, Martin Luther, Jr. *The Papers of Martin Luther King, Jr.*, Volume V, edited by Clayborne Carson, Tenisha Armstrong, Susan Carson, Adrienne Clay, and Kieran Taylor. Berkeley: University of California Press, 2005.

Krock, Arthur. *Memoirs: Sixty Years on the Firing Line.* New York: Funk & Wagnalls, 1968.

Leaming, Barbara. *Jack Kennedy: Education of a Statesman.* New York: W. W. Norton & Co., 2007.

———. *Jacqueline Bouvier Kennedy Onassis: The Untold Story.* New York: Thomas Dunne Books, 2014.

Matthews, Chris. *Jack Kennedy: Elusive Hero.* New York: Simon & Schuster, 2012.

———. *Kennedy & Nixon: The Rivalry That Shaped Postwar America.* New York: Simon & Schuster, 1996.

Nasaw, David. *The Patriarch: The Remarkable Life and Turbulent Times of Joseph P. Kennedy.* New York: Penguin, 2012.

Neff, James. *Vendetta: Bobby Kennedy Versus Jimmy Hoffa.* New York: Little, Brown, 2015.

Newfield, Jack. *RFK: A Memoir.* New York: E. P. Dutton, 1969.

O'Donnell, Helen. *The Irish Brotherhood: John F. Kennedy, His Inner Circle, and the Improbable Rise to the Presidency.* Berkeley: Counterpoint, 2015.

O'Donnell, Kenneth P., and David E. Powers. *Johnny, We Hardly Knew Ye: Memories of John Fitzgerald Kennedy.* New York: Open Road Media, 2013.

Oliphant, Thomas, and Curtis Wilkie. *The Road to Camelot: Inside JFK's Five-Year Campaign.* New York: Simon & Schuster, 2017.

Oshinsky, David M. *A Conspiracy So Immense: The World of Joe McCarthy.* New York: Oxford University Press, 2005.

Pietrusza, David. *1960: LBJ vs. JFK vs. Nixon: The Epic Campaign That Forged Three Presidencies.* New York: Sterling Publishing, 2008.

Pitts, David. *Jack and Lem: John F. Kennedy and Lem Billings: The Untold Story of an Extraordinary Friendship.* New York: Da Capo, 2007.

Reeves, Richard. *President Kennedy: Profile of Power.* New York: Simon & Schuster, 2011.

Sabato, Larry J. *The Kennedy Half-Century: The Presidency, Assassination, and Lasting Legacy of John F. Kennedy.* New York: Bloomsbury, 2013.

Sandbrook, Dominic. *Eugene McCarthy: The Rise and Fall of Postwar American Liberalism.* New York: Alfred A. Knopf, 2007.

Schlesinger, Arthur M., Jr. *Journals: 1952–2000.* New York: Penguin, 2007.

———. *Robert Kennedy and His Times.* New York: Ballantine, 1978.

———. *A Thousand Days: John F. Kennedy in the White House.* Boston: Houghton Mifflin, 1965.

Shesol, Jeff. *Mutual Contempt: Lyndon Johnson, Robert Kennedy and the Feud That Defined a Decade.* New York: W. W. Norton, 1997.

Smith, Jean Kennedy. *The Nine of Us: Growing Up Kennedy.* New York: HarperCollins, 2016.

Steel, Ronald. *In Love with Night: The American Romance with Robert Kennedy.* New York: Thorndike Press, 2000.

Stein, Jean. *American Journey: The Times of Robert Kennedy.* New York: Harcourt Brace, 1970.

Thomas, Evan. *Robert Kennedy: His Life.* New York: Simon & Schuster, 2000.

vanden Heuvel, William Jacobus, and Milton Gwirtzman. *On His Own: Robert F. Kennedy, 1964–1968.* New York: Doubleday, 1970.

White, Theodore H. *The Making of the President 1972*. New York: HarperCollins, 2010.

Whittaker, Jim. *A Life on the Edge: Memoirs of Everest and Beyond*. Seattle: Mountaineers Books, 2013.

Wofford, Harris. *Of Kennedys and Kings: Making Sense of the Sixties*. Pittsburgh: University of Pittsburgh Press, 1980.

INDEX

Page numbers in *italics* refer to photographs.

ABOUT THE AUTHOR

Chris Matthews is the host of MSNBC's *Hardball*. He is the author of *Hardball: How Politics Is Played—Told by One Who Knows the Game*, *Kennedy & Nixon: The Rivalry That Shaped Postwar America*, *Jack Kennedy: Elusive Hero*, and *Tip and the Gipper: When Politics Worked*.